Stanley's Adventures in the Wilds of Africa

J. T. Headley
& W. F. Johnson

Stanley's Adventures in the Wilds of Africa

The present edition is a reproduction of previous publication of this classic work. Minor typographical errors may have been corrected without note; however, for an authentic reading experience the spelling, punctuation, and capitalization have been retained from the original text.

ISBN: 978-1-64439-375-8

PREFACE

For centuries Africa has been "the dark continent" of our globe. The sea-washed edges of this immense tract have been known time immemorial. Egypt, at its northeastern corner, is the oldest of the governments of the earth; while the nations skirting the Red and the Mediterranean seas were actors in the earliest recorded history. But Africa as a whole has been an unknown land.

That it was a fertile land, was demonstrated by the treasures brought from its depths by those mighty rivers, the Nile, the Niger and the Congo. That it was populous, was proven by the fact that its native tribes had furnished to the world without, forty millions of slaves in the period of two centuries. Both the slave-hunter and the slave told wondrous tales of the inner depths of the land, but these were mere hints as to the actual facts of the case. Africa remained a mystery and a riddle, that seemingly were never to be penetrated.

For many years explorations in Africa were made simply to gratify curiosity, or from a desire to penetrate beyond lines reached by other men. All the results desired or expected were amusement or fame. But in later years African explorations have assumed an entirely different aspect. From Livingstone, who first began to open up "the dark continent," to Cameron and Stanley who pierced its very heart, all explorations have tended to one great end—the civilization and Christianization of the vast population that inhabits it. No matter what the ruling motive may have been in each case, whether, as in Livingstone, to introduce Christianity; or, in Baker, to put a stop to the slave trade; or, in Stanley, to unlock the mystery of ages, still the tendency has been the same: to bring Africa into the family of continents instead of being the earth's "pariah;" to throw light on this black spot of our planet, and make those who inhabit it practically and morally, what they are really, a portion of the human race.

Mungo Park, Denham and Clapperton made explorations of considerable value early in the present century, but Livingstone with thirty years of toil in Africa was the real pioneer of successful work. In 1840, at the age of twenty-five, he embarked as a missionary to South Africa, thus entering the land where he lived and died, and which he never left save on two brief visits to his native land.

After Livingstone's last return to Africa, circumstantial reports of his death were received. These were subsequently contradicted and other reports of death came. He wrote but few letters and some of these failed to reach their destination; his fate, therefore, remained in painful uncertainty until Bennett sent Stanley to discover him, dead or alive.

This commission led to the two expeditions of Stanley, the thrilling events of which are narrated in this volume.

CONTENTS

CHAPTER I

HENRY M. STANLEY

Stanley is one of those characters which forcibly illustrate the effect of republican institutions in developing strong men. Despotism cannot fetter thought—that is free everywhere—but it can and does restrain its outworking into practical action. Free institutions do not make great men, but they allow those endowed by nature with extraordinary gifts free scope for action. This fact never had, perhaps, a more striking illustration than in the French Revolution. The iron frame-work of despotism had rested so long over the heads of the people that it had become rusted in its place, and no individual force or strength could rend it asunder. But when the people, in their fury, shattered it into fragments, there was exhibited the marvelous effects of individual character. A lieutenant of artillery vaulted to the throne of France and made marshals and dukes and kings of plebeians. A plebeian himself, he took to his plebeian bed the daughter of the Cæsars. He took base-born men and pitted them against nobles of every degree, and the plebeians proved themselves the better men. In other words, he put men against titles, and the tiles went down before the men. Thus, no matter how despotic he became, he and his marshals and new-made kings were the most terrible democracy. The mighty changes that were then wrought show what results may be expected when the whole world shall be thus set free, and every man be allowed to strike his best and strongest blow. When the race is thus let loose on the planet we inhabit, we shall see the fulfillment of that prophecy, "a nation shall be born in a day."

The same truth is apparent in our own country, though its exhibitions are not so sudden and startling. Indeed they could not be, because this freedom of action has no restraints to break through, and hence no violent effort is required. Every man grows and expands by degrees without let or hindrance. In a despotism, Webster would probably have taught school in a log school-house all his days, and the "mill-boy of the slashes" never would have made the forum of a nation ring with his eloquence, nor the "rail-splitter" have become the foremost man of his time, nor the "tanner-boy" the president of the republic. Republican institutions never made any of those men—they simply allowed them to make themselves.

Stanley is among the latest and most extraordinary examples

of this. It is folly to point to such men as he, as a stimulus to youthful ambition. No amount of study or effort can make such a boy or man as he was and is. The energy, daring, self-confidence, promptness and indomitable will were born in him, not acquired. The Latin proverb, Poeta nascitur, non fit, "the poet is born, not made," is not truer of the poet than of a character such as his. His peculiarities may be pointed out for the admiration of others, his good qualities may teach youth how perseverance, and determination, and work will elevate a man, whatever be his walk in life. One born with a combination of qualities like Stanley's, must have room given him or he will make room. He has such an abundance of energy and will-power that they must have scope for action. A despotism could not have repressed him. He would either have become a wanderer or adventurer in strange lands, or he would have headed a revolution and vaulted to power or to a scaffold, as others had done before him.

But although Stanley developed his character under free institutions, he was not born under them, he being a native of Wales. He was born near Denbigh, in 1840. His father's name was Rowland. When three years old, he was sent to the poor-house at St. Asaph, to get an education. Here the poor, unpromising lad remained till he had finished such an education as this institution could furnish, and then he sought employment as a teacher, and for a year was employed as such at Mold, Flintshire. But the strong instincts of his nature then began to show themselves. He felt that a school-teacher's life, however honorable and useful, could not be his, and, therefore, with his scant earnings, he shipped as cabin-boy in a vessel bound for New Orleans. Having arrived in safety, he began to look about for employment. By what lucky chance it happened we do not know, but he fell into the hands of a merchant named Stanley, who became so attached to the frank, energetic, ambitious youth, that he finally adopted him and gave him his name. Thus the Welsh boy Rowland, became the American youth Stanley.

Fortune had certainly smiled on him, and his future seemed secure. As the partner, and eventually heir of his benefactor, as he doubtless would become, fortune, ease and a luxurious life lay before him. But even here, so pleasantly situated and cared for, the same restless spirit that has since driven him over the world, exhibited itself, and he wandered off into the wilds of Arkansas, and in his log-cabin on the banks of the Wichita River, with the pine-trees moaning above him, he dwelt for a long time, among the strange, wild dreams of his imaginative and daring youth. His adopted father mourned him as dead, never expecting to behold him again. But the youth made his way to the Mississippi, and going on board a flat-boat, became the companion of the rough western characters to be found on these boats, and slowly floated down to New Orleans and was received by his overjoyed father as one risen from the dead.

But just here, fortune, which seemed to have had him in her special care, took him another step forward by apparently deserting him. His adopted father suddenly died without making his will. His place and prospective heirship both disappeared together, and the curtain was let down between him and a pleasant, successful future. Doubtless that father intended to provide for his adopted son, but now all the property went to the natural legal heirs, and he was once more thrown upon the world. In the delirium of an African fever, tossing in his hammock, far from the haunts of civilization, there came back to him remembrances of his life at this point. We learn that impelled by his roving disposition he wandered away among the California miners, and at last among the Indians, and sat by their council fires. He seemed destined to see every phase of human life, to become acquainted with the roughest characters, to prepare him for the wildest of all men, the African savage. This kind of life also toughened and hardened the fibre of the youth, so that he settled down into the man with a constitution of iron, without which he could not have endured the trials he has since undergone, and still retain his health and physical powers unworn.

At this time a new field opened before him. The civil war broke out, and being a Southern man, he enlisted in the Confederate army. This was a kind of service just adapted to his peculiar character, one in which a man with the courage, daring, energy, promptness and indomitable will that he possessed, was sure to win fame and promotion. But before he had time to exhibit these qualities, fate, that seemed against him to human eyes, again advanced him a step toward success by causing him to be taken prisoner by the Union troops. As a prisoner he was worthless, and the Union cause really having his sympathies, he proposed to enlist in the Northern army.

Whether the military authorities were afraid of this sudden conversion or not daring to give too much freedom of action to one who showed by his whole bearing and language, that there was no undertaking too daring for him to attempt, we are not told, but they put him where he would probably have little chance to show what stuff he was made of, and he was placed on the iron-clad ship Ticonderoga. It is said, he was released as prisoner and volunteered to enlist in the navy. Be that as it may, though totally unfit for service of any kind on board of a man-of-war, he soon became acting ensign.

At the close of the war he looked about for some field of active service, and what little war he had seen seemed to fit his peculiar character, and hearing that the Cretans were about to attempt to throw off the Turkish yoke, he resolved to join them. He proceeded thither with two other Americans, after having first made an engagement with the New York Herald, as its correspondent. Disgusted, it is said, with the insurgent leaders, he abandoned his purpose, and having a sort of roving commission from Mr. Bennett, he determined to travel in the East. But he and his fellow-travelers were attacked by Turkish brigands, and robbed of all their money and clothing. They laid their complaint before Mr. Morris, then our minister at Constantinople, who in turn laid it before the Turkish government, and at the same time advanced them funds to supply their wants.

After various journeyings Stanley returned to England. Here a strong desire seized him to visit the place of his nativity in Wales, the house where he was born, and the humble dwelling where he received the first rudiments of his education at St. Asaph. One can imagine the feelings with which this bronzed young man, who had traveled so far and wide, entered the quiet valley from which he had departed so long ago to seek his fortune. It speaks well for his heart, that his sympathies turned at once toward the poor-house of which he had been an inmate in his childhood. Remembering that the greatest boon that could have been conferred at that time on him would have been a good, generous dinner, he resolved to give those poor children one. The daring young adventurer, in the presence of those simple, wonderstruck children, would have made a noble subject for a picture. We venture to say that Mr. Stanley enjoyed that unobtrusive meal in that quiet Welsh valley more than he has ever enjoyed a banquet with nobles and princes; and as the shadows of life lengthen he will look back on it with more real pleasure. He addressed the little ones of the Institution, giving them a familiar talk, telling them that he was once one of that household, accompanying his words with good advice, saying for their encouragement, and to stimulate them to noble endeavors, that all he had been in the past and all he hoped to be in the future, he attributed to the education which was begun in that poor-house.

This was a real episode in his eventful life, and, though it doubtless soon passed away in the more stirring scenes on which he entered, yet the remembrance of it still lingers around that quiet, retired Welsh valley, and, to-day, the name of Stanley is a household word there, and is the pride and glory of its simple inhabitants. And

4

as time goes on and silvers those dark hairs, and the "almond-tree flourishes" and "desire fails because man goeth to his long home," he, too, will remember it as a green oasis he once longed to see and found in the arid desert.

In 1867, when he was twenty-seven years of age, he returned to the United States and, in the next year, accompanied the English army in its campaign against Theodore, king of Abyssinia, which was set on foot to revenge the wrongs this tyrant had committed against the subjects and representatives of the British government. Stanley went as correspondent of the New York Herald, and gave a vivid and clear account of the painful march and skirmishes up to the last great battle in the king's stronghold, where, with a gallant dash, the fortress was taken, the king killed and the war ended. With that promptness in acting, which is one of his chief characteristics, he at once dispatched the news of the victory and the ending of the campaign to London, outstripping the government dispatches sent by the commander-in-chief, so that one morning the readers of the London newspapers knew that of which the government was ignorant. This, of course, was a genuine surprise. A young American newspaper correspondent, without a vessel at his command, had, nevertheless, by his enterprise, beaten the government messenger, and steady old conservative England was disgusted to find its time-honored custom reversed, which was that the government should first give notice of successes to the public, leaving to newspaper correspondents to fill up the minor details. But an enterprising young American had furnished the important news, leaving the British government the secondary duty of supplying these details. Notwithstanding the admiration of the enterprise that had accomplished this great feat, there was a ludicrous aspect to the affair, in the position in which it placed official personages, that raised a quiet laugh on both continents. Stanley's letters contain the best history of that expedition that has been written. This was still another onward step in the great work before him, of which he, as yet had no intimation.

The next year, 1868, he returned to the United States, and in the following year was sent by the Herald into Spain, to follow the fortunes of the civil war there, as correspondent. Like everything else that he undertook, he performed his duties more than faithfully. Exposure, danger, hardships, nothing interfered when there was a prospect of acquiring valuable information. It mattered not to him whether he was on the margin or in the vortex of battle— he never thought of anything but the object before him and toward which he bent all his energies. His letters from the seat of war not only gave the best description of the battles fought and of the military position of affairs, but, also, of the political state of the kingdom. But while he was here, considering himself fixed down for an indefinite period, for Spain is proverbial for the protracted duration of its civil wars, Mr. Bennett, in Paris, was planning an expedition to go in search of Dr. Livingstone, buried, alive or dead, somewhere in the heart of Africa. The sympathies of everybody were enlisted in his fortunes, yet the British government, though he had done so much to enhance the fame of his native country, refused to stir a step toward ascertaining his fate, discovering his whereabouts, or relieving him if in want.

The Royal Geographical Society, ashamed of the apathy and indifference of the government, had started a subscription to raise funds from private sources to defray the expenses of an expedition to go in search of him. In the meantime this American editor, scorning alike state patronage or private help, conceived the bold project of finding him himself. Looking around for a suitable leader to command an expedition, his eye rested upon Stanley in Spain. And here should be noted the profound sagacity of Mr. Bennett in selecting such a leader for this desperate expedition, that was to go no one knew where, and end no one knew how.

Most people thought it was a mammoth advertisement of the New York Herald, nothing more. If he was in earnest why did he not select some one of the many African explorers who were familiar with the regions of Central Africa, and had explored in the vicinity of where Livingstone was, by the best judges, supposed to be, if alive? Men, for instance, like Speke, Baker, Burton, Grant and others. This certainly would have given great eclat to the expedition, and, if it failed in its chief object, would unquestionably have furnished new facts for the geographer and the man of science. But to send one who made no pretensions to science, no claims to be a meteorologist, botanist, geologist, or to be familiar with astronomical calculations, all of which are indispensable to a great explorer, seemed absurd.

But Mr. Bennett had no intention of making new scientific or geographical discoveries. He had but one object in view—to find Dr. Livingstone—and on the true Napoleonic system of selecting the best man to accomplish a single object, he, with Napoleonic sagacity, fixed on Stanley. The celebrated men who would have given greater distinction to the enterprise would, doubtless, divide up their time and resources between scientific research and the chief object of the expedition, and thus cause delays that might defeat it; or, with more or less of the martinet about them, push their researches only to a reasonable extent and be content with reports instead of personal investigation. But he wanted a man who

6

had but one thing to do, and not only that, but a man who would accomplish the errand on which he was sent or die in the attempt. This was to be no mere well-regulated expedition, that was to turn back when all reasonable efforts had been made. It was one that, if desperate straits should come, would resort to desperate means, and he knew that with Stanley at its head this would be done. He knew that Stanley would fetch out Livingstone, dead or alive, or leave his own bones to bleach in the depths of Africa. Stanley was comparatively young, it was true, and had always accompanied, never led, expeditions. He knew nothing of Africa, or how an expedition should be organized or furnished—it mattered not. Bennett knew he had resources within himself—nerves that never flinch, courage that no amount of danger could daunt, a will that neither an African fever nor a wasted form could break down, and a resolution of purpose that the presence of death itself could not shake, while, to complete all, he had a quickness and accuracy of judgment in a perilous crisis, followed by equally quick and right action, which would extricate him out of difficulties that would overwhelm men who had all his courage, will and energy, but were slower in coming to a decision.

This latter quality is one of the rarest ever found even in the strongest men; to think quick and yet think right, to come to a right decision as if by impulse, is a power few men possess. To go swift and yet straight as the cannon ball or lightning's flash, gives to any man's actions tenfold power. In this lay the great secret of Napoleon's success. His campaigns were started, while those of others were under discussion, and the thunder and tumult of battle cleared his preceptions and judgment so that no unexpected disaster could occur that he was not ready to meet. This quickness and accuracy of thought and action is one of the prominent characteristics of Stanley, and more than once saved his life and his expedition.

On the 16th day of October, 1869, as he was sitting in his hotel at Madrid, having just returned from the carnage of Valencia, a telegram was handed him. The thunder of cannon and tumult of battle had scarce ceased echoing in his ear when this telegram startled him from his reverie: "Come to Paris on important business." In a moment all was hurry and confusion, his books and pictures were packed, his washed and unwashed clothes were stowed away, and in two hours his trunks were strapped and labeled "Paris." The train started at 3 o'clock, and he still had some time to say good-bye to his friends, and here by mere accident comes out one of the most pleasing traits of his character. Of the friends he is thus to leave, he merely refers to those of the American legation, but dwells with regret on the farewell he must give to two little children, whom he calls his "fast friends." Like a sudden burst of sunlight on a landscape, this unconscious utterance reveals a heart as tender as it is strong, and increases our interest in the man quite as much as in the explorer. At 3 o'clock he was thundering on toward Paris, ready, as he said, to go to the battle or the banquet, all the same. His interview with Mr. Bennett reveals the character of both these men so clearly that we give it in Stanley's own words:

"At 3 P. M. I was on my way, and being obliged to stop at Bayonne a few hours, did not arrive at Paris until the following night. I went straight to the 'Grand Hotel,' and knocked at the door of Mr. Bennett's room.

"'Come in,' I heard a voice say. Entering, I found Mr. Bennett in bed.

"'Who are you?' he asked.

"'My name is Stanley,' I answered.

"'Ah, yes, sit down; I have important business on hand for you.'

"After throwing over his shoulders his robe de chambre, Mr. Bennett asked: 'Where do you think Livingstone is?'

"'I really do not know, sir.'

"'Do you think he is alive?'

"'He may be, and he may not be,' I answered.

"'Well, I think he is alive, and that he can be found, and I am going to send you to find him.'

"'What,' said I, 'do you really think I can find Dr. Livingstone? Do you mean me to go to Central Africa?'

"'Yes; I mean that you shall go and find him, wherever you hear that he is, and get what news you can of him; and, perhaps'—delivering himself thoughtfully and deliberately—'the old man may be in want. Take enough with you to help him, should he require it. Of course, you will act according to your own plans, and you will do what is best—but find Livingstone!'

"Said I, wondering at the cool order of sending one to Central Africa to search for a man whom I, in common with most other men, believed to be dead: 'Have you considered seriously the great expense you are liable to incur on account of this little journey?'

"'What will it cost?' he asked abruptly.

"'Burton and Speke's journey to Central Africa cost between £3,000 and £5,000, and I fear it cannot be done under £2,500.'

"'Well, I will tell you what you will do. Draw a thousand pounds now, and when you have gone through that, draw another thousand, and when that is spent draw another thousand, and when you have finished that draw another thousand, and so on—but find Livingstone!'

"Surprised, but not confused, at the order, for I knew that Mr. Bennett, when he had once made up his mind, was not easily drawn aside from his purpose, I yet thought, seeing it was such a gigantic scheme, that he had not quite considered in his own mind the pros and the cons of the case, I said: 'I have heard that, should your father die, you would sell the Herald, and retire from business.'

"'Whoever told you so is wrong, for there is not money enough in the United States to buy the New York Herald. My father has made it a great paper, but I mean to make it a greater. I mean, that it shall be a newspaper in the true sense of the word; I mean that it shall publish whatever news may be useful to the world, at no matter what cost.'

"'After that,' said I, 'I have nothing more to say. Do you mean me to go straight on to Africa to search for Dr. Livingstone?'

"'No; I wish you to go to the inauguration of the Suez Canal first, and then proceed up the Nile. I hear Baker is about starting for Upper Egypt. Find out what you can about his expedition, and, as you go up, describe, as well as possible, whatever is interesting for tourists, and then write up a guide—a practical one—for Lower Egypt; tell us about whatever is worth seeing, and how to see it.

"'Then you might as well go to Jerusalem; I hear that Captain Warren is making some interesting discoveries there. Then visit Constantinople, and find out about the khedive and sultan.

"'Then—let me see—you might as well visit the Crimea and those old battle-grounds. Then go across the Caucasus to the Caspian Sea. I hear there is a Russian expedition bound for Khiva. From thence you may get through Persia to India; you could write an interesting letter from Persepolis.

"'Bagdad will be close on your way to India; suppose you go there and write up something about the Euphrates Valley Railway. Then, when you have come to India, you may go after Dr. Livingstone. Probably you will hear by that time that Livingstone is on his way to Zanzibar; but, if not, go into the interior and find him, if alive. Get what news you can; and if you find that he is dead, bring all possible proofs you can of his being dead. That is all. Good-night, and God be with you.'

"'Good-night, sir,' I said, 'what is in the power of human nature I will do; and on such an errand as I go upon, God will be with me.'

"I lodged with young Edward King, who is making such a name in New England. He was just the man who would have delighted to tell the journal he was engaged upon what young Mr.

Bennett was doing, and what errand I was bound upon. I should have liked to exchange opinions with him upon the probable results of my journey, but dared not do so. Though oppressed with the great task before me, I had to appear as if only going to be present at the Suez Canal. Young King followed me to the express train bound for Marseilles, and at the station we parted—he to go and read the newspapers at Bowles's Reading-room, I to Central Africa and—who knows? There is no need to recapitulate what I did before going to Central Africa."

He started on his travels, and we hear of him first in Constantinople, from our minister there, Mr. Morris, who had relieved him and his companions when plundered by Turkish brigands. One of Mr. Stanley's traveling companions who had been robbed with himself, accused him, in a published letter, of dishonesty regarding the money our minister had advanced. It is not necessary to go into this accusation or a refutation of it now. It is sufficient to say that Mr. Morris declared the whole charge false, and as the shortest and most complete refutation of such a charge, we give Mr. Morris's own views of Mr. Stanley:

"The uncouth young man whom I first knew had grown into a perfect man of the world, possessing the appearance, the manners and the attributes of a perfect gentleman. The story of the adventures which he had gone through and the dangers he had passed during his absence, were perfectly marvelous, and he became the lion of our little circle. Scarcely a day passed but he was a guest at my table, and no one was more welcome, for I insensibly grew to have a strong attachment for him myself." In speaking further on of his projected travels, he said he advised him to go to Persia, which Stanley suddenly came to the conclusion to follow out. "He therefore," he says, "busied himself in procuring letters of introduction to the Russian authorities in the Caucasus, in Georgia and in other countries through which he would have to pass."

This is quite enough to put to rest the scandal, which at one time produced quite a sensation, that Stanley had cheated Mr. Morris and misappropriated the funds advanced by him. No explanations are required after this indorsement.

Of this long and hazardous journey, the columns of the Herald gave all the principal details. There is nothing in them that illustrates the peculiar characteristics of Stanley more than, or even so much as, his subsequent acts, hence his brief summary of this tour, that seems to have had no definite object whatever, except to give the correspondent of the Herald something to do, until the proper moment to start on the expedition for Livingstone, is, perhaps, the best account that could be given, so far as the general reader is concerned. All we can say is, it seems a very roundabout way in which to commence such an expedition.

"I went up the Nile and saw Mr. Higginbotham, chief engineer in Baker's expedition, at Philæ, and was the means of preventing a duel between him and a mad young Frenchman, who wanted to fight Mr. Higginbotham with pistols, because Mr. Higginbotham resented the idea of being taken for an Egyptian through wearing a fez cap. I had a talk with Captain Warren at Jerusalem, and descended one of the pits with a sergeant of engineers to see the marks of Tyrian workmen on the foundation-stones of the Temple of Solomon. I visited the mosques of Stamboul with the minister resident of the United States, and the American consul-general. I traveled over the Crimean battle-grounds with Kinglake's glorious books for reference. I dined with the widow of General Liprandi, at Odessa. I saw the Arabian traveler, Palgrave, at Trebizond, and Baron Nicolay, the civil governor of the Caucasus, at Tiflis. I lived with the Russian embassador while at Teheran, and wherever I went through Persia I received the most hospitable welcome from the gentlemen of the Indo-European Telegraph Company; and, following the example of many illustrious men, I wrote my name upon one of the Persepolitan monuments. In the month of August, 1870, I arrived in India."

In completing this sketch of Mr. Stanley's life and character, it is necessary only to add that his after career fully justified the high estimate Mr. Bennett had placed on his extraordinary qualities. These were tested to their utmost extent in his persistent, determined search after the man he was sent to find. But we believe that Livingstone, when found, with whom Stanley passed some months, exerted a powerful influence on the character which we have attempted to portray. Stanley was comparatively young, full of life and ambition, with fame, greater probably than he had ever anticipated, now within his reach. Yet, here in the heart of Africa, he found a man well on in years, of a world-wide fame, yet apparently indifferent to it.

This man who had spent his life in a savage country, away from home and all the pleasures of civilized society, who expected to pass the remnant of his days in the same isolated state, was looking beyond this life. He was forgetting himself, in the absorbing purpose to benefit others. Fame to him was nothing, the welfare of a benighted race everything. This was a new revelation to the ambitious young man. Hitherto he had thought only of himself, but here was a man, earnest, thoughtful, sincere, who was living to carry out a great idea—no less than the salvation of a continent—nay more than this, who was working not for himself, but for a Master,

11

and that Master, the God of the universe. He remained with him in close companionship for months, and intimate relations with a man borne up by such a lofty purpose, inspired by such noble feelings, and looking so far away beyond time for his reward, could not but have an important influence on a man with Stanley's noble and heroic qualities. It was a new revelation to him. He had met, not a successful, bold explorer, but a Christian, impelled and sustained by the great and noble idea of regenerating a race and honoring the God of man and the earth. Such a lengthened companionship with a man of this character could but lift Stanley to a higher plane, and inspire him with a loftier purpose than that of a mere explorer.

But while this expedition brought out all the peculiar traits we have spoken of, yet his later expedition developed qualities which circumstances had not previously shown. When from this he emerged on the Atlantic coast with his company, he was hailed with acclamations and a British vessel was placed at his disposal in which to return home. But the ease and comfort offered him, and the applause awaiting him, were nothing compared with the comfort and welfare of the savage band that had for so long a time been his companions and his only reliance in the perils through which he had passed. True, they had often been intractable, disobedient and trustless, but still they had been his companions in one of the most perilous marches ever attempted by man, and with that large charity that allowed for the conduct of these untutored, selfish animals of the desert, he forgot it all and would do nothing, think of nothing, till their wants were supplied and their welfare secured. He would see them safe back to the spot from which he took them, and did, before he took care of himself. A noble nature there asserted itself, and we doubt not that every one of those poor ignorant savages would go to the death for that brave man to whom their own welfare was so dear.

In this sketch of Mr. Stanley, as it appears to us from the record of his life, we have omitted to notice those faults which are incident to poor human nature, in whatever person it is enshrined. But perhaps this is as good a place as any to notice the charge brought against him by some persons in the English press, of having killed natives, not in self-defense but to carry out his explorations; they asserting that neither for fame nor science, nor for any other motive, had a man a right to take the life of his fellow-man. Without going into an argument on this point, or bringing forward the circumstances of this particular case, leaving that to be explained in the narrative, as it will appear in subsequent pages, we wish simply to say that the philanthropy and Christianity, in behalf of which the charge is made, is pure Pharisaism. Those writers asserted that life should be taken only in self-defense. But in their eyes it is right, from mere covetousness to seize territory in India, and thus provoke the rightful owners to rise in defense of their own, which act converts them into assailants that must be killed in self-defense.

But this man having passed through friendly territory, suddenly finds himself stopped by hostile savages, who declare that he must retrace his three months' journey and turn back, not because they are to be despoiled of their land, or wronged in their persons, but from mere savage maliciousness and hate. Mr. Stanley quietly insists on continuing his journey, desiring no conflict, but finding them determined to kill him and break up his expedition, he anticipates their movements and shoots down some of them, and lo, these writers who defend the slaughter of tens of thousands of men in India, so that England may enjoy her wholesale robbery, nay, who threaten Europe with bloody war at the mere hint that others may want to share her unjust possessions—these writers call on the English people to refuse to give Stanley a public reception, because he killed a half-dozen savages who wanted to kill him. He should have waited, they say, till they fired the first shot; as he did not his conduct should be investigated by the philanthropic subjects of Her Majesty the Queen.

CHAPTER II

DESCRIPTION OF AFRICA

All there was of civilization in the world was found at one time in Africa. Art and science had their home there, while now as a whole it is regarded as the most benighted and barbarous portion of the earth and is, not inaptly, called "the dark continent." With a breadth at the equator of four thousand five hundred miles, with the exception of thin lines of sea-coast on each side, this vast space has been as much unknown as the surface of a distant planet. The Barbary States and Egypt on the Mediterranean and Red Seas, some Portuguese settlements on the Indian Ocean, the English and Dutch colonies of South Africa, a few trading ports and the English and American colonies in Guinea, constituted Africa, so far as the

13

knowledge of the civilized world went. And yet within these outer rims lay real Africa, and there lived its immense population.

The vast Desert of Sahara on the north, stretching down to the equator, presented an impenetrable barrier to explorers entering from that direction, while along the eastern and western coasts they were beaten back by savage tribes or fell victims to the diseases of the country. Matted forests, wild beasts and venomous reptiles were added to the other obstacles that beset their path, so that only now and then an adventurous explorer penetrated the continent itself.

The Nile, piercing to the equator, seemed the most natural avenue by which to enter this region, but the slave hunters by their cruelty, and the petty wars they had engendered among the various tribes, made the presence of a white man in their midst the occasion of hostile demonstrations. The lofty mountains and broad rivers that came out of this vast unknown region added to the mysterious interest that enveloped it. Though certain death awaited the daring traveler who endeavored to penetrate far into the interior, fresh victims were found ready to peril their lives in the effort to solve the mystery of Central Africa. The paths of these travelers, when traced on the map, appears like mere punctures of the great continent. Missionary effort could only effect a lodgment along the coast, while colonies remained stationary on the spot where they were first planted.

Although holding the entire southern portion the English colony could make but little headway against the tribes that confronted them on the north. The most adventurous men urged not by curiosity or desire of knowledge, but cupidity, penetrated the farthest into the interior, but, instead of throwing light on those dark places, they made them seem more dark and terrible by the miserable naked and half-starved wretches they brought out to civilization, to become more wretched still by the life of slavery to which they were doomed.

Hence it could not be otherwise than that the name of white man should be associated with everything revolting and cruel, and that his presence among these wild barbarians should awaken feelings of vengeance. A white man, to those inland tribes, represented wrong and cruelty alone. The very word meant separation of wives, and husbands, and families, and carrying away to a doom whose mystery only enhanced its actual horrors. Hence the white man's rapacity and cruelty put an effectual bar to his curiosity and enterprise. The love of knowledge and physical science was thwarted by the love of sin and wrong, and the civilized world, instead of wondering at the ignorance and barbarity that kept back all research and all benevolent effort, should wonder that any one

14

bearing the slightest relationship to the so-called outside civilized world, should have been allowed to exist for a day where these wronged, outraged savages bore sway.

It is not a little singular that the first real encroachment of these forbidden regions was not made by daring explorers either for adventure or geographical knowledge, or to extend commerce, but by a poor missionary, whose sole object was to get the Gospel introduced among these uncounted millions of heathen. Livingstone really broke the spell that hung over tropical Africa, and set on foot movements that are to work a change in the continent more important and momentous than the imagination of man can at present conceive.

It is the tropical region of Africa that gives birth to its largest rivers, is covered by its most magnificent forests, is crossed by its loftiest mountains, and where dwell its teeming millions. And this is the unknown part of the continent and the central point toward which all explorers press.

This tropical Africa extends from about ten degrees above to ten degrees below the equator, and from ten to thirty-five east longitude, or in round numbers, nearly a thousand miles above and below the equator, to two thousand or more east and west between these parallels of latitudes. With an ordinary map before him, and with Zanzibar on the east and Congo on the west as great landmarks, the reader will get a very clear idea of the ground aimed at and touched, or pierced and crossed by the more recent explorers, and the thorough final explorations of which will unlock the hidden mystery of Africa, and open all there is of interest to both the Christian and commercial world. That to the former there is a field to be occupied that will tax the self-sacrifice and benevolence of the Christian world, there can be no doubt; while to the commercial world a field of equal magnitude and importance will be laid open.

From the mere punctures into the borders of this unknown land, and the two slight trails recently made across it, there remains no doubt that from sixty to one hundred millions of men are here living in the lowest and most degraded condition of heathenism, while the country is burdened with those articles which the commercial world needs and can make of vast benefit to man.

A glance at the map will reveal what a vast territory remains to be explored and what a mighty population exists there, yet to come into contact with the civilized world. It is probable that that unexplored region between the equator and the great Desert of Sahara will reveal even greater wonders than have yet been discovered.

It is a little strange that the enterprise and the curiosity of man should urge him to make repeated costly and vain attempts to reach the north pole, where there are neither inhabitants nor articles of commerce, while one of the largest continents on our globe, crowded with people and rich in the very products most needed by man, should be allowed to remain so long a sealed book.

What little of Africa has been traversed reveals untold wealth waiting the enterprising hand of commerce to bring it forth to civilization. A partial list of the products of this rich country will show what a mine of wealth it is destined to be. Sugar-cane, cotton, coffee, oil palm, tobacco, spices, timber, rice, wheat, Indian corn, India rubber, copal, hemp, ivory, iron, copper, silver, gold and various other articles of immense value are found here, and some of them in the greatest profusion.

Thus it will be seen that this vast continent, which from creation seemed destined only to be the abode of wild beasts and reptiles, and of man as wild and savage as the animals amid which he dwelt, and who when brought into contact with civilization becomes more debased, if possible, by the bondage in which he is kept, contains almost everything that civilization needs, and in a future which now seems near, it will be traversed by railroads and steamboats, and the solitudes that have echoed for thousands of years to the howl of wild beasts and the yells of equally wild men, will resound with the hum of peaceful industry and the rush and roar of commerce. The miserable hut will give way to commodious habitations, and the disgusting rites of heathenism to the worship of the true God. Reaching to the temperate zones, north and south, it presents every variety of climate and yields every variety of vegetation. What effect the great revolution awaiting this continent will have on the destiny of the world, none can tell. He would have been considered a mad prophet who would have predicted one-half of the changes that the discovery of the American continent, less than four hundred years ago, has wrought. None can doubt that the Creator of these continents had some design in letting this one, which constitutes nearly a fourth part of our planet, remain in darkness and mystery and savage debasement so long, and now, by the effort of one missionary, cause it to be thrown open to the world.

CHAPTER III

STANLEY'S SEARCH FOR LIVINGSTONE

We have seen how suddenly Mr. Stanley was called from Spain, to take charge of an expedition in search of Livingstone, how he was sent to see Baker who was about to enter Africa from the north, and how he was first sent east. But the time came at last for him to enter upon his work in earnest, and he sailed from Bombay, on the 12th of October, for Zanzibar. On board the barque was a Scotchman, named Farquhar, acting as first mate. Taking a fancy to him, Stanley engaged him to accompany the expedition to find Livingstone.

Nearly three months later, on the 6th of January, he landed at Zanzibar, one of the most fruitful islands of the Indian Ocean, rejoicing in a sultan of its own. It is the great mart to which come the ivory, gum, copal, hides, etc., and the slaves of the interior. Stanley immediately set about preparing for his expedition. The first things to decide were: How much money is required? How many pigeons as carriers? How many soldiers? How much cloth? How many beads? How much wire? What kinds of cloth is required for the different tribes?

After trying to figure this out from the books of other travelers, he decided to consult an Arab merchant who had fitted out several caravans for the interior. In a very short time he obtained more information than he had acquired from books in his long three months' voyage from India.

Money is of no use in the heart of Africa. Goods of various kinds are the only coin that can purchase what the traveler needs, or pay the tribute that is exacted by the various tribes. He found that forty yards of cloth per day would keep one hundred men supplied with food. Thus, three thousand six hundred and fifty yards of cloth would support one hundred men twelve months. Next to cloths, beads were the best currency of the interior. Of these he purchased twenty sacks of eleven varieties in color and shape. Next came the brass wire, of which he purchased three hundred and fifty pounds, of about the thickness of telegraph wire. Next came the provisions and outfit of implements that would be needed—medicines, arms, donkeys, and last of all, men.

A man by the name of Shaw, a native of England, who came to Zanzibar as third mate of an American ship, from which he was discharged, applied for work, and was engaged by Stanley in getting what he needed together and to accompany him on the expedition. He agreed to give him three hundred dollars per annum, and placed him next in rank to Farquhar. He then cast about for an escort of twenty men. Five who had accompanied Speke, and were called "Speke's Faithfuls," among whom, as a leader, was a man named Bombay, were first engaged. He soon got together eighteen more men as soldiers, who were to receive three dollars a month. Each was to have a flint-lock musket, and be provided with two hundred rounds of ammunition. Bombay was to receive eighty dollars a year, and the other "faithfuls" forty dollars.

Knowing that he was to enter a region of vast inland lakes, and that much delay and travel might be avoided by the possession of a large boat, he purchased one and stripped it of all its covering, to make the transportation easier. He also had a cart constructed to fit the goat-paths of the interior and to aid in transportation.

When all his purchases were completed and collected together, he found that the combined weight would be about six tons. His cart and twenty donkeys would not suffice for this, and so the last thing of all, was to procure carriers, or pagosi, as they were called. He himself was presented with a blooded bay horse by an American merchant at Zanzibar, named Gordhue, formerly of Salem.

On the 4th of February, 1871, twenty-eight days from his arrival at Zanzibar, Mr. Stanley's equipment was completed and he set sail for Bagomayo, twenty-five miles distant on the mainland, from which all caravans start for the interior, and where he was to hire his one hundred and forty or more pagosi or carriers. He was immediately surrounded with men who attempted in every way to fleece him, and he was harassed, and betrayed and hindered on every side. But, at length, all difficulties were overcome—the goods packed in bales weighing seventy-two pounds each—the force divided into five caravans, and in six weeks after he entered Bagomayo, Stanley himself was ready to start. The first caravan had departed February 18th; the second, February 21st; the third, February 25th; the fourth, on March 11th, and the last on March 21st. All told, the number comprised in all the caravans of the "Herald Expedition," was one hundred and ninety.

It was just seventy-three days after Stanley landed at Zanzibar, that he passed out of Bagomayo on his bay horse, with his last caravan, accompanied by twenty-eight carriers and twelve soldiers, under Bombay, while his Arab boy, Selim, the interpreter, had charge of the cart and its load.

Out through a narrow lane shaded by trees, they passed, the American flag flying in front, and all in the highest spirits. Stanley had left behind him the quarreling, cheating Arabs, and all his troubles with them. The sun, speeding to the west, was beckoning him on; his heart beat high with hope and ambition; he had taken a new departure in life, and with success would come the renown he so ardently desired. He says, "loveliness glowed around me; I saw fertile fields, rich vegetation, strange trees; I heard the cry of cricket and pewit, and jubilant sounds of many insects, all of which seemed to tell me, 'you are started.' What could I do but lift up my face toward the pure, glowing sky, and cry, 'God be thanked?'"

The first camp was three miles and a half distant. The next three days were employed in completing the preparations for the long land journey and for meeting the rainy season, now very near, and on April 4th, a start was made for Unyanyembe, the great half-way house, which he resolved to reach in three months.

The road was a mere foot-path, leading through fields in which naked women were at work, who looked up and laughed and giggled as they passed. Passing on, they entered an open forest, abounding in deer and antelope. Reaching the turbid Kingemi, a bridge of felled trees was soon made; Stanley, in the meantime amusing himself with shooting hippopotami, or rather shooting at them, for his small bullets made no more impression on their thick skulls than peas would have done. Crossing to the opposite shore, he found the traveling better. They arrived at Kikoka, a distance of but ten miles, at 5 o'clock in the afternoon, having been compelled to unload the animals during the day, to cross the river and mud pools. This was slow marching, and at this rate of speed it would take a long time to reach the heart of Africa. The settlement was a collection of rude huts. Though bound to the same point that Speke and Burton had reached, Ujiji, Stanley took a different route from them, and one never traveled by a white man before.

On the 27th, he left this place and moved westward over a rolling, monotonous country, until they came to Rosako, the province of Ukwee. Just before his departure the next morning, Magonga, the leader of the fourth caravan, came up and told him that three of his carriers were sick, and asked for some medicine. He found the three men in great terror, believing they were about to die, and crying out like children, "Mama, mama." Leaving them, with orders to hurry on as soon as possible, he departed. The country everywhere was in a state of nature except in the neighborhood of villages. Sheltered by the dense forests, he toiled on but was so anxious about the fourth caravan left behind that, after marching nine miles he ordered a halt and made a camp. It soon swarmed with insects, and he set to work to examine them and see if they were the tsetsé, said to be fatal to horses in Africa. Still waiting for the caravan, he went hunting, but soon found himself in such an impenetrable jungle and swamp, filled with alligators, that he resolved never to make the attempt again. The second and third days passing without the arrival of the caravan, he sent Shaw and Bombay back after it, who brought it up on the fourth day. Leaving it to rest in his own camp, he pushed on five miles to the village of Kingaru, set in a deep, damp, pestiferous-looking hollow, surrounded by pools of water. To add to the gloominess of the scene, a pouring rain set in, which soon filled their camping-place with lakelets and rivulets of water. Toward evening the rain ceased, and the villagers began to pour in with their vendibles. Foremost was the chief, bringing with him three measures of matama and a half a measure of rice, which he begged Stanley to accept. The latter saw through the trickery of this meagre present, in offering which the chief called him the "rich sultan." Stanley asked him why, if he was a rich sultan, the chief of Kingaru did not bring him a rich present, that he might give him a rich one in return. "Ah," replied the blear-eyed old fox, "Kingaru is poor, there is no matama in the village." "Well," said Stanley, "if there is no matama in the village, I can give but a yard of cloth," which would be equivalent to his present. Foiled in his sharp practice the chief had to be content with this.

At this place he lost one of his horses. The burial of the carcass not far from the encampment, raised a terrible commotion in the village, and the inhabitants assembled in consultation as to how much they must charge him for burying a horse in their village without permission, and soon the wrinkled old chief was also at the camp, and the following dialogue took place, which is given as an illustration of the character of the people with whom he was to have a year's trading intercourse:

White Man—"Are you the great chief of Kingaru?"

Kingaru—"Huh-uh—yes."

W. M.—"The great, great chief?"

Kingaru—"Huh-uh—yes."

W. M.—"How many soldiers have you?"

Kingaru—"Why?"

W. M.—"How many fighting men have you?"

Kingaru—"None."

W. M.—"Oh! I thought you might have a thousand men with you, by your going to fine a strong white man who has plenty of guns and soldiers two doti for burying a dead horse."

Kingaru (rather perplexed)—"No; I have no soldiers. I have only a few young men."

W. M.—"Why do you come and make trouble, then?"

20

Kingaru—"It was not I; it was my brothers who said to me, 'Come here, come here, Kingaru, see what the white man has done! Has he not taken possession of your soil, in that he has put his horse into your ground without your permission? Come, go to him and see by what right!' Therefore have I come to ask you who gave you permission to use my soil for a burying-ground?"

W. M.—"I want no man's permission to do what is right. My horse died; had I left him to fester and stink in your valley, sickness would visit your village, your water would become unwholesome, and caravans would not stop here for trade; for they would say, 'This is an unlucky spot, let us go away.' But enough said; I understand you to say you do not want him buried in your ground; the error I have fallen into is easily put right. This minute my soldiers shall dig him out again and cover up the soil as it was before, and the horse shall be left where he died." (Then shouting to Bombay). "Ho, Bombay, take soldiers with jeinbes to dig my horse out of the ground; drag him to where he died and make everything ready for a march to-morrow morning."

Kingaru, his voice considerably higher and his head moving to and fro with emotion, cries out, "Akuna, akuna, Bana"—no, no, master. "Let not the white man get angry. The horse is dead and now lies buried; let him remain so, since he is already there, and let us be friends again."

The matter had hardly been settled, when Stanley heard deep groans issuing from one of the animals. On inquiry, he found that they came from the bay horse. He took a lantern and visited him, staying all night and working to save his life. It was in vain—in the morning he died, leaving him now without any horse, which reduced him to donkey riding. Three days passed, and the lagging caravan had not come up. In the meantime, one of his carriers deserted, while sickness attacked the camp, and out of his twenty-five men, ten were soon on the sick list. On the 4th, the caravan came up, and on the following morning was dispatched forward, the leader being spurred on with the promise of a liberal reward if he hurried to Unyanyembe. The next morning, to rouse his people, he beat an alarm on a tin pan, and before sunrise they were on the march, the villagers rushing like wolves into the deserted camp to pick up any rags or refuse left behind. The march of fifteen miles to Imbike showed a great demoralization in his men, many of them not coming up till nightfall. One of the carriers had deserted on the way, taking with him a quantity of cloth and beads. The next morning, before starting, men were sent in pursuit of him. They made that day, the 8th, but ten miles to Msuwa. Though the journey was short, it was the most fatiguing one of all. As it gives a vivid description of the difficulties experienced in traveling through this country, we quote Stanley's own language:

"It was one continuous jungle, except three interjacent glades of narrow limits, which gave us three breathing pauses in the dire task of jungle-traveling. The odor emitted from its fell plants was so rank, so pungently acrid, and the miasma from its decayed vegetation so dense, that I expected every moment to see myself and men fall down in paroxysms of acute fever. Happily this evil was not added to that of loading and unloading the frequently falling packs. Seven soldiers to attend seventeen laden donkeys, were entirely too small a number while passing through a jungle; for while the path is but a foot wide, with a wall of thorny plants and creepers bristling on each side, and projecting branches darting across it, with knots of spiky twigs, stiff as spike-nails, ready to catch and hold anything above four feet in height, it is but reasonable to suppose that donkeys, standing four feet high, with loads measuring across, from bale to bale, four feet, would come to grief.

"This grief was of frequent recurrence here, causing us to pause every few minutes for re-arrangements. So often had this task to be performed, that the men got perfectly discouraged, and had to be spoken to sharply before they would set to work. By the time I reached Msuwa, there was nobody with me and the ten donkeys I drove but Mabruk, who perseveringly, though generally stolid, stood to his work like a man. Bombay and Uledi were far behind with the most jaded donkeys. Shaw was in charge of the cart, and his experiences were most bitter, as he informed me he had expended the whole vocabulary of stormy abuse known to sailors, and a new one which he had invented ex tempore. He did not arrive until two o'clock next morning, and was completely worn out. Truly, I doubt if the most pious divine, in traveling through that long jungle, under those circumstances, with such oft-recurring annoyances, Sisyphean labor, could have avoided cursing his folly for coming hither."

A halt was made here, that men and animals might recuperate. The chief of this village was "a white man in everything but color," and brought him the choicest mutton. He and his subjects were intelligent enough to comprehend the utility of his breech-loading guns, and by their gestures illustrated their comprehension of the deadly effects of those weapons in battle.

On the 10th, somewhat recuperated, the caravan left this hospitable village and crossed a beautiful little plain, with a few cultivated fields, from which the tillers stared in wonder at the unwonted spectacle it presented. But here Stanley met one of those sights common in that part of the world, but which, it is to be hoped, will soon be seen no more. It was a chained slave-gang, bound east. He says the slaves did not appear to be in the least down-hearted, on the contrary, they were jolly and gay. But for the chains, there was no difference between master and slave. The chains were heavy, but as men and women had nothing else to carry, being entirely naked, their weight, he says, could not have been insupportable.

He camped at 10 A. M., and fired two guns, to show they were ready to trade with any of the natives in the region. The halting-place was Kisemo, only twelve miles from Msuwa which was the centre of a populous district, there being no less than five villages in the vicinity fortified by stakes and thorny abattis, as formidable, in their way, as the old fosse and draw-bridge of feudal times. "The belles of Kisemo," he says, "are of gigantic posterioral proportions," and are "noted for their variety in brass wire, which is wound in spiral rings round their wrists and ankles, and for the varieties of style which their wisped heads exhibit; while their poor lords, obliged to be contented with dingy, torn clouts and split ears, show what wide sway Asmodeus holds over this terrestrial sphere—for it must have been an unhappy time when the hard besieged husbands gave way before their hotly-pressing spouses. Besides these brassy ornaments on their extremities, the women of Kisemo frequently wear lengthy necklaces, which run in rivers of colors down their black bodies." But a more comical picture is seldom presented than that of one of those highly-dressed females, "with their huge posterior development, while grinding out corn. This is done in a machine very much like an old-fashioned churn, except the dasher becomes a pestle and the churn a mortar. Swaying with the pestle, as it rises and falls, the breast and posteriors correspond to the strokes of the dasher in a droll sort of sing-song, which gave to the whole exhibition the drollest effect imaginable."

A curious superstition of the natives was brought to light here by Shaw removing a stone while putting up his tent. As he did so, the chief rushed forward, and putting it back in its place, solemnly stood upon it. On being asked what was the matter, he carefully lifted it, pointed to an insect pinned by a stick to the ground, which he said had been the cause of a miscarriage of a female of the village.

In the afternoon the messengers came back with the deserter and all the stolen goods. Some of the natives had captured him and were about to kill him and take the goods, when the messengers came up and claimed both. He was given up, his captors being content with receiving a little cloth and a few beads in return. Stanley, with great sagacity, caused the thief to be tried by the other

23

carriers, who condemned him to be flogged. They were ordered to carry out their own sentence, which they did amid the yells of the culprit.

Before night a caravan arrived, bringing, among other things, a copy of the Herald, containing an account of a Presidential levee in Washington, in which the toilette of the various ladies were given. While engrossed in reading in his tent, Stanley suddenly became aware that his tent-door was darkened, and looking up, he saw the chief's daughters gazing with wondering eyes on the great sheets of paper he was scanning so closely. The sight of these naked beauties, glittering in brass wire and beads, presented a ludicrous contrast to the elaborately-dressed belles of whom he had been reading in the paper, and made him feel, by contrast, in what a different world he was living.

On the 12th, the caravan reached Munondi, on the Ungerangeri River. The country was open and beautiful, presenting a natural park, while the roads were good, making the day's journey delightful. Flowers decked the ground, and the perfume of sweet-smelling shrubs filled the air. As they approached the river, they came upon fields of Indian corn and gardens filled with vegetables, while stately trees lined the bank. On the 14th, they crossed the river and entered the Wakami territory. This day and the next the road lay through a charming country. The day following, they marched through a forest between two mountains rising on either side of them, and on the 16th reached the territory of Wosigahha. As he approached the village of Muhalleh he was greeted with the discharge of musketry. It came from the fourth caravan, which had halted here. Here also good news awaited him. An Arab chief, with a caravan bound east, was in the place, and told him that he had met Livingstone at Ujiji, and had lived in the next hut to him for two weeks. He described him as looking old, with long, gray mustache and beard, just recovered from illness, and looking very wan. He said, moreover, that he was fully recovered, and was going to visit a country called Monyima. This was cheering news, indeed, and filled Stanley's heart with joy and hope. The valley here, with its rich crops of Indian corn, was more like some parts of the fertile west than a desert country. But the character of the natives began to change. They became more insolent and brutal, and accompanied their requests with threats.

Continuing their journey along the valley of the river, they suddenly, to their astonishment, came upon a walled town containing a thousand houses. It rose before them like an apparition with its gates and towers of stone and double row of loop-holes for musketry. The fame of Stanley had preceded him, being carried by the caravans he had dispatched ahead, and a thousand or more of the inhabitants came out to see him. This fortified town was established by an adventurer famous for his kidnapping propensities. A barbaric orator, a man of powerful strength and of cunning address, he naturally acquired an ascendency over the rude tribes of the region, and built him a capital, and fortified it and became a self-appointed sultan. Growing old, he changed his name, which had been a terror to the surrounding tribes, and also the name of his capital, and just before death, bequeathed his power to his eldest daughter, and in her honor named the town Sultana, which name it still bears. The women and children hung on the rear of Stanley's caravan, filled with strange curiosity at sight of this first white man they had ever seen, but the scorching sun drove them back one by one, and when Stanley pitched his camp, four miles farther on, he was unattended. He determined to halt here for two days to overhaul his baggage and give the donkeys, whose backs had become sore, time to recuperate. On the second day, he was attacked with the African fever, similar to the chills and fever of the west and southwest. He at once applied the remedies used in the Western States, using powerful doses of quinine, and in three days he pronounced himself well again.

CHAPTER IV

WILD EXPERIENCES

Stanley had now traveled one hundred and nineteen miles in fourteen marches, occupying one entire month lacking one day, and making, on an average, four miles a day. This was slow work. The rainy season now set in, and day after day it was a regular downpour. Stanley was compelled to halt, while disgusting insects, beetles, bugs, wasps, centipedes, worms and almost every form of the lower animal life, took possession of his tent, and gave him the first real taste of African life.

On the morning of the 23d of April, he says the rain held up for a short time and he prepared to cross the river, now swollen and turbid. The bridge over which he carried his baggage was of the most primitive kind, while the donkeys had to swim. The passage

25

occupied five hours, yet it was happily accomplished without any casualties. Reloading his baggage and wringing out his clothes, he set out again, leaving the river and following a path that led off in a northerly direction.

With his heart light and cheerful by being once more on the march and out of the damp and hateful valley, which was made still more hateful by the disgusting insect life that filled his tent, he ascended to higher ground, and passed with his caravan through successive glades, which opened one after another between forest clumps of trees hemmed in distantly by isolated peaks and scattered mountains. "Now and then," he says, "as we crested low eminences, we caught sight of the blue Usagara Mountains, bounding the horizon westerly and northerly, and looked down on a vast expanse of plain which lay between. At the foot of the lengthy slope, well watered by bubbling springs and mountain rills, we found a comfortable Khembi with well-made huts, which the natives call Simbo. It lies just two hours, or five miles, northwest from the Ungerengeri crossing."

We here get incidentally the rapidity with which he traveled, where the face of the country and the roads gave him the greatest facilities for quick marching, two "hours or five miles," he says, which makes his best time two and a half miles an hour. In this open, beautiful country no villages or settlements could be seen, though he was told there were many in the mountain inclosures, the inhabitants of which were false, dishonest and murderous.

On the morning of the 24th, as they were about to leave, Simbo, his Arab cook, was caught for the fifth time pilfering, and it being proved against him, Stanley ordered a dozen lashes to be inflicted on him as a punishment, and Shaw was ordered to administer them. The blows being given through his clothes, did not hurt him much, but the stern decree that he, with his donkey and baggage, should be expelled from camp and turned adrift in the forests of Africa, drove him wild, and leaving donkey and everything else, he rushed out of camp and started for the mountains. Stanley, wishing only to frighten him, and having no idea of leaving the poor fellow to perish at the hands of the natives, sent a couple of his men to recall him. But it was of no use; the poor, frightened wretch kept on for the mountains, and was soon out of sight altogether. Believing he would think better of it and return, his donkey was tied to a tree near the camping-ground, and the caravan started forward and having passed through the Makata Valley, which afterward became of sorrowful memory, it halted at Rehenneko at the base of the Usagara Mountains.

This valley is a wilderness covered with bamboo, and palm,

26

and other trees, with but one village on its broad expanse, through which the hartbeest, the antelope and the zebra roam. In the lower portions, the mud was so deep that it took ten hours to go ten miles, and the company was compelled to encamp in the woods when but half-way across. Bombay with the cart did not get in till near midnight, and he brought the dolorous tale that he had lost the property-tent, an axe, besides coats, shirts, beads, cloth, pistol and hatchet and powder. He said he had left them a little while that he might help lift the cart out of a mud-hole and during his absence they disappeared. This told to Stanley at midnight roused all his wrath, and he poured a perfect storm of abuse on the cringing Arab, and he took occasion to overhaul his conduct from the start. The cloth if ever found, he said, would be spoiled, the axe, which would be needed at Ujiji to construct a boat, was an irreparable loss, to say nothing of the pistol, powder and hatchet, and worse than all, he had not brought back the cook, whom he knew there was no intention to abandon, and Stanley then and there told him he would degrade him from office and put another man in his place, and then dismissed him, with orders to return at daylight and find the missing property. Four more were now dispatched after the missing cook, and Stanley halted three days to wait the return of his men. In the meantime, provisions ran low, and though there was plenty of game, it was so wild that but little could be obtained, he being able to secure but two potfuls in two days' shooting, but these were quail, grouse and pigeons. On the fourth day, becoming exceedingly anxious, he dispatched Shaw and two more soldiers after the missing men. Toward night he returned, sick with ague, bringing the soldiers with him, but not the missing cook. The soldiers reported that they had marched immediately back to Simbo and having searched in vain in the vicinity for the missing man, they went to the bridge over the river to inquire there. They were told, so they said, that a white donkey had crossed the river in another place driven by some Washensi. Believing the cook had been murdered by those men who were making off with his property, they hastened to the walled town and told the warriors of the western gate that two Washensi, who had murdered a man belonging to the white man, must have passed the place, with a white donkey. They were immediately conducted to the sultana, who had much of the spirit of her father, to whom they told their story. Of the results, Stanley says:

"The sultana demanded of the watchmen of the towers if they had seen the two Washensi with the white donkey. The watchmen answered in the affirmative, upon which she at once dispatched twenty of her musketeers in pursuit to Muhalleh. These returned before night, bringing with them the two Washensi and the donkey, with the cook's entire kit. The sultana, who is evidently possessed of her father's energy, with all his lust for wealth, had my messengers, the two Washensi, the cook's donkey and property at once brought before her. The two Washensi were questioned as to how they became possessed of the donkey and such a store of Kisunga clothes, cloth and beads; to which they answered that they had found the donkey tied to a tree with the property on the ground close to it; that seeing no owner or claimant anywhere in the neighborhood, they thought they had a right to it, and accordingly had taken it with them. My soldiers were then asked if they recognized the donkey and property, to which questions they unhesitatingly made answer that they did. They further informed Her Highness that they were not only sent after the donkey, but also after the owner, who had deserted their master's service; that they would like to know from the Washensi what they had done with him. Her Highness was also anxious to know what the Washensi had done with the Hindi, and accordingly, in order to elicit the fact, she charged them with murdering him, and informed them she but wished to know what they had done with the body.

"The Washensi declared most earnestly that they had spoken the truth, that they had never seen any such man as described; and if the sultana desired, they would swear to such a statement. Her Highness did not wish them to swear to what in her heart she believed to be a lie, but she would chain them and send them in charge of a caravan to Zanzibar to Lyed Burghosh, who would know what to do with them. Then turning to my soldiers, she demanded to know why the Musungu had not paid the tribute for which she had sent her chiefs. The soldiers could not answer, knowing nothing of such concerns of their master's. The heiress of Kisabengo, true to the character of her robber sire, then informed my trembling men that, as the Musungu had not paid the tribute, she would now take it; their guns should be taken from them, together with that of the cook; the cloth and beads found on the donkey she would also take, the Hindi's personal clothes her chiefs should retain, while they themselves should be chained until the Musungu himself should return and take them by force.

"And as she threatened, so was it done. For sixteen hours my soldiers were in chains in the market-place, exposed to the taunts of the servile populace. It chanced the next day, however, that Sheikh Thani, whom I met at Kingaru, and had since passed by five days, had arrived at Limbamwanni, and proceeding to the town to purchase provisions for the crossing of the Makata wilderness, saw my men in chains and at once recognized them as being in my employ. After hearing their story, the good-hearted sheikh sought the presence of the sultana, and informed her that she was doing very wrong—a wrong that could only terminate in blood. 'The Musungu is strong,' he said, 'very strong. He has got ten guns which shoot forty times without stopping, carrying bullets half an hour's distance; he has got several guns which carry bullets that burst and tear a man in pieces. He could go to the top of that mountain and kill every man, woman and child in the town before one of your soldiers could reach the top. The road will then be stopped, Lyed Burghosh will march against your country, the Wadoe and Wakami will come and take revenge on what is left; and the place that your father made so strong will know the Waseguhha no more. Set free the Musungu's soldiers; give them their food and grain for the Musungu; return the guns to the men and let them go, for the white man may even now be on his way here.'

"The exaggerated report of my power, and the dread picture sketched by the Arab sheikh, produced good effect, inasmuch as Kingaru and the Mabrukis were at once released from durance, furnished with food sufficient to last our caravan four days, and one gun with its accoutrements and stock of bullets and powder, was returned, as well as the cook's donkey, with a pair of spectacles, a book in Malabar print and an old hat which belonged to one whom we all now believed to be dead. The sheikh took charge of the soldiers as far as Simbo; and it was in his camp, partaking largely of rice and ghee, that Shaw found them, and the same bountiful hospitality was extended to him and his companions."

Stanley was now filled with keen regrets for the manner in which he had punished the cook, and mentally he resolved that no matter what a member of his caravan should do in the future he would never drive him out of camp to perish by assassins. Still he would not yet believe that the man was murdered. But he was furious at the treatment of his soldiers by the black Amazon of Limbamwanni, and the tribute she exacted, especially at the seizure of the guns, and if he had been near the place would have made reprisals. But he had already lost four days, and so, next morning, although the rain was coming down in torrents, he broke camp and set forth. Shaw was still sick, and so the whole duty of driving the floundering caravan devolved upon himself. As fast as one was flogged out of the mire in which he had stuck, another would fall in. It took two hours to cross the miry plain, though it was but a mile and a half wide. He was congratulating himself on having at last got over it, when he was confronted by a ditch which the heavy rains had converted into a stream breast deep. The donkeys had all to be unloaded, and led through the torrent, and loaded again on the farther side. They had hardly got under way when they came upon another stream, so deep that it could not be forded, over which they had to swim, and float across their baggage. They then floundered on until they came to a bend of the river, where they pitched their camp, having made but six miles the whole day. This River Makata is only about forty feet in width in the dry season, but at this time it was a wide, turbid stream. Its shores, with its matted grass, decayed vegetable matter and reeking mists, seemed the very home of the ague and fever. It took five hours to cross it the next morning. The rain then came down in such torrents that traveling became impossible, and the camp was pitched. Luckily this proved the last day of the rainy season.

It was now the 1st of May, and the expedition was in a pitiable plight. Shaw was still sick, and one man was down with the small-pox. Bombay, too, was sick, and others complaining. Doctoring the sick as well as he knew how, and laying the whip lustily on the backs of those who were shamming, Stanley at length got his caravan in motion and began to cross the Makata plain, now a swamp thirty-five miles broad. It was plash, plash, through the water in some places three or four feet deep, for two days, until they came in sight of the Rudewa River. Crossing a branch of this stream, a sheet of water five miles broad stretched out before the tired caravan. The men declared it could not be crossed, but Stanley determined to try, and after five hours of the most prostrating effort they reached dry ground. The animals, however, began to sicken from this day on, while Stanley himself was seized with dysentery caused by his exposure, and was brought to the verge of the grave. The expedition seemed about to end there on the borders of the Makata swamp.

On the 4th, they came to the important village of Rehenneko, the first near which they had encamped since entering the district of Usagara. It was a square, compact village, of about one thousand inhabitants, surrounded by a mud wall and composed of cane-topped huts, which the natives moved from place to place at pleasure. The peculiar ceremonies of the queen's court were very interesting to witness. They rested here four days to recruit. On the 8th, they started forward and began to ascend the mountain. Having reached the summit of the first range of hills, Stanley paused to survey the enchanting prospect. The broad valley of Makata stretched out before him, laced with streams sparkling in the sun, while over it waved countless palm-trees, and far away, blue in the distance, stretched a mighty range of mountains. "Turning our faces west," he says, "we found ourselves in a mountain world, fold rising above fold, peak behind peak, cone jostling cone; away to the north, to the west, to the south, the mountain tops rolled away like so many vitrified waves, not one adust or arid spot was visible in all this scene."

The change from the pestilential swamps, through which they had been so long floundering, was most grateful, but the animals suffered greatly, and before they reached their first camping-ground, two had given out. The 9th, they descended into the valley of Mukondokno, and there struck the road traversed by Speke and Burton in 1817. Reaching the dirty village, Kiora, Stanley found there his third caravan, led by Farquhar. By his debaucheries on the way he had made himself sick and brought his caravan into a sad condition. As he heard Stanley's voice, he came staggering out of his tent, a bloated mass of human flesh that never would have been recognized as the trim mate of the vessel that brought Stanley from India. After he examined him as to the cause of his illness, he questioned him about the condition of the property intrusted to his care. Not able to get an intelligent answer out of him, he resolved to overhaul the baggage. On examination, he found that he had spent enough for provisions on which to gormandize to have lasted eight months, and yet he had been on the route but two and a half months. If Stanley had not overtaken him, everything would have been squandered, and of all the bales of cloth he was to take to Unyanyembe not one bale would have been left. Stanley was sorely puzzled what to do with the miserable man. He would die if left at Kiora; he could not walk or ride far, and to carry him seemed well-nigh impossible.

On the 11th, however, the two caravans started forward, leaving Shaw to follow with one of the men. But he lagged behind, and had not reached the camp when it was roused next morning. Stanley at once dispatched two donkeys, one for the load that was on the cart and the other for Shaw, and with the messenger the following note: "You will, upon the receipt of this order, pitch the cart into the nearest ravine, gully or river, as well as all the extra pack saddles; and come at once, for God's sake, for we must not starve here." After waiting four hours, he went back himself and met them, the carrier with the cart on his head, and Shaw on the donkey, apparently ready, at the least jolt, to tumble off. They, however, pushed on, and arrived at Madete at four o'clock. Crossing the river about three, and keeping on, they, on the 14th, from the top of a hill caught sight of Lake Ugenlo. The outline of it, he says, resembles England without Wales. It is some three miles long by two wide, and is the abode of great numbers of hippopotami, while the buffalo, zebra, boar and antelope come here by night to quench their thirst. Its bosom is covered with wild fowl of every description. Being obliged to halt here two days on account of the desertion of the

31

cooper, with one of the carbines, Stanley explored the lake, and tried several shots at the lumbering hippopotami without effect.

The deserter having returned of his own free will, the caravan started forward, cursed by the slow progress of the peevish, profane and violent Shaw. The next day at breakfast, a scene occurred that threatened serious consequences. When Shaw and Farquhar took their places, Stanley saw by their looks that something was wrong. The breakfast was a roast quarter of goat, stewed liver, some sweet potatoes, pancakes and coffee. "Shaw," said Stanley, "please carve and serve Farquhar." Instead of doing so, he exclaimed, in an insulting tone, "What dog's meat is this?" "What do you mean?" demanded Stanley. "I mean," replied the fellow, "that it is a downright shame the way you treat us," and then he complained of being compelled to walk and help himself, instead of having servants to wait upon him as he was promised. All this was said in a loud, defiant tone, interlarded with frequent oaths and curses of the "damned expedition," etc. When he had got through, Stanley, fixing his black, resolute eye on him, said: "Listen to me, Shaw, and you, Farquhar, ever since you left the coast have had donkeys to ride. You have had servants to wait upon you; your tents have been set up for you; your meals have been cooked for you; you have eaten with me of the same food I have eaten; you have received the same treatment I have received. But now all Farquhar's donkeys are dead; seven of my own have died, and I have had to throw away a few things, in order to procure carriage for the most important goods. Farquhar is too sick to walk, he must have a donkey to ride; in a few days all our animals will be dead, after which I must have over twenty more pagosi to take up the goods or wait weeks and weeks for carriage. Yet, in the face of these things, you can grumble, and curse, and swear at me at my own table. Have you considered well your position? Do you realize where you are? Do you know that you are my servant, sir, not my companion?"

"Servant, be ——" said he.

Just before Mr. Shaw could finish his sentence he had measured his length on the ground.

"Is it necessary for me to proceed further to teach you?" said Stanley.

"I tell you what it is, sir," he said, raising himself up, "I think I had better go back. I have had enough, and I do not mean to go any farther with you. I ask my discharge from you."

"Oh, certainly. What—who is there? Bombay, come here."

After Bombay's appearance at the tent-door, Stanley said to him: "Strike this man's tent," pointing to Shaw; "he wants to go back. Bring his gun and pistol here to my tent, and take this man and his baggage two hundred yards outside of the camp, and there leave him."

In a few minutes his tent was down, his gun and pistol in Stanley's tent, and Bombay returned to make his report, with four men under arms.

"Now go, sir. You are at perfect liberty to go. These men will escort you outside of camp, and there leave you and your baggage."

He walked out, the men escorting him and carrying his baggage for him.

After breakfast, Stanley explained to Farquhar how necessary it was to be able to proceed; that he had had plenty of trouble, without having to think of men who were employed to think of him and their duties; that, as he (Farquhar) was sick, and would be probably unable to march for a time, it would be better to leave him in some quiet place, under the care of a good chief, who would, for a consideration, look after him until he got well. To all of which Farquhar agreed.

Stanley had barely finished speaking before Bombay came to the tent-door, saying: "Shaw would like to speak to you."

Stanley went out to the door of the camp, and there met Shaw, looking extremely penitent and ashamed. He commenced to ask pardon, and began imploring to be taken back, and promising that occasion to find fault with him again should never arise.

Stanley held out his hand, saying: "Don't mention it, my dear fellow. Quarrels occur in the best of families. Since you apologize, there is an end of it."

That night, as Stanley was about falling asleep, he heard a shot, and a bullet tore through the tent a few inches above his body. He snatched his revolver and rushed out from the tent, and asked the men around the watch-fires, "Who shot?" They had all jumped up, rather startled by the sudden report.

"Who fired that gun?"

One said the "Bana Mdogo"—little master.

Stanley lit a candle and walked with it to Shaw's tent.

"Shaw, did you fire?"

There was no answer. He seemed to be asleep, he was breathing so hard.

"Shaw! Shaw! did you fire that shot?"

"Eh—eh?" said he, suddenly awakening; "me?—me fire? I have been asleep."

Stanley's eye caught sight of his gun lying near him. He seized it—felt it—put his little finger down the barrel. The gun was warm; his finger was black from the burnt gunpowder.

"What is this?" he asked, holding his finger up; "the gun is warm; the men tell me you fired."

"Ah—yes," he replied, "I remember it. I dreamed I saw a thief pass my door, and I fired. Ah—yes—I forgot, I did fire. Why, what's the matter?"

"Oh, nothing," said Stanley. "But I would advise you, in future, in order to avoid all suspicion, not to fire into my tent; or, at least, so near me. I might get hurt, you know, in which case ugly reports would get about, and that, perhaps, would be disagreeable, as you are probably aware. Good-night."

All had their thoughts about this matter, but Stanley never uttered a word about it to any one until he met Livingstone. The doctor embodied his suspicions in the words: "He intended murder!"

Mr. Livingstone was evidently right in his conjecture, and Mr. Stanley wrong about the intent of Shaw. In the first place, the coincidence in time between the punishment inflicted on Shaw and this extraordinary shot, in which the ball took the still more extraordinary direction of going through Stanley's tent, that is, to say the least, very difficult to explain. In the second place, his drowsy condition when questioned, and finally remembering so much as that he dreamed a thief was passing his door, is more than suspicious. The fact that, as Mr. Stanley says, he could have had much better opportunities of killing him than this, we regard of very little weight. Opportunities that are absolutely certain of success without suspicion or detection, are not so common as many suppose. Besides, an opportunity so good that the would-be murderer could desire nothing better might occur, and yet the shot or stab not prove fatal. In this case it doubtless never occurred to this man that any one would run his finger down his gun-barrel to see if it was hot from a recent discharge, while no man could tell, in the middle of the night, who fired the shot. It is true, that the wretch knew that the chances were against such a random fire proving fatal, but he knew it was better to take them than the almost certain discovery if he adopted any other method. If, for instance, he had in a lonely place fired at Stanley and the shot had not proved mortal, or if mortal, not immediately so, he well knew what would have been his fate, in the heart of Africa, where justice is administered without the form of law.

On the 16th of May the little caravan started off again, and after a march of fifteen miles, camped at Matamombo, in a region where monkeys, rhinoceros, steinboks and antelopes abounded. The next day's march extended fifteen miles, and was through an almost impenetrable jungle. Here he came upon the old Arab sheikh,

Thani, who gave him the following good advice: "Stop here two or three days, give your tired animals some rest, and collect all the carriers you can; fill your insides with fresh milk, sweet potatoes, beef, mutton, ghee, honey, beans, matama, madeira nuts, and then, Inshalla! we shall go through Ugogo without stopping anywhere." Stanley was sensible enough to take this advice. He at once commenced on this certainly very prodigal bill of fare for Central Africa. How it agreed with him after the short trial of a single day, may be inferred from the following entry in his diary:

"Thank God! after fifty-seven days of living upon matama porridge and tough goat, I have enjoyed with unctuous satisfaction a real breakfast and a good dinner."

Here upon the Mpwapwa, he found a place to leave the Scotchman, Farquhar, until he should be strong enough to join him at Unyanyembe. But when he proposed this to the friendly chief, he would consent only on the condition that he would leave one of his own men behind to take care of him. This complicated matters, not only because he could not well spare a man, but because it would be difficult to find one who would consent to undertake this difficult task. This man, whom Stanley had thought would be a reliable friend and a good companion in his long, desolate marches, had turned out a burden and a nuisance. His wants were almost endless, and instead of using the few words in the language of the natives to make them known, he would use nothing but the strongest Anglo-Saxon, and when he found he was not understood, would fall to cursing in equally good round English oaths, and if the astonished natives did not understand this, relapse into regular John Bull sullenness. When, therefore, Stanley opened up the subject to Bombay, the latter was horrified. He said the men had made a contract to go through, not to stop by the way; and when Stanley, in despair, turned to the men, they one and all refused absolutely to remain behind with the cursing, unreasonable white man, one of them mimicking his absurd conduct so completely, that Stanley himself could not help laughing. But the man must be left behind, and somebody must take care of him; and so Stanley had to use his authority, and notwithstanding all his protestations and entreaties, Sako, the only one who could speak English, was ordered to stay.

Having engaged twelve new carriers, and from the nearest mountain summit obtained an entrancing view of the surrounding region for a hundred miles, he prepared to start, but not before, notwithstanding the good milk it furnished, giving Mpwapwa a thorough malediction for its earwigs. "In my tent," he says, "they might be counted by thousands; in my slung cot by hundreds; on my clothes they were by fifties; on my neck and head they were by

35

scores. The several plagues of locusts, fleas and lice sink into utter insignificance compared with this damnable one of earwigs." Their presence drove him almost insane. Next to these come the white ants, that threatened in a short time to eat up every article of baggage.

He now pushed on toward the Ugogo district, famous for the tribute it exacted from all caravans.

CHAPTER V

TRIALS BY THE WAY

On the 22d of May the two other caravans of Stanley joined him, only three hours' march from Mpwapwa, so that the one caravan numbered some four hundred souls, but it was none too large to insure a safe transit through dreaded Ugogo. A waterless desert thirty miles across, and which it would take seventeen hours to traverse, now lay before them. On the way, Stanley was struck down with fever and, borne along in a hammock, was indifferent to the herds of giraffes, and zebras, and antelopes that scoured the desert plain around him. The next morning the fever had left him and mounting, he rode at the head of his caravan, and at 8 A. M. had passed the sterile wilderness and entered the Ugogo district. He had now come into a land of plenty, but one also of extortion. The tribute that all passing caravans had to pay to the chiefs or sultans of this district was enormous. At the first village the appearance of this white man caused an indescribable uproar. The people came pouring out, men and women, naked, yelling, shouting, quarreling and fighting, making it a perfect babel around Stanley, who became irritated at this unseemly demonstration. But it was of no use. One of his men asked them to stop, but the only reply was "shut up," in good native language. Stanley, however, was soon oblivious of their curiosity or noise, as heavy doses of quinine to check a chill sent him off into a half doze.

The next day, a march of eight miles brought him to the sultan of the district. Report did not exaggerate the abundance of provisions to be found here. Now came the pay of tribute to the exorbitant chief. After a great deal of parley, which was irritating and often childish, Stanley satisfied the sultan's greed, and on the 27th of May he shook the dust of the place from his feet and pushed westward. As he passed the thickly-scattered villages and plenteous fields, filled with tillers, he did not wonder at the haughty bearing of the sultan, for he could command force enough to rob and destroy every caravan that passed that way. Twenty-seven villages lined the road to the next sultan's district, Matomhiru. This sultan was a modern Hercules, with head and shoulders that belonged to a giant. He proved, however, to be a much more reasonable man than the last sultan, and, after a little speechifying, the tribute was paid and the caravan moved off toward Bihawena. The day was hot, the land sterile, crossed with many jungles, which made the march slow and difficult. In the midst of this desolate plain were the villages of the tribe, their huts no higher than the dry, bleached grass that stood glimmering in the heat of the noonday sun. Here he was visited by three natives, who endeavored to play a sharp game on him, which so enraged Stanley that he would have flogged them out of camp with his whip, but one of his men told him to beware, for every blow would cost three or four yards of cloth. Not willing to pay so dearly to gratify his temper he forbore. The sultan was moderate in his demands, and from him he received news from his fourth caravan, which was in advance, and had had a fight with some robbers, killing two of them.

The water here was so vile that two donkeys died from drinking of it, while the men could hardly swallow it. Stanley, nervous and weak from fever, paid the extravagant tributes demanded of him, without altercation. From here to the next sultan was a long stretch of forest, filled with elephants, rhinoceros, zebras, deer, etc. But they had no time to stop and hunt. At noon they had left the last water they should find until noon of the next day, even with sharp marching, and hence, no delay could be permitted. The men without tents bivouacked under the trees, while Stanley tossed and groaned all night in a paroxysm of fever, but his courage in no way weakened. At dawn the caravan started off through the dark forest, in which one of the carriers fell sick and died.

At 7 A. M. they drew near Nyambwa, where excellent water was found. The villagers here crowded around them with shouts and yells, and finally became so insolent that Stanley grabbed one of them by the neck and gave him a sound thrashing with his donkey-whip. This enraged them, and they walked backward and forward like angry tom-cats, shouting, "Are the Wagogo to be beaten like slaves?" and they seemed by their ferocious manner determined to avenge their comrade, but the moment Stanley raised his whip and advanced they scattered. Finding that the long lash, which cracked like a pistol, had a wholesome effect, whenever they crowded upon him so as to impede his progress, he laid it about him without mercy, which soon cleared a path.

The Sultan Kimberah was a small, queer and dirty old man, a great drunkard, and yet the most powerful of all the Ugogo chiefs. Here they had considerable trouble in arranging the amount of tribute, but at length everything was settled and the caravan passed on and entered on a vast salt plain containing a hundred or more square miles, from the salt springs of which the Wagogo obtained their salt. At Mizarza, the next camping-place, Stanley was compelled to halt and doctor himself for the fever which was wearing him to skin and bones. Early in the morning he began to take his quinine, and kept repeating the doses at short intervals until a copious perspiration told him he had broken the fever which had been consuming him for fourteen days. During this time, the sultan of the district, attracted by Stanley's lofty tent, with the American flag floating above it, visited him. He was so astonished at the loftiness and furnishing of the tent, that in his surprise he let fall the loose cloth that hung from his shoulders and stood stark naked in front of Stanley, gaping in mute wonder. Admonished by his son—a lad fifteen years old—he resumed his garb and sat down to talk. Stanley showed him his rifles and other fire-arms, which astonished him beyond measure.

On the 4th of June, the caravan was started forward again, and after three hours' march it came upon another district, containing only two villages occupied by pastoral Wahumba and Wahehe. These live in cow-dung cone huts, shaped like Tartar tents. Stanley says:

"The Wahumba, so far as I have seen them, are a fine and well-formed race. The men are positively handsome, tall, with small heads, the posterior parts of which project considerably. One will look in vain for a thick lip or flat nose amongst them; on the contrary, the mouth is exceedingly well cut, delicately small; the nose is that of the Greeks, and so universal was the peculiar feature, that I at once named them the Greeks of Africa. Their lower limbs have not the heaviness of the Wagogo and other tribes, but are long and shapely, clean as those of an antelope. Their necks are long and slender, on which their small heads are poised most gracefully. Athletes from their youth, shepherd bred, and intermarrying among themselves, thus keeping the race pure, any of them would form a fit subject for a sculptor who would wish to immortalize in marble an Antrinus, a Hylas, a Daphnis, or an Apollo. The women are as beautiful as the men are handsome. They have clear ebon skins, not coal black, but of an inky hue. Their ornaments consist of spiral

38

rings of brass pendent from the ears, brass ring collars about the neck, and a spiral cincture of brass wire about their loins, for the purpose of retaining their calf and goat skins, which are folded about their bodies, and depending from the shoulder, shade one-half of the bosom, and fall to the knees.

"The Wahehe may be styled the Romans of Africa.

"Resuming our march, after a halt of an hour, in four hours more we arrived at Mukondoku proper.

"This extremity of Ugogo is most populous. The villages which surround the central tembe, where the Sultan Swaruru lives, amount to thirty-six. The people who flocked from these to see the wonderful men whose faces were white who wore the most wonderful things on their persons, and possessed the most wonderful weapons: guns which 'bum-bummed' as fast as you could count on your fingers, formed such a mob of howling savages, that I, for an instant, thought there was something besides mere curiosity which caused such a commotion, and attracted such numbers to the roadside. Halting, I asked what was the matter, and what they wanted, and why they made such a noise? One burly rascal, taking my words for a declaration of hostilities, promptly drew his bow, but as prompt as he had fixed his arrow my faithful Winchester with thirteen shots in the magazine was ready and at my shoulder, and but waited to see the arrow fly to pour the leaden messengers of death into the crowd. But the crowd vanished as quickly as they had come, leaving the burly Thersites, and two or three irresolute fellows of his tribe, standing within pistol range of my leveled rifle. Such a sudden dispersion of the mob which, but a moment before, was overwhelming, caused me to lower my rifle and indulge in a hearty laugh at the disgraceful flight of the men-destroyers. The Arabs, who were as much alarmed at their boisterous obtrusiveness, now came up to patch a truce, in which they succeeded to everybody's satisfaction.

"A few words of explanation, and the mob came back in greater numbers than before; and the Thersites who had been the cause of the momentary disturbance were obliged to retire abashed before the pressure of public opinion. A chief now came up, whom I afterwards learned was the second man to Swaruru, and lectured the people upon their treatment of the 'white strangers.'"

The tribute-money was easily settled here. On the 7th of June, the route was resumed. There were three roads leading to Uyanzi, and which of the three to take caused long discussion and much quarreling, and when Stanley settled the matter and the caravan started off on the road to Kiti, an attempt was made to direct it to another road, which Stanley soon discovered and prevented only by his prompt resort to physical arguments.

At last they reached the borders of Uyanzi, glad to be clear of the land of Ugogo, said to be flowing with milk and honey but which had proved to Stanley a land of gall and bitterness. The forest they entered was a welcome change from the villages of the Ugogo, and two hours after leaving them they came, with the merry sound of horns, to a river in a new district. Continuing on, they made the forest ring with cheers, and shouts, and native songs. The country was beautiful, and the scenery more like cultivated England in former times than barbaric Africa.

Passing thus merrily on, they had made twenty miles by five o'clock. At one o'clock next morning the camp was roused, and by the light of the moon the march was resumed, and at three o'clock they arrived at a village to rest till dawn. They had reached a land of plenty and fared well. Kiti was entered on the 10th of June. Here cattle and grain could be procured in abundance.

A valley fifteen miles distant was the next camp, and a march of three hours and a half brought them to another village, where provisions were very cheap. They were now approaching Unyanyembe, their first great stopping-place, and where the term of service of many of Stanley's men expired. They marched rapidly now,—to-day through grain-fields, to-morrow past burnt villages, the wreck of bloody wars.

At last, with banners flying and trumpets and horns blowing, and amid volleys of small arms, the caravan entered Unyanyembe.

Of the three routes from the coast to this place, Stanley discarded the two that had before been traveled by Speke and Burton and Grant and chose the third, with the originality of an American, and thus saved nearly two hundred miles' travel.

Mr. Stanley, after reaching this first great objective point, goes back and gives a general description of the regions he has traversed. To the geographer, it may be of interest, but not to the general reader. But the following, taken from his long account, will give the reader a clear idea of the country traversed and of its inhabitants. Beginning with Wiami River, emptying into the Indian Ocean near Zanzibar, he says:

"First it appears to me that the Wiami River is available for commerce and, by a little improvement, could be navigated by light-draft steamers near to the Usagara Mountains, the healthy region of this part of Africa, and which could be reached by steamers in four days from the coast, and then it takes one into a country where ivory, sugar, cotton, indigo and other productions can be obtained."

Besides, he says:

"Four days by steamer bring the missionary to the healthy uplands of Africa, where he can live amongst the gentle Wasagara without fear or alarm; where he can enjoy the luxuries of civilized life without fear of being deprived of them, amid the most beautiful and picturesque scenes a poetic fancy could imagine. Here is the greenest verdure, purest water; here are valleys teeming with grain-stalks, forests of tamarind, mimosa, gum-copal tree; here is the gigantic moule, the stately mparamnsi, the beautiful palm; a scene such as only a tropic sky covers. Health and abundance of food are assured to the missionary; gentle people are at his feet, ready to welcome him. Except civilized society, nothing that the soul of man can desire is lacking here.

"From the village of Kadetamare a score of admirable mission sites are available, with fine health-giving breezes blowing over them, water in abundance at their feet, fertility unsurpassed around them, with docile, good-tempered people dwelling everywhere at peace with each other, and with all travelers and neighbors.

"As the passes of the Olympus unlocked the gates of the Eastern empires to the hordes of Othman; as the passes of Kumaylé and Sura admitted the British into Abyssinia; so the passes of the Mukondokwa may admit the Gospel and its beneficent influences into the heart of savage Africa.

"I can fancy old Kadetamare rubbing his hands with glee at the sight of the white man coming to teach his people the words of the 'Mulungu'—the Sky Spirit; how to sow, and reap, and build houses; how to cure their sick, how to make themselves comfortable—in short, how to be civilized. But the missionary, to be successful, must know his duties as well as a thorough sailor must know how to reef, hand and steer. He must be no kid-glove, effeminate man, no journal writer, no disputatious polemic, no silken stole and chasuble-loving priest, but a thorough, earnest laborer in the garden of the Lord,—a man of the David Livingstone, or of the Robert Moffatt stamp.

"The other river, the Rufiji, or Ruhwha, is a still more important stream than Wiami. It is a much longer river, and discharges twice as much water into the Indian Ocean. It rises near some mountains about one hundred miles southwest of Nbena. Kisigo River, the most northern and most important affluent of the Ruhwha, is supposed to flow into it near east longitude thirty-five degrees; from the confluence to the sea, the Ruhwha has a length of four degrees of direct longitude. This fact, of itself, must prove its importance and rank among the rivers of East Africa.

"After Zanzibar, our début into Africa is made via Bagomayo. At this place we may see Wangindo, Wasawahili, Warori, Wagogo,

41

Wanyamwezi, Waseguhha and Wasagara; yet it would be a difficult task for any person, at mere sight of their dresses or features, to note the differences. Only by certain customs or distinctive marks, such as tattooing, puncturing of the lobes of the ears, ornaments, wearing the hair, etc., which would appear, at first, too trivial to note, could one discriminate between the various tribal representatives. There are certainly differences, but not so varied or marked as they are reported.

"The Wasawahili, of course, through their intercourse with semi-civilization, present us with a race, or tribe, influenced by a state of semi-civilized society, and are, consequently, better dressed and appear to better advantage than their more savage brethren farther west. As it is said that underneath the Russian skin lies the Tartar, so it may be said that underneath the snowy dish-dasheh, or shirt of the Wasawahili, one will find the true barbarian. In the street or bazaar he appears semi-Arabized; his suavity of manner, his prostrations and genuflexions, the patois he speaks, all prove his contact and affinity with the dominant race, whose subject he is. Once out of the coast towns, in the Washensi villages, he sheds the shirt that had half civilized him, and appears in all his deep blackness of skin, prognathous jaws, thick lips—the pure negro and barbarian. Not keenest eye could detect the difference between him and the Washensi, unless his attention had been drawn to the fact that the two men were of different tribes.

"The next tribe to which we are introduced are the Wakwere, who occupy a limited extent of country between the Wazaramo and the Wadoe. They are the first representatives of the pure barbarian the traveler meets, when but two days' journey from the sea-coast. They are a timid tribe and a very unlikely people to commence an attack upon any body of men for mere plunder's sake. They have not a very good reputation among the Arab and Wasawahili traders. They are said to be exceedingly dishonest, of which I have not the least doubt. They furnished me with good grounds for believing these reports while encamped at Kingaru, Hera and Imbiki. The chiefs of the more eastern part of Ukwere profess nominal allegiance to the Dwians of the Mrima. They have selected the densest jungles wherein to establish their villages. Every entrance into one of their valleys is jealously guarded by strong wooden gates, seldom over four and a half feet high, and so narrow, sometimes, that one must enter sideways.

"These jungle islets which in particular dot the extent of Ukwere, present formidable obstacles to a naked enemy. The plants, bushes and young trees which form their natural defense, are generally of the aloetic and thorny species, growing so dense, interlaced one with the other, that the hardest and most desperate robber would not brave the formidable array of sharp thorns which bristle everywhere.

"Some of these jungle islets are infested with gangs of banditti, who seldom fail to take advantage of the weakness of a single wayfarer, more especially if he be a Mgwana—a freeman of Zanzibar, as every negro resident of the island of Zanzibar is distinguished by the Washensi natives of the interior.

"I should estimate the population of Ukwere, allowing about one hundred villages to this territory (which is not more than thirty miles square, its bounds on the south being the Rufu River, and on the north the River Wiami), at not more than five thousand souls. Were all these banded together under the command of one chief, the Wakwere might become a powerful tribe.

"After the Wakwere we come to the Wakami, a remnant of the once grand nation which occupied the lands from the Ungerengeri to the Great Makata River. Frequent wars with the Wadoe and Waseguhha have reduced them to a narrow belt of country, ten rectilinear miles across, which may be said to be comprised between Kiva Peak and the stony ridge bounding the valley of the Ungerengeri on the east, within a couple of miles from the east bank of the river.

"They are as numerous as bees in the Ungerengeri Valley. The unsurpassed fertility has been a great inducement to retain for these people the distinction of a tribe. By the means of a spyglass one may see, as he stands on the top of that stony ridge looking down into the fair valley, clusters of brown huts visible amid bosky clumps, fullness and plenty all over the valley, and may count easily over a hundred villages.

"From Ukami, we pass Southern Udoe, and find a warlike, fine-looking people, with a far more intelligent cast of features, and a shade lighter than the Wakami and Wakwere—a people who are full of traditions of race, a people who have boldly rushed to war upon the slightest encroachment upon their territories, and who have bravely defended themselves against the Waseguhha and Wakami, as well as against nomadic marauders from Uhumba.

"Udoe, in appearance, is amongst the most picturesque countries between the sea and Unyanyembe. Great cones shoot upward above the everlasting forest, tipped by the light, fleecy clouds, through which the warm, glowing sun darts its rays, bathing the whole in sunlight, which brings out those globes of foliage, which rise in tier after tier to the summits of the hills, colors which would mock the most ambitious painter's efforts at imitation. Udoe first evokes the traveler's love of natural beauty after leaving the sea, her roads lead him up along the sharp spines of hilly ridges, whence he may look down upon the forest-clad slopes, declining on either side of him into the depths of deep valleys, to rise up beyond into aspiring cones which kiss the sky, or into a high ridge with deep, concentric folds, which almost tempt one to undergo much labor in exploring them for the provoking air of mystery in which they seem to be enwrapped.

"What a tale this tribe could relate of the slave-trader's deeds. Attacked by the joint forces of the Waseguhha from the west and north, and the slave-traders of Whinde and Sa'adani from the east, the Wadoe have seen their wives and little ones carried into slavery a hundred times, and district after district taken from their country, and attached to Useguhha. For the people of Useguhha were hired to attack their neighbors, the Wadoe, by the Whinde slave-traders, and were also armed with muskets and supplied with ammunition by them, to effect large and repeated captures of Wadoe slaves. The people of this tribe, especially women and children, so superior in physique and intelligence to the servile races by which they were surrounded, were eagerly sought for as concubines and domestics by the lustful Mohammedans.

"This tribe we first note to have distinctive tribal marks—by a line of punctures extending lengthwise on each side of the face, and a chipping of the two inner sides of the two middle teeth of the upper row.

"The arms of this tribe are similar to the arms of the Wakami and Wakwere, and consist of a bow and arrows, a shield, a couple of light spears or assegais, a long knife, a handy little battle-axe and a club with a large knob at the end of it, which latter is dexterously swung at the head of an enemy, inflicting a stunning and sometimes a fatal blow.

"Emerging from the forest of Mikeseh, we enter the territory of the Waseguhha, or Wasegura, as the Arabs wrongly call this country. Useguhha extends over two degrees in length, and its greatest breadth is ninety geographical miles. It has two main divisions, that of Southern Useguhha, from Uruguini to the Wiami River, and Northern Useguhha, under the chieftain Moto, from the Wiami River to Umagassi and Usumbara.

"Mostly all the Waseguhha warriors are armed with muskets, and the Arabs supply them with enough ammunition, in return for which they attack Waruguru, Wadoe and Wakwenni, to obtain slaves for the Arab market, and it is but five years since the Waseguhha organized a successful raid into the very heart of the Wasagara Mountains, during which they desolated the populated part of the Makata plain, capturing over five hundred valuable slaves.

"Formerly wars in this country were caused by blood feuds between different chiefs; they are now encouraged by the slave buyers of the Mirma, for the purpose of supplying these human chattels for the market of Zanzibar. The Waseguhha are about the most thorough believers in witchcraft, yet the professors of this dark science fare badly at their hands. It is a very common sight to see cinereous piles on the roadside, and the waving garments suspended to the branches of trees above them, which mark the fate of the unfortunate 'Waganga' or medicine man. So long as their predictions prove correct and have a happy culmination, these professors of 'uchawi'—magic art—are regarded with favor by the people; but if an unusual calamity overtakes a family, and they can swear that it is the result of the magician's art, a quorum of relentless inquisition is soon formed, and a like fate to that which overtook the 'witches' in the dark days of New England surely awaits him.

"Enough dead wood is soon found in their African forests, and the unhappy one perishes by fire, and, as a warning to all false professors of the art, his loin-cloth is hung up to a tree above the spot where he met his doom.

"In Southern Usagara, the people are most amiable; but in the north, in those districts adjacent to the Wahumba, the people partake of the ferocious character of their fierce neighbors. Repeated attacks from the Waseguhha kidnappers, from the Wadirigo or Wahehe robbers on the southwest, from Wagogo on the west and from Wahumba on the north, have caused them to regard strangers with suspicion; but after a short acquaintance they prove to be a frank, amiable and brave people. Indeed, they have good cause to be distrustful of the Arabs and the Wangwana of Zanzibar. Mbumi, Eastern Usagara, has been twice burned down, within a few years, by the Arabian Waseguhha kidnappers; Rehemeko has met the same fate, and it was not many years ago since Abdullah bin Nasib carried fire and sword from Misonghi to Mpwapwa. Kanyaparu, lord of the hills around Chunyo, Kunyo, once cultivated one-fourth of the Marenga, Mkali; but is now restricted to the hill-tops, from fear of the Wadirigo marauders.

"The Wasagara, male and female, tattoo the forehead, bosom and arms. Besides inserting the neck of a gourd in each ear—which carries his little store of 'tumbac' or tobacco, and lime, which he has obtained by burning land shells—he carries quite a number of primitive ornaments around his neck, such as two or three snowy cowrie-shells, carved pieces of wood, or a small goat's horn, or some

45

medicine consecrated by the medicine man of the tribe, a fund of red or white beads, or two or three pieced Lungomazzi egg-beads, or a string of copper coins, and sometimes small brass chains, like a cheap Jack watch-chain. These things they have either made themselves or purchased from Arab traders for chickens or goats. The children all go naked; youths wear a goat or sheep-skin; grown men and women, blessed with progeny, wear domestic or a loin-cloth of Kaniki, or a barsati, which is a favorite colored cloth in Usagara; chiefs wear caps such as are worn by the Wamrima Diwans, or the Arab tarboosh.

"Next on our line of march, appears the Wagogo, a powerful race, inhabiting the region west of Usagara to Uyanzi, which is about eighty miles in breadth and about one hundred in length.

"The traveler has to exercise great prudence, discretion and judgment in his dealings with them. Here he first heard the word 'houga' after passing Limbomwenni, a word which signifies tribute, though it formerly meant a present to a friend. Since it is exacted from him with threats, that if it is not paid they will make war on him, its best interpretation would be, 'forcibly extorted tribute or toll.'

"Naturally, if the traveler desires to be mulcted of a large sum, he will find the Wagogo ready to receive every shred of cloth he gives them. Moumi will demand sixty cloths, and will wonder at his own magnanimity in asking such a small number of cloths from a great Musungu (white man). The traveler, however, will be wise if he permits his chief men to deal with them, after enjoining them to be careful, and not commit themselves too hastily to any number or amount of gifts.

"They are, physically and intellectually, the best of the races between Unyamwezi and the sea. Their color is a rich dark brown. There is something in their frontal aspect which is almost leonine. Their faces are broad and intelligent. Their eyes are large and round. Their noses are flat, and their mouths are very large; but their lips, though thick, are not so monstrously thick as those our exaggerated ideal of a negro has. For all this, though the Wagogo is a ferocious man, capable of proceeding to any length upon the slightest temptation, he is an attractive figure to the white traveler. He is proud of his chief, proud of his country, sterile and unlovable though it be; he is proud of himself, his prowess, his weapons and his belongings; he is vain, terribly egotistic, a bully, and a tyrant, yet the Wagogo is capable of forming friendships, and of exerting himself for friendship's sake. One grand vice in his character, which places him in a hostile light to travelers, is his exceeding avarice and greed for riches; and if the traveler suffers by this, he is not likely to be amiably disposed toward him.

"This sturdy native, with his rich complexion, his lion front, his menacing aspect, bullying nature, haughty, proud and quarrelsome, is a mere child with a man who will devote himself to the study of his nature, and not offend his vanity. He is easily angered, and his curiosity is easily aroused. A traveler with an angular disposition is sure to quarrel with him—but, in the presence of this rude child of nature, especially when he is so powerful, it is to his advantage and personal safety to soften those angles of his own nature. The Wagogo 'Rob Roy' is on his native ground, and has a decided advantage over the white foreigner. He is not brave, but he is at least conscious of the traveler's weakness, and he is disposed to take advantage of it, but is prevented from committing an act because it is to his advantage to keep the peace. Any violence to a traveler would close the road; caravans would seek other ways, and the chiefs would be deprived of much of their revenues.

"The Wagogo warrior carries as his weapons a bow and a sheaf of murderous-looking arrows, pointed, pronged and barbed; a couple of light, beautifully-made assegais; a broad, sword-like spear, with a blade over two feet long; a battle-axe, and a rungu or knob-club. He has also a shield, painted with designs in black and white, oval-shaped, sometimes of rhinoceros, or elephant, or bull-hide. From the time he was a toddling urchin he has been familiar with his weapons, and by the time he was fifteen years old he was an adept with them.

"He is armed for battle in a very short time. The messenger from the chief darts from village to village, and blows his ox-horn, the signal for war. The warrior hears it, throws his hoe over his shoulder, enters his house, and in a few seconds issues out again, arrayed in war-paint and full fighting costume. Feathers of the ostrich, or the eagle, or the vulture nod above his head; his long crimson robe streams behind him, his shield is on his left arm, his darting assegai in his left hand, and his ponderous man-cleaver—double-edged and pointed, heading a strong staff—is in his right hand; jingling bells are tied around his ankles and knees; ivory wristlets are on his arms, with which he sounds his approach. With the plodding peasant's hoe he has dropped the peasant's garb, and is now the proud, vain, exultant warrior—bounding aloft like a gymnast, eagerly sniffing the battle-field. The strength and power of the Wagogo are derived from their numbers.

"Though caravans of Wagogo are sometimes found passing up and down the Unyamwezi road, they are not so generally employed as the Wanyamwezi in trade. Their villages are thus always full of warriors. Weak tribes, or remnants of tribes are very glad to be admitted under their protection. Individuals of other tribes, also, who have been obliged to exile themselves from their own tribes, for some deed of violence, are often found in the villages of the Wagogo. In the north, the Wahumba are very numerous; in the south may be found the Wahehe and Wakimbu, and in the east may be found many a family from Usagara. Wanyamwi are also frequently found in this country. Indeed, these latter people are like Scotchmen, they may be found almost everywhere throughout Central Africa, and have a knack of pushing themselves into prominence.

"As in Western Usagara, the houses of the Wagogo are square, arranged around the four sides of an area—to which all the doors open. The roofs are all flat, on which are spread the grain, herbs, tobacco and pumpkins. The back of each department is pierced with small holes for observation and for defense.

"The tembe is a fragile affair as constructed in Wagogo; it merely consists of a line of slender sticks daubed over with mud, with three or four strong poles planted at intervals to support the beams and rafters, on which rests the flat clay roof. A musket-ball pierces the wattled walls of a Wagogo tembe through and through. In Uyanzi, the tembe is a formidable affair, because of the abundance of fine trees, which are cut down and split into rails three or four inches thick.

"The tembe is divided into apartments, separated from each other by a wattled wall. Each apartment may contain a family of grown-up boys and girls, who form their beds on the floor, out of dressed hides. The father of the family, only, has a kitanda, or fixed cot, made of ox-hide, stretched over a frame, or of the bark of the myombo tree. The floor is of tamped mud, and is exceedingly filthy, smelling strongly of every abomination. In the corners, suspended to the rafters, are the fine, airy dwellings of black spiders of very large size, and other monstrous insects.

"Rats, a peculiarly long-headed, dun-colored species, infest every tembe. Cows, goats, sheep and cats are the only domestic animals permitted to dwell within the tembe.

"The Wagogo believe in the existence of a God, or sky spirit, whom they call Mulungu. Their prayers are generally directed to him when their parents die. A Wagogo, after he has consigned his father to the grave, collects his father's chattels together, his cloth, his ivory, his knife, his jeinbe (hoe), his bows and arrows, his spear and his cattle, and kneels before them, repeating a wish that Mulungu would increase his worldly wealth, that he would bless his labors and make him successful in trade. They venerate, and often perform a dance in honor of the moon.

48

"The following conversation occurred between myself and a Wagogo trader:

"'Who do you suppose made your parents?'

"'Why, Mulungu, white man.'

"'Well, who made you?'

"'If God made my father, God made me, didn't He?'

"'That's very good. Where do you suppose your father has gone to, now that he is dead?'

"'The dead die,' said he, solemnly, 'they are no more. The sultan dies, he becomes nothing—he is then no better than a dead dog; he is finished, his words are finished—there are no words from him. It is true,' he added, seeing a smile on my face, 'the sultan becomes nothing. He who says other words is a liar. There.'

"'But then he is a very great man, is he not?'

"'While he lives only—after death he goes into the pit, and there is no more to be said of him than any other man.'

"'How do you bury a Wagogo?'

"'His legs are tied together, his right arm to his body, and his left is put under his head. He is then rolled on his left side in the grave. His cloth he wore during his life is spread over him. We put the earth over him, and put thorn-bushes over it, to prevent the fize (hyena) from getting at him. A woman is put on her right side in a grave apart from the man.'

"'What do you do with the sultan, when he is dead?'

"'We bury him, too, of course; only he is buried in the middle of the village, and we build a house over it. Each time they kill an ox, they kill before his grave. When the old sultan dies, the new one calls for an ox, and kills it before his grave, calling on Mulungu to witness that he is the rightful sultan. He then distributes the meat in his father's name.'

"'Who succeeds the sultan? Is he the eldest son?'

"'Yes, if he has a son; if childless, the great chief next to him in rank. The msagira is the next to the sultan, whose business it is to hear the cause of complaint, and convey it to the sultan, who, through the sultan, dispenses justice, he receives the honga, carries it to the mtemi (sultan), places it before him, and when the sultan has taken what he wishes, the rest goes to the msagiri. The chiefs are called manya-para; the msagiri is the chief manya-para.'

"'How do the Wagogo marry?'

"'Oh, they buy their women.'

"'What is a woman worth?'

"'A very poor man can buy his wife from her father for a couple of goats.'

"'How much has the sultan got to pay?'

49

"'He has got to pay about one hundred goats, or so many cows, so many sheep and goats, to his bride's father. Of course, he is a chief. The sultan would not buy a common woman. The father's consent is to be obtained, and the cattle have to be given up. It takes many days to finish the talk about it. All the family and friends of the bride have to talk about it before she leaves her father's house.'

"'In cases of murder, what do you do to the man that kills another?'

"'The murderer has to pay fifty cows. If he is too poor to pay, the sultan gives permission to the murdered man's friends or relatives to kill him. If they catch him, they tie him to a tree, and throw spears at him—one at a time first; they then spring on him, cut his head off, then his arms and limbs, and scatter them about the country.'

"'How do you punish a thief?'

"'If he is found stealing, he is killed at once, and nothing is said about it. Is he not a thief?'

"'But, suppose you do not know who the thief is?'

"'If a man is brought before us accused of stealing, we kill a chicken. If the entrails are white, he is innocent; if yellow, he is guilty.'

"'Do you believe in witchcraft?'

"'Of course we do, and punish the man with death who bewitches cattle or stops rain.'

"Sacrifices of human life as penalty for witchcraft and kindred superstitions—indeed for many trivial offenses—are painfully numerous among nearly all the tribes.

"Next to Wagogo is Uyanzi, or the 'Magunda Mkali'—the Hot Field.

"Uyanzi or Magunda Mkali is at present very populous. Along the northern route—that leading via Munieka—water is plentiful enough, villages are frequent and travelers begin to perceive that the title is inappropriate. The people who inhabit the country are Wakimbu from the south. They are good agriculturists, and are a most industrious race. They are something like the Wasagara in appearance, but do not obtain a very high reputation for bravery. Their weapons consist of light spears, bows and arrows, and battle-axes. Their tembes are strongly made, showing considerable skill in the art of defensive construction. Their bomas are so well made, that one would require cannon to effect an entrance, if the villages were at all defended. They are skillful, also, in constructing traps for elephants and buffaloes. A stray lion or leopard is sometimes caught by them."

CHAPTER VI

ADVENTURES IN GREAT VARIETY

Stanley received a noiseless ovation in Unyanyembe as he walked with the governor to his house. Soldiers and men by the hundreds, hovered round their chief, staring at him, while the naked children peered between the legs of the parents. Tea was served in a silver tea-pot and a sumptuous breakfast was furnished, which Stanley devoured as only a hungry man can, who has been shut up for so many months in the wilds of Africa.

Then pipes and tobacco were produced, and amid the whiffs of smoke came out all the news that Stanley had brought from Zanzibar, while the gratified sheikh smoked and listened. When Stanley took his leave to look after his men his host accompanied him to show him the house he was to occupy while he remained. It was commodious and quite luxurious after his long life in a tent.

All the caravans had arrived, and he received the reports of the chief of each, while the goods were unpacked and examined. One had had a fight with the natives and beaten them, another had shot a thief, and the fourth had lost a bale of goods. On the whole, Stanley was satisfied and thankful there had been no more serious misfortunes. Food was furnished with lavish prodigality, and while he was surfeiting himself, he ordered a bullock to be slain for his men, now reduced to twenty-five in number.

On the second day of his arrival, the chief Arabs of Tabna came to visit him. This is the chief Arab settlement of Central Africa, and contains a thousand huts and about five thousand inhabitants. The Arabs are a fine, handsome set of men, and living amid rich pastures, they raise large herds of cattle and goats, and vegetables of all kinds, while their slaves bring back in caravans from Zanzibar the luxuries of the East, not only coffee, spices, wines, salmon, etc., but Persian carpets, rich bedding, and elegant table service. Some of them sport gold watches and chains. Each one keeps as many concubines as he can afford, the size of his harem being limited only by his means.

These magnates from Tabna after finishing their visit, invited Stanley to visit their town and partake of a feast they had prepared for him. Three days after, escorted by eighteen of his men, he returned the visit. He arrived in time to attend a council of war which was being held, as to the best manner of asserting their rights against a robber-chief named Mirambo. He had carried war through several tribes and claimed the right to waylay and rob Arab caravans. This must be stopped, and it was resolved to make war against him in his stronghold. Stanley agreed to accompany them, taking his caravan a part of the way and leaving it until Mirambo was defeated, and the way to Ujiji cleared.

Returning to Unyanyembe, he found the caravan which had been made up to carry supplies to Livingstone in November 1st, 1870. Having gone twenty-five miles from Zanzibar, to Bagomayo, it had stayed there one hundred days, when, hearing that the English consul was coming, it had started off in affright just previous to Stanley's arrival. Whether owing to his great change in diet or some other cause, Stanley was now stricken down with fever and for a week tossed in delirium. Selim, his faithful servant, took care of him. When he had recovered, the servant also was seized with it.

But by the 29th of July all the sick had recovered, and the caravan was loaded up for Ujiji. But Bombay was absent and they had to wait from eight o'clock till two in the afternoon, he stubbornly refusing to leave his mistress. When he arrived and was ordered to his place he made a savage reply. The next moment Stanley's cane was falling like lightning on his shoulders. The poor fellow soon cried for mercy. The order "March" was then given, and the guide, with forty armed men behind him, led off with flags streaming. At first, in dead silence, they moved on, but soon struck up a monotonous sort of chorus, which seemed to consist mostly of "Hoy, hoy," and was kept up all day. The second day he arrived at Masangi, where he was told the Arabs were waiting for him at Mfuto, six hours' march distant. The next morning, he arrived at the place where the Arab army was gathered, numbering in all two thousand two hundred and twenty-five men, of whom fifteen hundred were armed with guns. With banners flying and drums beating, they, on the 3d of August, marched forth, but in a few hours Stanley was again stricken down with fever.

The next day the march was resumed, and at eleven o'clock Zimbize, the stronghold of the enemy, came in view. The forces quickly surrounded it. A general assault followed and the village was captured, the inhabitants fleeing toward the mountains, pursued closely by the yelling Arabs. Only twenty dead bodies were found within. The next day, two more villages were burned and the day after, a detachment five hundred strong scoured the country around, carrying devastation and ruin in their path. At this critical period of the campaign, Stanley was still down with fever, and while he lay in his hammock, news came that the detachment of five hundred men had been surprised and killed. Mirambo had turned and ambushed them, and now the boasting of the morning was turning into despondency. The women made the night hideous with shrieks and lamentations over their slain husbands. The next day there was a regular stampede of the Arabs, and when Stanley was able to get out of his tent only seven men were left to him; all the rest had returned to Mfuto, and soon after to Tabna twenty-five miles distant.

It was plain that it was useless to open the direct road to Ujiji, which lay through Mirambo's district. In fact, it seemed impossible to get there at all, and the only course left was to return to the coast and abandon the project of reaching Livingstone altogether. But what would Livingstone do locked up at Ujiji? He might perhaps go north and meet Baker, who was moving with a strong force southward. But he was told by a man that Livingstone was coming to Nyano Lake toward the Tanganika, on which Ujiji is situated, at the very time it was last reported he was murdered. He was then walking, dressed in American sheeting, having lost all his cloth in Lake Leemba. He had a breech-loading double-barreled rifle with him and two revolvers. Stanley felt that he could not give up trying to reach him now, when it was so probable that he was within four hundred miles of him.

On the 13th, a caravan came in from the east and reported Farquhar dead at the place where he had been left. Ten days after, Mirambo attacked Tabna and set it on fire. Stanley, at this time, was encamped at Kwihara, in sight of the burning town. The refugees came pouring in, and Stanley, finding the men willing to stand by him, began to prepare for defense, and counting up his little force found he had one hundred and fifty men. He was not attacked, however, and five days after, Mirambo retreated. The Arabs held councils of war and urged Stanley to become their ally, but he refused, and finally took the bold resolution of organizing a flying caravan, and by a southern route and quick marching, reach Ujiji. This was August 27th, and the third month he had been in Unyanyembe. Having got together some forty men in all, he gave a great banquet to them prior to their departure, which an attack of fever caused him to postpone. On the 20th of September, though too weak to travel, he mustered his entire force outside the town and found, that by additional men which the Arabs had succeeded in securing, it now numbered fifty-four men. When all was ready Bombay was again missing, and when found and brought up, excused himself, as of old, by saying he was bidding his "misses" good-bye. As he seemed inclined to pick a quarrel with Stanley, the latter not being in the most amiable mood and wishing to teach the others a lesson, gave him a sound thrashing.

Soon, everything being ready, the word "march" passed down

the line and Stanley started on his last desperate attempt to push on to Ujiji, not much farther than from Albany to Buffalo as the crow flies, but by the way he would be compelled to go, no one knew how far, nor what time it would take to reach it. But Stanley had good reason to believe that Livingstone was alive, and from the reports he could get of his movements that he must be at or near Ujiji, and therefore to Ujiji he was determined to go, unless death stopped his progress. He had been set on a mission, and although the conditions were not that he should surmount impossibilities, still he would come as near to that as human effort could. Though sick with fever, and with that prostration and utter loss of will accompanying it, he nevertheless with that marvelous energy that is never exhibited except in rare exceptional characters, kept his great object in view. That never lost its hold on him under the most disastrous circumstances, neither in the delirium of fever nor in the utter prostration that followed it. This tenacity of purpose and indomitable will ruling and governing him, where in all other men it would have had no power, exhibit the extraordinary qualities of this extraordinary man. We do not believe that he himself was fully aware of this inherent power, this fixedness of purpose that makes him different from all other men. No man possessing it is conscious of it any more than an utterly fearless man is conscious of his own courage. The following touching extract from his journal at this time lets in a flood of light on the character and the inner life of this remarkable man:

"About 10 P. M. the fever had gone. All were asleep in the tembe but myself, and an unutterable loneliness came on me as I reflected on my position, and my intentions, and felt the utter lack of sympathy with me in all around. Even my own white assistant, with whom I had striven hard, was less sympathizing than my little black boy Kalulu. It requires more nerve than I possess to dispel all the dark presentiments that come upon the mind. But, probably, what I call presentiments are simply the impress on the mind of the warnings which these false-hearted Arabs have repeated so often. This melancholy and loneliness which I feel, may probably have their origin from the same cause. The single candle which barely lights up the dark shade which fills the corners of my room, is but a poor incentive to cheerfulness. I feel as though I were imprisoned between stone walls. But why should I feel as if baited by these stupid, slow-witted Arabs, and their warnings and croakings? I fancy a suspicion haunts my mind, as I write, that there lies some motive behind all this.

"I wonder if these Arabs tell me all these things to keep me here, in the hope that I may be induced another time to assist them in their war against Mirambo! If they think so, they are much mistaken, for I have taken a solemn, enduring oath—an oath to be kept while the least hope of life remains in me—not to be tempted to break the resolution I have formed, never to give up the search until I find Livingstone alive, or find his dead body; and never to return home without the strongest possible proofs that he is alive or that he is dead. No living man or living men shall stop me—only death can prevent me. But death—not even this; I shall not die—I will not die—I cannot die!

"And something tells me, I do not know what it is—perhaps it is the everliving hopefulness of my own nature; perhaps it is the natural presumption born out of an abundant and glowing vitality, or the outcome of an overweening confidence in one's self—anyhow and everyhow, something tells me to-night I shall find him, and—write it larger—Find him! Find him! Even the words are inspiring. I feel more happy. Have I uttered a prayer? I shall sleep calmly to-night."

There is nothing in this whole terrible journey so touching, and revealing so much, as this extract from his journal does. It shows that he is human, and yet far above common human weakness. Beset with difficulties, his only white companion dead or about to be left behind, the Arabs themselves and the natives telling him he cannot go on, left all alone in a hostile country, his men deserting him, he pauses and ponders. To make all these outer conditions darker, he is smitten down with fever that saps the energies, unnerves the heart and fills the imagination with gloomy forebodings, and makes the soul sigh for rest. It is the lowest pit of despondency into which a man may be cast. He feels it, and all alone, fever-worn and sad, he surveys the prospect before him. There is not a single soul on which to lean—not a sympathizing heart to turn to while fever is burning up his brain, and night, moonless and starless, is settling down around him. He would be less than human not to feel the desolation of his position, and for a moment to sink under this accumulation of disastrous circumstances. He does feel how utterly hopeless and sad is his condition; and all through the first part of this entry in his journal, there is something that sounds like a mournful refrain; yet at its close, out of his gloomy surroundings, up from his feverish bed speaks the brave heart in trumpet tones, showing the indomitable will that nothing can break, crying out of the all-enveloping gloom, "no living man or living men shall stop me—only death can prevent me." There spoke one of the few great natures God has made. The closing words of that entry in his journal ring like a bugle-note from his sick-bed, and foretell his triumph.

But, at last, they were off. Shaw, the last white man left to Stanley, had been sick and apparently indifferent whether he lived or died; but all after a short march became enlivened, and things looked more promising. But Stanley was soon again taken sick with the fever and the men began to be discouraged. Staggering from his sick-bed he found that twenty of his men had deserted. Aroused at this new danger he instantly dispatched twenty men after them, while he sent his faithful follower, Selim, to an Arab chief to borrow a long slave-chain. At night, the messengers returned with nine of the missing men. Stanley then told them that he had never used the slave-chain, but now he should on the first deserters. He had resolved to go to Ujiji, where he believed Dr. Livingstone was, and being so near the accomplishment of the mission he was sent on, he was ready to resort to any measures rather than fail. Deferring the use of the chain at present, he started forward and encamped at Iresaka. In the morning, two more men were missing. Irritated but determined, this resolute man halted, sent back for the fugitives, caught them, and when brought back, flogged them severely and chained them. Notwithstanding this severe treatment, the next morning another man deserted, while to add to his perplexities and enhance the difficulties that surrounded him, a man who had accompanied him all the way from the coast asked to be discharged. Several others of the expedition were now taken sick and became unable to proceed; and it seemed, notwithstanding the resolute will of the leader, that the expedition must break up. But fortunately, that evening men who had been in caravans to the coast entered the village where they were encamped with wondrous stories of what they had seen, which revived the spirits of all, and the next morning they started off, and after three hours' march through the forest came to Kigandu. Shaw, the last white man now left to him, between real and feigned sickness had become such a burden, that he determined to leave him behind, as the latter had often requested.

That night, the poor wretch played on an old accordion "Home, Sweet Home," which, miserable as it was, stirred the depths of Stanley's heart for the man now about to be left alone amid Arabs and natives in the most desperate crisis of the undertaking. But it could not be helped. Speed was everything on this new route, or Mirambo would close it also. So on the morning of the 27th he ordered the horn to sound "get ready," and Shaw being sent back to Kwihara, Stanley set off on his southern unknown route to Ujiji and entered the dark forests and pressed rapidly forward. In seven hours he reached the village of Ugunda which numbers two thousand souls. It was well fortified against the robber, Mirambo. Around their principal village, some three thousand square acres were under cultivation, giving them not only all the provisions they wanted for their own use, but also enough for passing caravans. They could also furnish carriers for those in want of them. On the 28th, they arrived at a small village well supplied with corn, and the next day reached Kikura a place impregnated with the most deadly of African fevers. Over desert plains, now sheering on one side to avoid the corpse of a man dead from small-pox, the scourge of Africa, and again stumbling on a skeleton, the caravan kept on till they came to the cultivated fields of Manyara.

A wilderness one hundred and thirty-five miles in extent stretched out before them from this place, and Stanley was inclined to be very conciliatory toward the chief of the village, in order to get provisions for the long and desperate march before him. But the chief was very sullen and wholly indifferent to the presents the white man offered him. With adroit diplomacy, Stanley sent to him some magnificent royal cloths, which so mollified the chief that abundant provisions were soon sent in, followed by the chief himself with fifty warriors bearing gifts quite equal to those which Stanley sent him, and they entered the tent of the first white man they had ever seen. Looking at him for some time in silent surprise, the chiefs burst into an incontrollable fit of laughter, accompanied with snapping their fingers. But when they were shown the sixteen-shooters and revolvers their astonishment knew no bounds, while the double-barreled guns, heavily charged, made them jump to their feet with alarm, followed by convulsions of laughter. Stanley then showed them his chest of medicine, and finally gave them a dose in the form of brandy. They tasted it, making wry faces, when he produced a bottle of concentrated ammonia, saying that it was for snake bites. One of the chiefs asked for some of it. It was suddenly presented to his nose, when his features underwent such indescribable contortions that the other chiefs burst into convulsions of laughter, clapped their hands, pinched each other and went through all sorts of ludicrous gesticulations. When the chief recovered himself, the tears in the meanwhile rolling down his cheeks, he laughed and simply said, "strong medicine." The others then took a sniff and went off into paroxysms of laughter.

Wednesday, October 4th, found them traveling toward the Gombe River. They had hardly left the waving corn-fields, when they came in sight of a large herd of zebras. Passing on, the open forest resembled a magnificent park, filled with buffalo, zebra, giraffe, antelope and other tropical animals, while the scenery on every side was entrancing. These noble animals, coursing in their wild freedom through those grand, primeval forests, presented a magnificent sight. Stanley, thoroughly aroused, crept back to his camp, which had been pitched on the Gombe River, and prepared for a right royal hunt. He says:

"Here, at last, was the hunter's paradise! How petty and insignificant appeared my hunts after small antelope and wild boar; what a foolish waste of energies, those long walks through damp grasses and thorny jungles. Did I not well remember my first bitter experience in African jungles, when in the maritime region? But this—where is the nobleman's park that can match this scene? Here is a soft, velvety expanse of young grass, grateful shade under close, spreading clumps, herds of large and varied game browsing within easy rifle-shot. Surely I must feel amply compensated now for the long southern detour I have made, when such a prospect as this opens to the view! No thorny jungles and rank-smelling swamps are to daunt the hunter, and to sicken his aspirations after true sport. No hunter could aspire after a nobler field to display his prowess.

"Having settled the position of the camp, which overlooked one of the pools found in the depression of the Gombe Creek, I took my double-barreled smooth bore, and sauntered off to the parkland. Emerging from behind a clump, three fine, plump spring-bok were seen browsing on the young grass just within one hundred yards. I knelt down and fired; one unfortunate antelope bounded forward instinctively and fell dead. Its companions sprang high into the air, taking leaps about twelve feet in length, as if they were quadrupeds practicing gymnastics, and away they vanished, rising up like India-rubber balls, until a knoll hid them from view. My success was hailed with loud shouts by the soldiers, who came running out from the camp as soon as they heard the reverberation of the gun, and my gun-bearer had his knife at the throat of the beast, uttering a fervent 'Bismillah' as he almost severed the head from the body.

"Hunters were now directed to proceed east and north to procure meat, because in each caravan it generally happens that there are fundi whose special trade it is to hunt for meat for the camp. Some of these are experts in stalking, but often find themselves in dangerous positions, owing to the near approach necessary before they can fire their most inaccurate weapons with any certainty.

"After luncheon, consisting of spring-bok steak, hot corn-cake and a cup of Mocha coffee, I strolled toward the southwest, accompanied by Kalulu and Majwara, two boy gun-bearers. The tiny perpusilla started up like rabbits from me as I stole along through the underbrush; the honey-bird hopped from tree to tree chirping its call, as if it thought I was seeking the little sweet treasure, the hiding-place of which it only knew; but, no! I neither desired perpusilla nor the honey. I was on the search for something great

58

this day. Keen-eyed fish-eagles and bustards poised on trees above the sinuous Gombe thought, and probably with good reason, that I was after them, judging by the ready flight with which both species disappeared as they sighted my approach. Ah, no! nothing but hartbeest, zebra, giraffe, eland and buffalo this day.

"After following the Gombe's course for about a mile, delighting my eyes with long looks at the broad and lengthy reaches of water, to which I was so long a stranger, I came upon a scene which delighted the innermost recesses of my soul; five, six, seven, eight, ten zebras switching their beautiful striped bodies, and biting one another, within about one hundred and fifty yards. The scene was so pretty, so romantic, never did I so thoroughly realize that I was in Central Africa. I felt momentarily proud that I owned such a vast dominion, inhabited by such noble beasts. Here I possessed, within reach of a leaden ball, any one I chose of the beautiful animals, the pride of the African forests. It was at my option to shoot any one of them. Mine they were, without money and without price; yet, knowing this, twice I dropped my rifle, loath to wound the royal beasts, but—crack! and a royal one was on his back, battling the air with his legs. Ah, it was such a pity! but hasten, draw the keen, sharp-edged knife across the beautiful stripes which fold around the throat, and—what an ugly gash! it is done, and I have a superb animal at my feet. Hurrah! I shall taste of Ukonongo zebra to-night.

"I thought a spring-bok and zebra enough for one day's sport, especially after a long march. The Gombe, a long stretch of deep water, winding in and out of green groves, calm, placid, with lotus leaves resting lightly on its surface, all pretty, picturesque, peaceful as a summer's dream, looked very inviting for a bath. I sought out the most shady spot under a wide-spreading mimosa, from which the ground sloped smooth as a lawn to the still, clear water. I ventured to undress, and had already stepped to my ankles in the water, and had brought my hands together for a glorious dive, when my attention was attracted by an enormously long body which shot into view, occupying the spot beneath the surface which I was about to explore by a 'header.' Great heavens, it was a crocodile! I sprang back instinctively, and this proved my salvation, for the monster turned away with the most disappointed look, and I was left to congratulate myself upon my narrow escape from his jaws, and to register a vow never to be tempted again by the treacherous calm of an African river."

CHAPTER VII

THE END APPROACHES

The following extract from Stanley's journal, written up that night after his hunting tour, shows that this strong, determined, fearless man was not merely a courageous lion, but that he possessed also the eye of an artist and the soul of a poet. With a few strokes of his pen, he sketches a picture on the banks of the forest-lined river, full of life and beauty:

"The adventures of the day were over; the azure of the sky had changed to a deep gray; the moon was appearing just over the trees; the water of the Gombe was like a silver belt; hoarse frogs bellowed their notes loudly by the margin of the creek; the fish-eagles uttered their dirge-like cries as they were perched high on the tallest trees; elands snorted their warning to the herd in the forest; stealthy forms of the carnivora stole through the dark woods outside of our camp. Within the high inclosure of bush and thorn which we had raised about our camp, all was jollity, laughter and radiant, genial comfort. Around every camp-fire, dark forms of men were seen squatted: one man gnawed at a luscious bone; another sucked the rich marrow in a zebra's leg bone; another turned the stick, garnished with huge cabobs, to the bright blaze; another held a large rib over a flame; there were others busy stirring, industriously, great black potfuls of ugali, and watching anxiously the meat simmering, and the soup bubbling, while the firelight flickered and danced bravely, and cast a bright glow over the naked forms of the men, and gave a crimson tinge to the tall tent that rose in the centre of the camp, like a temple sacred to some mysterious god; the fires cast their reflections upon the massive arms of the trees, as they branched over our camp; and, in the dark gloom of their foliage, the most fantastic shadows were visible. Altogether, it was a wild, romantic and impressive scene."

They halted here for two days, the men hunting and gormandizing. Like all animals, after gorging themselves they did not want to move, and when on the 7th of October Stanley ordered the caravan to be put in motion, the men refused to stir. Stanley at once walked swiftly toward them with his double-barreled gun, loaded with buck-shot, in his hand. As he did so he saw the men seize their guns. He, however, kept resolutely on till within thirty yards of two men, whose heads were peering above an ant-hill, their guns pointed across the road,—then suddenly halting, he took deliberate aim at them, determined come what would to blow out their brains. One of them, a giant, named Azmani, instantly brought up his gun with his finger on the trigger. "Drop that gun or you are a dead man," shouted Stanley. They obeyed and came forward, but he saw that murder was in Azmani's eyes. The other man, at the second order, laid down his gun and, with a blow from Stanley that sent him reeling away, sneaked off. But the giant, Azmani, refused to obey, and Stanley aiming his piece at his head and touching the trigger was about to fire. The former quickly lifted his gun up to his shoulder to shoot. In another second he would have fallen dead at Stanley's feet. At this moment an Arab, who had approached from behind, struck up the wretch's gun and exclaimed, "Man, how dare you point your gun at the master?" This saved his life, and perhaps Stanley's also. It required nerves of iron in a man thus to stand up all alone in the heart of an African forest surrounded by savages and defy them all, and cow them all. But the trouble was over, peace was concluded, and the men with one accord agreed to go on. The two instigators of this mutiny were Bombay and a savage, named Ambari. Snatching up a spear Stanley immediately gave the former a terrible pounding with the handle. Then turning on the latter, who stood looking on with a mocking face, he administered the same punishment to him, after which he put them both in chains.

For the next fourteen days, nothing remarkable occurred in the march, which had been in a southwesterly direction. Near a place called Mrera, Stanley, for the first time saw a herd of wild elephants, and was deeply impressed with their lordly appearance. Here Selim was taken sick and the caravan halted for three days, Stanley spending the interval in mending his shoes.

He now had four districts to traverse, which would occupy him twenty-five days. Taking a northwesterly route having, as he thought, got around the country of Mirambo, he pushed forward with all speed. Buffaloes, leopards and lions were encountered; the country was diversified, and many of the petty chiefs grasping and unfriendly, so that it was a constant, long, wearisome fight with obstacles from the beginning to the end of each week. But, on November 3d, a caravan of eighty came into Stanley's camp from the westward. The latter asked the news. They replied that a white man had just arrived at Ujiji. This was startling news indeed.

"A white man!" exclaimed Stanley.

"Yes, a white man."

"How is he dressed?"

"Like the master," pointing to him.

"Is he young or old?"

"He is old, with white hair on his face; and he is sick."

"Where has he come from?" was the next anxious inquiry.

"From a very far country, away beyond Uguh-ha."

"And is he now stopping at Ujiji?"

"Yes, we left him there eight days ago."

"How long is he going to stay there?"

"Don't know."

"Was he ever there before?"

"Yes; he went away a long time ago."

Stanley gave a shout of exultation, exclaiming: "It is Livingstone!"

Then came the thought, it may be some other man. Perhaps it is Baker, who has worked his way in there before me. It was a crushing thought, that after all his sufferings, and sickness, and toils, he should have been anticipated, and that there was now nothing left for him but to march back again. "No!" he exclaimed to himself: "Baker has no white hair on his face." But he could now wait no longer, and turning to his men, he asked them if they were willing to march to Ujiji without a single halt. If they were, he would, on their arrival, present each two doti of cloth. They all shouted, "Yes!" Stanley jots down: "I was madly rejoiced, intensely eager to resolve the burning question, 'Is it Dr. Livingstone?' God grant me patience; but I do wish there was a railroad, or at least, horses, in this country. With a horse I could reach him in twelve hours."

But new dangers confronted him. The chiefs became more exhorbitant in their demands and more hostile in their demonstrations, and but for Stanley's eagerness to get on, he would more than once have fought his way through some of those pertinacious tribes. But his patience, at last, gave out, for he was told after he had settled the last tribute that there were five more chiefs ahead who would exact tribute. This would beggar him, and he asked two natives if there was no way of evading the next chief, named Wahha.

"This rather astonished them at first, and they declared it to be impossible; but finally, after being pressed, they replied that one of their number should guide us at midnight, or a little after, into the jungle which grew on the frontiers of Uhha and Uvinza. By keeping a direct west course through this jungle until we came to Ukavanga, we might be enabled—we were told—to travel through Uhha without further trouble. If I were willing to pay the guide twelve doti, and if I were able to impose silence on my people while passing through the sleeping village, the guide was positive I could reach Ujiji without paying another doti. It is needless to add that I accepted the proffered assistance at such a price with joy.

"But there was much to be done. Provisions were to be purchased, sufficient to last four days, for the tramp through the jungle and men were at once sent with cloth to purchase grain at any price. Fortune favored us, and before 8 P. M. we had enough for six days.

"November 7th.—I did not go to sleep at all last night, but a little after midnight, as the moon was beginning to show itself, by gangs of four the men stole quietly out of the village; and by 3 A. M. the entire expedition was outside the bonna and not the slightest alarm had been made. After whistling to the new guide, the expedition began to move in a southern direction along the right bank of the Kanenzi River. After an hour's march in this direction, we struck west across the grassy plain, and maintained it, despite the obstacles we encountered which were sore enough to naked men. The bright moon lighted our path; dark clouds now and then cast immense long shadows over the deserted and silent plain, and the moonbeams were almost obscured, and at such times our position seemed awful—

"'Till the moon,
Rising in clouded majesty, at length
Apparent queen, unveiled her peerless light,
And o'er the dark her silver mantle threw.'

"Bravely toiled the men, without murmur, though their legs were bleeding from the cruel grass. 'Ambrosial morn' at last appeared, with all its beautiful and lovely features. Heaven was born anew to us, with comforting omens and cheery promise. The men, though fatigued at the unusual travel, sped forward with quicker pace as daylight broke, until at 8 A. M. we sighted the swift Rusugi River, where a halt was ordered in a clump of jungle for breakfast and rest. Both banks of the river were alive with buffalo, eland and antelope, but though the sight was very tempting, we did not fire, because we dared not. The report of a gun would have alarmed the whole country. I preferred my coffee, and the contentment which my mind experienced at our success.

"An hour after we had rested, some natives carrying salt from the Malagarazi were seen coming up the right bank of the river. When abreast of our hiding-place they detected us, and dropping their salt-bags, they took to their heels at once, shouting out as they ran, to alarm some villages that appeared some four miles north of us. The men were immediately ordered to take up their loads, and in a few minutes we had crossed the Rusugi, and were making direct for a bamboo jungle that appeared in our front. Almost as soon as we entered, a weak-brained woman raised a series of piercing yells. The men were appalled at this noisy demonstration, which would call down upon our heads the vengeance of the Wahha for evading the tribute, to which they thought themselves entitled. In half an hour we should have hundreds of howling savages about us in the jungle, and probably a general massacre would ensue. The woman screamed fearfully again and again, for no cause whatever. Some of the men, with the instinct of self-preservation, at once dropped their bales and loads and vanished into the jungle. The guide came rushing back to me, imploring me to stop her noise. The woman's husband, livid with rage and fear, drew his sword and asked permission to cut her head off at once. Had I given the least signal, the woman had paid with her life for her folly. I attempted to hush her cries by putting my hand over her mouth, but she violently wrestled with me, and continued her cries worse than ever. There remained nothing else for me to do but to try the virtue of my whip over her shoulders. I asked her to desist after the first blow. 'No!' She continued her insane cries with increased force and volume. Again my whip descended on her shoulders. 'No, no, no.' Another blow. 'Will you hush?' 'No, no, no,' louder and louder she cried, and faster and faster I showered the blows for the taming of this shrew. However, seeing I was as determined to flog as she was to cry, she desisted before the tenth blow and became silent. A cloth was folded over her mouth, and her arms were tied behind her; and in a few moments, the runaways having returned to their duty, the expedition moved forward again with redoubled pace."

That night they encamped at Lake Musunya, which swarmed with hippopotami. No tent nor hut was raised, nor fire kindled, and Stanley lay down with his rifle slung over his shoulders, ready to act on a moment's notice. Before daylight they were off again, and at early dawn emerged from the jungle and stretched rapidly across a naked plain. Reaching the Rugufa River, they halted in a deep shade, when suddenly Stanley heard a sound like distant thunder. Asking one of his men if it were thunder, the latter replied no, that it was the noise made by the waves of Tanganika breaking into the caverns on its shore. Was he, indeed, so near this great inland sea, of which Ujiji was the chief harbor?

Pressing on three hours longer they encamped in the forest. Two hours before daylight they again set out, the guide promising that by next morning they should be clear of the hostile district. On this Stanley exclaims, "Patience, my soul! A few hours more and then the end of all this will be known. I shall be face to face with that white man with the white beard on his face, whoever he may be." Before daylight they started again, and emerging from the forest on to the high road, the guides, thinking they had passed the last village of the hostile tribe, set up a shout, but soon, to their horror, came plump upon its outskirts. Fate seemed about to desert him at the last moment, for if the village was roused he was a doomed man. Keeping concealed amid the trees, Stanley ordered the goats to be killed lest their bleating should lead to discovery, the chickens to be killed also, and then they plunged into the jungle, Stanley being the last man to follow. It was a narrow escape. After an half-hour's march, finding they were not pursued, they again took to the road. One more night in the encampment and then the end would come. Next morning they pushed on with redoubled speed, and in two hours, from the top of a mountain Stanley, with bounding heart, beheld Lake Tanganika, a vast expanse of burnished silver, with dark mountains around it and the blue sky above it. "Hurrah," shouted Stanley, and the natives took up the shout, till the hills and forest rang with their exultant cries. The long struggle was near over; the goal toward which he had been so long straining was almost won.

CHAPTER VIII

STANLEY MEETS LIVINGSTONE

Stanley's excitement at this supreme moment of his life can never be described or even imagined. When he started from Zanzibar, he knew he had thrown the dice which were to fix his fate. Successful, and his fame was secure, while failure meant death; and all the chances were against him. How much he had taken upon himself no one but he knew; into what gloomy gulfs he had looked before he started, he alone was conscious. Of the risks he ran, of the narrow escapes he had made, of the toils and sufferings he had endured, he alone could form an estimate. With the accumulation of difficulties and the increasing darkness of his prospects, the one great object of his mission had increased in importance, till great though it was, it became unnaturally magnified so that, at last, it filled all his vision, and became the one, the great, the only object in life worth pursuing. For it he had risked so much, toiled so long and suffered so terribly, that the whole world, with all its interests, was secondary to it. Hope had given way to disappointment and disappointment yielded to despair so often, that his strong nature had got keyed up to a dangerous pitch. But now the reward was near. Balboa, when alone he ascended the summit that was to give him a sight of the great Pacific Ocean, was not more intensely excited than was Stanley when he labored up the steep mountain that should give him a view of the Tanganika.

The joy, the exultation of that moment, outbalanced a life of common happiness. It was a feeling that lifts the soul into a region where our common human nature never goes, and it becomes a memory that influences and shapes the character forever. Such a moment of ecstasy—of perfect satisfaction—of exultant, triumphant feeling that asks nothing better—that brings perfect rest with the highest exaltation, can happen to any man but once in a life-time. To attempt to give any description of this culmination of all his effort, and longing, and ambition, except in his own words, would be not only an act of injustice to him, but to the reader.

The descent to Ujiji and the interview with Livingstone is full of dramatic interest and the description of it should not be made by a third party, for to attempt to improve on it would be presumption and would end only in failure. We, therefore, give it in Mr. Stanley's own words, that glow with vivid life from beginning to end, and this shall be his chapter:

"We are descending the western slope of the mountain, with the valley of the Linche before us. Something like an hour before noon we have gained the thick matite brake, which grows on both banks of the river; we wade through the clear stream, arrive on the other side, emerge out of the brake, and the gardens of the Wajiji are around us—a perfect marvel of vegetable wealth. Details escape my hasty and partial observation. I am almost overpowered with my own emotion. I notice the graceful palms, neat plats, green with vegetable plants, and small villages, surrounded with frail fences of the matite cane.

"We push on rapidly, lest the news of our coming might reach the people of Bunder Ujiji before we come in sight and are ready for them. We halt at a little brook, then ascend the long slope of a naked ridge, the very last of the myriads we have crossed. This alone prevents us from seeing the lake in all its vastness. We arrive at the summit, travel across and arrive at its western rim, and—pause, reader—the port of Ujiji is below us, embowered in the palms, only five hundred yards from us. At this grand moment we do not think of the hundreds of miles we have marched, of the hundreds of hills we have ascended and descended, of the many forests we have traversed, of the jungles and thickets that annoyed us, of the fervid salt plains that blistered our feet, of the hot suns that scorched us, nor the dangers and difficulties now happily surmounted. At last the sublime hour has arrived! our dreams, our hopes, our anticipations are about to be realized. Our hearts and our feelings are with our eyes, as we peer into the palms and try to make out in which hut or house lives the white man, with the gray beard, we heard about on the Malagarazi.

"'Unfurl the flags and load the guns.'

"'Ay, Wallah, ay, Wallah, bana!' responded the men, eagerly.

"'One—two—three—fire.'

"A volley from nearly fifty guns roars like a salute from a battery of artillery; we shall note its effect, presently, on the peaceful-looking village below.

"'Now, Kirangozi, hold the white man's flag up high, and let the Zanzibar flag bring up the rear. And you men keep close together, and keep firing until we halt in the market-place, or before the white man's house. You have said to me often that you could smell the fish of the Tanganika. I can smell the fish of the Tanganika now. There are fish, and beer, and a long rest awaiting for you. March!'

"Before we had gone one hundred yards our repeated volleys had the desired effect. We had awakened Ujiji to the fact that a caravan was coming, and the people were witnessed running up in hundreds to meet us. The mere sight of the flags informed every one immediately that we were a caravan, but the American flag, borne aloft by the gigantic Asmani, whose face was one broad smile on this day, rather staggered them at first. However, many of the people who now approached us remembered the flag. They had seen it float above the American consulate, and from the mast-heads of many a ship in the harbor of Zanzibar, and they were soon heard welcoming the beautiful flag with cries of 'Bindera Kisungu!'—a white man's flag! 'Bindera Mericani!'—the American flag! These cries resounded on all sides.

"Then we were surrounded by them—by Wajiji, Wanyamzi, Wangwana, Warundi, Waguhha, Wamanyuema and Arabs, and were almost deafened with the shout of 'Yambo, yambo, bona! Yambo bona, Yambo bona, Yambo bona!' To all and each of my men the welcome was given.

"We were now about three hundred yards from the village of Ujiji, and the crowds are dense about me. Suddenly I hear a voice on my right say: 'Good morning, sir!'

"Startled at hearing this greeting in the midst of such a crowd of black people, I turn sharply around in search of the man, and see him at my side with the blackest of faces, but animated and joyous—

a man dressed in a long white shirt, with a turban of American sheeting around his woolly head, and I ask: 'Who the mischief are you?'

"'I am Susi, the servant of Dr. Livingstone,' said he, smiling and showing a gleaming row of teeth.

"'What! is Dr. Livingstone here?'

"'Yes, sir.'

"'In this village?'

"'Yes, sir.'

"'Are you sure?'

"'Sure, sure, sir. Why I just left him.'

"'Good-morning, sir,' said another voice.

"'Hallo,' said I, 'is this another one?'

"'Yes, sir.'

"'Well, what is your name?'

"'My name is Chumah, sir.'

"'What are you, Chumah, the friend of Weko-tani?'

"'Yes, sir.'

"'And is the doctor well?'

"'Not very well, sir.'

"'Where has he been so long?

"'In Manyuema.'

"'Now you, Susi, run and tell the doctor I am coming.'

"'Yes, sir,' and off he darted like a madman.

"By this time we were within two hundred yards of the village, and the multitude was getting denser, and almost preventing our march. Flags and streamers were out; Arabs and Wangwana were pushing their way through the natives in order to greet us, for according to their account we belonged to them. But the great wonder of all was, 'How did you come from Unyanyembe?'

"Soon Susi came running back and asked me my name; he had told the doctor that I was coming, but the doctor was too surprised to believe him, and when the doctor asked him my name Susi was rather staggered.

"But during Susi's absence the news had been conveyed to the doctor that it was surely a white man that was coming, whose guns were firing and whose flag could be seen; and the great Arab magnates of Ujiji—Mohammed bin Sali, Sayd bin Majid, Abid bin Suliman, Mohammed bin Gharib and others—had gathered together before the doctor's house, and the doctor had come out on his veranda to discuss the matter and await my arrival.

"In the meantime, the head of the expedition had halted and the Kirangozi were out of the ranks, holding the flag aloft, and Selim said to me, 'I see the doctor, sir. Oh, what an old man! He has got a white beard.' And I—what would I not have given for a bit of friendly wilderness where, unseen, I might vent my joy in some mad freak, such as idiotically biting my hand, turning a somersault, or slashing some trees, in order to allay those exciting feelings that were well-nigh uncontrollable. My heart beats fast, but I must not let my face betray my emotions, lest it shall detract from the dignity of a white man appearing under such extraordinary circumstances.

"So I did that which I thought was most dignified, I pushed back the crowds, and, passing from the rear, walked down a living avenue of people until I came in front of the semi-circle of Arabs, in front of which stood the white man with the gray beard. As I advanced slowly toward him I noticed he was pale, looked wearied, had a gray beard, wore a bluish cap with a faded gold band around it, had on a red-sleeved waistcoat and a pair of gray tweed trousers. I would have run to him, only I was a coward in such a mob—would have embraced him, only, he being an Englishman, I did not know how he would receive me; so I did what cowardice and false pride suggested was the best thing—walked deliberately to him, took off my hat and said, 'Dr. Livingstone, I presume?'

"'Yes,' said he, with a kind smile, lifting his hat slightly.

"I replace my cap on my head, and he puts on his cap, and we both grasp hands, and then I say aloud: 'I thank God, doctor, I have been permitted to see you.'

"He answered: 'I feel thankful I am here to welcome you.'

"I turned to the Arabs, took off my hat to them in response to the saluting chorus of 'Yambos,' I receive, and the doctor introduces them to me by name. Then oblivious of the crowds, oblivious of the men who shared with me my dangers, we—Livingstone and I—turn our faces toward his tembe. He points to the veranda, or rather mud platform, under the broad over-hanging eaves; he points to his own particular seat, which I see his age and experience in Africa have suggested, namely, a straw mat with a goat-skin over it, and another skin nailed against the wall to protect his back from contact with the cold mud. I protest against taking this seat, which so much more befits him than me, but the doctor will not yield: I must take it.

"We are seated—the doctor and I—with our backs to the wall. The Arabs take seats on our left. More than a thousand natives are in our front, filling the whole square densely, indulging their curiosity and discussing the fact of two white men meeting at Ujiji—one just come from Manyuema, in the west, the other from Unyanyembe, in the east.

"Conversation began. What about? I declare I have forgotten. Oh! we mutually asked questions of one another, such as: 'How did you come here?' and 'Where have you been all this long time? the world has believed you to be dead.' Yes, that was the way it began; but whatever the doctor informed me, and that which I communicated to him, I cannot exactly report, for I found myself gazing at him, conning the wonderful man, at whose side I now sat in Central Africa. Every hair of his head and beard, every wrinkle of his face, the wanness of his features, and the slightly wearied look he wore, were all imparting intelligence to me—the knowledge I craved for so much ever since I heard the words, 'Take what you want, but find Livingstone.' What I saw was deeply interesting intelligence to me, and unvarnished truths I was listening and reading at the same time. What did these dumb witnesses relate to me?

"Oh, reader, had you been at my side that day at Ujiji, how eloquently could be told the nature of this man's work! Had you been there but to see and hear! His lips gave me the details; lips that never lie. I cannot repeat what he said; I was too much engrossed to take my note-book out and begin to stenograph his story. He had so much to say that he began at the end, seemingly oblivious of the fact that five or six years had to be accounted for. But his account was oozing out; it was growing fast into grand proportions—into a most marvelous history of deeds.

"The Arabs rose up with a delicacy I approved, as if they intuitively knew that we ought to be left to ourselves. I sent Bombay with them to give them the news they also wanted so much to know about the affairs at Unyanyembe. Sayd bin Majid was the father of the gallant young man whom I saw at Masange, and who fought with me at Zimbizo, and who soon afterwards was killed by Mirambo's Ruga—Ruga in the forest of Wilyankuru; and knowing I had been there, he earnestly desired to hear the tale of the fight; but they all had friends at Unyanyembe, and it was but natural that they should be anxious to hear of what concerned them.

"After giving orders to Bombay and Asmani for the provisioning of the men of the expedition, I called 'Kaif-Halek,' or 'how do ye do,' and introduced him to Dr. Livingstone as one of the soldiers in charge of certain goods left at Unyanyembe, whom I had compelled to accompany me to Ujiji that he might deliver in person to his master, the letter-bag he had been intrusted with by Dr. Kirk.

"This was the famous letter-bag marked 'Nov. 1st, 1870,' which was now delivered into the doctor's hands, three hundred and sixty-five days after it left Zanzibar! How long, I wonder, had it remained at Unyanyembe, had I not been dispatched into Central Africa in search of the great traveler?

"The doctor kept the letter-bag on his knee, then, presently, opened it, looked at the letters contained there and read one or two of his children's letters, his face, in the meanwhile, lighting up.

"He asked me to tell him the news. 'No, doctor,' said I, 'read your letters first, which, I am sure, you must be impatient to read.'

"'Ah,' said he, 'I have waited years for letters, and I have been taught patience. I can surely afford to wait a few hours longer. No; tell me the general news; how is the world getting along?'

"'You probably know much already. Do you know that the Suez Canal is a fact—is opened and a regular trade carried on between Europe and India through it?'

"'I did not hear about the opening of it. Well, that is grand news! What else?'

"Shortly I found myself enacting the part of an annual periodical to him. There was no need of exaggeration—of any penny-a-line news, or of any sensationalism. The world had witnessed and experienced much the last few years. The Pacific Railroad had been completed; Grant had been elected President of the United States; Egypt had been flooded with savans; the Cretan rebellion had terminated; a Spanish revolution had driven Isabella from the throne of Spain, and a regent had been appointed; General Prim was assassinated; a Castelar had electrified Europe with his advanced ideas upon the liberty of worship; Prussia had humbled Denmark and annexed Schleswig-Holstein, and her armies were now around Paris; the 'Man of Destiny' was a prisoner at Wilhelmshöhe; the queen of fashion and the empress of the French was a fugitive; and the child born in the purple had lost forever the imperial crown intended for its head; the Napoleon dynasty was extinguished by the Prussians, Bismarck and Von Moltke, and France, the proud empire, was humbled to the dust.

"What could a man have exaggerated of these facts? What a budget of news it was to one who had emerged from the depths of the primeval forests of Manyuema! The reflection of the dazzling light of civilization was cast on him while Livingstone was thus listening in wonder to one of the most exciting passages of history ever repeated. How the puny deeds of barbarism paled before these! Who could tell under what new phases of uneasy life Europe was laboring even then, while we two of her lonely children rehearsed the tale of her late woes and glories? More worthily, perhaps, had the tongue of a lyric Demodocus recounted them; but in the absence of the poet, the newspaper correspondent performed his part as well and truthfully as he could.

"Not long after the Arabs had departed, a dishful of hot hashed-meat cakes was sent to us by Sayd bin Majid, and a curried chicken was received from Mohammed bin Sali, and Moeni Kheri sent a dishful of stewed goat meat and rice; and thus presents of food came in succession, and as fast as they were brought we set to. I had a healthy, stubborn digestion, the exercise I had taken had put it in prime order, but Livingstone—he had been complaining that he had no appetite, that his stomach refused everything but a cup of tea now and then—he ate also—ate like a vigorous, hungry man; and as he vied with me in demolishing the pancakes, he kept repeating, 'You have brought me new life.'

"'Oh, by George,' I said, 'I have forgotten something. Hasten, Selim, and bring that bottle; you know which; and bring me the silver goblets. I brought this bottle on purpose for this event, which I hoped would come to pass, though often it seemed useless to expect it.'

"Selim knew where the bottle was, and he soon returned with it—a bottle of Sillery champagne; and, handing the doctor a silver goblet brimful of the exhilarating wine, and pouring a small quantity into my own, I said: 'Dr. Livingstone, to your very good health, sir.'

"'And to yours,' he responded.

"And the champagne I had treasured for this happy meeting was drank with hearty good wishes to each other.

"But we kept on talking and talking, and prepared food was brought to us all that afternoon, and we kept on eating every time it was brought until I had eaten even to repletion, and the doctor was obliged to confess that he had eaten enough. Still, Halimah, the female cook of the doctor's establishment, was in a state of the greatest excitement. She had been protruding her head out of the cook-house, to make sure that there were really two white men sitting down in the veranda, when there used to be only one, who would not, because he could not, eat anything; and she had been considerably exercised in her mind over this fact. She was afraid the doctor did not properly appreciate her culinary abilities; but now she was amazed at the extraordinary quantity of food eaten, and she was in a state of delightful excitement. We could hear her tongue rolling off a tremendous volume of clatter to the wondering crowds who halted before the kitchen to hear the current of news with which she edified them. Poor, faithful soul. While we listen to the noise of her furious gossip, the doctor related her faithful services and the terrible anxiety she evinced when the guns first announced the arrival of another white man in Ujiji; how she had been flying about in a state of the utmost excitement, from the kitchen into his presence, and out again into the square, asking all sorts of questions; how she was in despair at the scantiness of the general larder and treasury of the strange household; how she was anxious to make up for their poverty by a grand appearance—to make up a sort of Barmecide feast to welcome the white man.

"'Why,' said she, 'is he not one of us? Does he not bring plenty of cloth and beads? Talk about the Arabs! Who are they, that they should be compared to white men? Arabs, indeed!'

"The doctor and I conversed upon many things, especially upon his own immediate troubles, and his disappointment upon his arrival at Ujiji when told that all his goods had been sold, and he was reduced to poverty. He had but twenty cloths or so left of the stock he had deposited with the man called sheriff, the half-caste, drunken tailor, who was sent by the British consul in charge of the goods. Besides which he had been suffering from an attack of the dysentery, and his condition was most deplorable. He was but little improved on this day, though he had eaten well, and already began to feel stronger and better.

"This day, like all others, though big with happiness to me, at last, was fading away. We, sitting with our faces looking to the east, as Livingstone had been sitting for days preceding my arrival, noted the dark shadow which crept up above the grove of palms beyond the village, and above the rampart of mountains which we had crossed that day, now looming through the fast-approaching darkness; and we listened, with our hearts full of gratitude to the great Giver of Good and Dispenser of all Happiness to the sonorous thunder of the surf of the Tanganika, and to the chorus which the night insects sang. Hours passed, and we were still sitting there with our minds busy upon the day's remarkable events, when I remembered that the venerable traveler had not yet read his letters.

"'Doctor,' I said, 'you had better read your letters. I will not keep you up any longer.'

"'Yes,' he answered, 'it is getting late, and I will go and read my friends' letters. Good-night, and God bless you.'

"'Good-night, my dear doctor, and let me hope, your news will be such as you desire.'"

Since the creation of the world there never has occurred such another interview. The feelings of Stanley that night, in the heart of Africa, can only be imagined. The strain had ended, the doubt and suspense were over—he had found Livingstone! he had succeeded; his most extravagant dreams had been realized; his wildest ambition was satisfied, and from that hour the adventurer, the newspaper correspondent, took his place among the great explorers of the world. But it was no stroke of luck,—it was the fitting reward of great risks and great endeavor.

CHAPTER IX

STANLEY'S HOMEWARD MARCH

Rest and repose were now enjoyed to the full by Stanley. His long struggles, his doubts and fears, his painful anxiety were over, and the end toward which he had strained with such unflagging resolution, the most disheartening circumstances, and which at times seemed to recede the more as he pressed forward, was at last reached. The sweet repose, the calm satisfaction and enjoyment which always come with the consciousness of complete success, now filled his heart, and he felt as none can feel but he who has at last won a long and doubtful battle. It was complete rest, the entire fruition of his hopes; and as he sat down there in the heart of Africa, beside Livingstone, he was doubtless for at least the first few days, the happiest man on the globe, and well he deserved to be. The goal was won, the prize secured, and for the time being his utmost desires were satisfied. Why should he not be happy?

His intercourse with Livingstone for the next four months will be marked by him as the brightest portion of his eventful life. Independent of all he had undergone to find this remarkable man, the man himself enlisted all his sympathies and awakened his most extravagant admiration and purest love, and a more charming picture can hardly be conceived than these two men, walking at sunset along the beach of the wild and lonely lake of Tanganika, talking over the strange scenes and objects of their strange, new world, or recalling home and friends far away amid all the comforts and luxuries of civilization. The man whom Stanley had at last found was almost as new and startling a revelation to him as the country in which he had found him. Simple, earnest, unselfish—nay, unambitious, so far as personal fame was concerned, borne up in all his sufferings and trials by one great and noble purpose, and conquering even savage hate by the power of goodness alone, he was an object of the profoundest interest. And no greater eulogium on the innate goodness and nobleness of Stanley's nature could be given than he unconsciously bestowed on himself by the deep attachment, nay, almost adoration, he expresses for this lonely, quiet, good man. He fastens to him at once, and casting off old prejudices and rejecting all former criticisms of his character, he impulsively becomes his champion, and crowns him the prince of men.

The talk between them at their first meeting in this far-off land, was long and pleasant, and when the good-night was given, it was with strange feelings that Stanley turned into his allotted sleeping place in a regular bed. After all the toils and almost unnatural excitement of the day, he soon sank into profound slumber. The next morning he awoke with a start, and looked about him for a moment in a dazed way. He was not on the ground, but in a bed; a roof, not a tent, was above him, while not a sound broke the stillness save the steady, monotonous roar of the surf beating on the shore. As he lay and listened, strange thoughts and varied emotions chased each other in rapid succession through his heart. At length he arose and dressed himself, intending before breakfast to take a stroll along the shore of the lake. But the doctor was up before him and met him with a cordial "Good-morning," and the hope that he had rested well.

Livingstone had sat up late reading the news that Stanley had brought him from the outside world, from which he had heard nothing for years.

"Sit down," said the venerable man, "you have brought me good and bad news," and then he repeated, first of all, the tidings he had received from his children.

In the excitement of the day before, the doctor had forgotten to inquire of Stanley the object of his coming, or where he was going, and the latter now said: "Doctor, you are probably wondering why I came here."

"It is true," was the reply, "I have been wondering."

That wonder was increased when Stanley said: "I came after you, nothing else."

"After me!" exclaimed the now utterly bewildered man.

"Yes," said Stanley, "after you. I suppose you have heard of the New York Herald?"

"Yes," said the doctor.

"Well, Mr. Bennett, son of the proprietor, sent me, at his own expense, to find you."

Poor Livingstone could hardly comprehend the fact that an American, and a stranger, should expend $25,000 to find him, a solitary Englishman.

Stanley lived now some four months in the closest intimacy with Livingstone. Removed from all the formalities of civilized life—the only two in that far-off land who could converse in the English language, and who were of the same lineage and faith—their relations of necessity became very intimate. All restraint was thrown off, and this noble man poured into the astonished ears of Stanley all he had thought, prayed for, endured and suffered for the last long five years. It was a new revelation to his hearer. It opened

75

up a new world; gave him a new and loftier conception of what human nature is capable of attaining, and he says: "I had gone over battle-fields, witnessed revolutions, civil wars, rebellions, emeutes and massacres; stood close to the condemned murderer to record his last struggles and last sighs; but never had I been called to record anything that moved me so much as this man's woes and sufferings, his privations and disappointments, which were now poured into my ear. Verily did I begin to believe that 'the gods above us do with just eyes survey the affairs of men.' I began to recognize the hand of an overruling Providence."

After resting for a week, during which time Stanley became thoroughly acquainted with Livingstone and learned to respect and love him more and more, the former asked the doctor if he would not like to explore the north end of the Tanganika Lake and among other things, settle the question whether the Rusizi River flowed into or out of the lake. The doctor gladly consented, and they set off in a canoe manned by sixteen rowers. The weather was fine, the scenery charming, and it seemed like floating through a fairyland. Day after day they kept on—landing at night on the picturesque shores, undisturbed, except in one or two instances, by the natives. The luxuriant banks were lined with villages, filled with an indolent, contented people. With no wants except food to eat, and the lake full of fish, they had nothing to stimulate them to activity or effort of any kind.

Islands came and went, mountains rose and faded on the horizon, and it was one long holiday to our two explorers. As the rowers bent steadily to their oars and the canoe glided softly through the rippling waters, they spent the time in admiring the beautiful scenery that kept changing like a kaleidoscope, or talking of home and friends and the hopes and prospects of the future. A hippopotamus would now and then startle them by his loud snort, as he suddenly lifted his head near the boat to breathe, wild fowl skittered away as they approached, a sweet fragrance came down from the hill-sides, and the tropical sky bent soft and blue above them. The conventionalities of life were far away and all was calm and peaceful, and seemed to Stanley more like a dream than a reality. They were thus voyaging along the coast twenty-eight days, during which time they had traversed over three hundred miles of water.

But at last the time came for Stanley to turn his footsteps homeward. He tried in vain to prevail on Livingstone to go home with him, but the latter, though anxious to see his children, resolutely refused, saying that he must finish his work. He, however, concluded to accompany Stanley as far as Unyanyembe, to meet the stores which had been forwarded to that place for him from Zanzibar. On the 27th of December, therefore, they set out by a new route. Nothing occurred in the long journey of special interest, except the shooting of a zebra or a buffalo, the meeting of a herd of elephants or giraffes, or a lion. It was a tedious and toilsome journey, during which Stanley suffered from attacks of fever, and Livingstone from lacerated feet. They were fifty-three days on the march, but at last Unyanyembe was reached. Stanley once more took possession of his old quarters. Here both found letters and papers from home, brought by a recent caravan, and once more they seemed put in communication with the outside world. Being well-housed and provided with everything they needed, they felt thoroughly comfortable.

The doctor's boxes were first broken open, and between the number of poor articles they contained and the absence of good ones which had been abstracted on the way, they proved something of a disappointment. Stanley then overhauled his own stores, of which there were seventy-four loads, the most valuable of which he intended to turn over to Livingstone. These also had been tampered with; still many luxuries remained, and they determined to have their Christmas dinner over again. Stanley arranged the bill of fare, and it turned out grandly. But now he saw that he must begin to prepare for his return to the coast, and so he left Livingstone to write up his journal and to finish the letters he was to send home. In overhauling the stores and making up the packages he should need on his return route, he was able to select and turn over to the doctor two thousand seven hundred and eighty-eight yards of cloth, nine hundred and ninety-two pounds of assorted beads, three hundred and fifty pounds of brass wire, besides bed, canvas boat, carpenters' tools, rifles, revolvers, ammunition, cooking utensils and various other articles of use, making in all about forty loads. These, with the doctor's personal stores, made Livingstone quite a rich man for Central Africa—in fact, he had a four years' supply.

At length the letters were all written, the loads strapped, and the next day fixed for Stanley to turn his face homeward and Livingstone his to the heart of Africa. At night the natives gave a great dance as a farewell compliment, and a wild, weird dance it was. Bombay wore a water-bucket on his head, while each carried or wore something grotesque or dangerous. The first was a war dance, and when it ended, a second and different one was started, accompanied by a chorus or song chanted in a slow, mournful tone, of which the burden was "Oh-oh-oh, the white man is going home."

That night as Stanley lay and pondered on the morrow, when he should see the "good man" for the last time, he was filled with the keenest sorrow. He had grown to love him like a father; and to see him turn back alone to the savage life he must encounter in his great work, seemed like giving him over to death.

It was a sad breakfast to which the two sat down next morning. But it was over at last and the parting hour came.

"Doctor," said Stanley, "I will leave two men with you for a couple of days, lest you may have forgotten something, and will wait for them at Tura; and now we must part—there is no help for it—good-bye."

"Oh," replied Livingstone, "I am coming with you a little way; I must see you off on the road;" and the two walked on side by side, their hearts burdened with grief.

At last Stanley said: "Now, my dear doctor, the best friends must part, you have come far enough, let me beg of you to turn back."

Livingstone stopped and, seizing Stanley's hand, said: "I am grateful to you for what you have done for me. God guide you safe home and bless you, my friend."

"And may God bring you safe back to us all, my friend," replied Stanley, with a voice choked with emotion. "Farewell."

They wrung each other's hands in silence for a minute, and then Stanley turned away to hide his tears, murmuring: "Good-bye, doctor; dear friend, good-bye."

He would not have been the man he is, not to have been overcome at this parting; alas, to be, as it proved, a final parting, so far as concerns meeting again in this life. But this was not all—the doctor's faithful servants would not be forgotten, and rushing forward, they seized Stanley's hands and kissed them for their good master's sake. The stern and almost tyrannical man, that neither danger nor suffering could move, completely broke down under this last demonstration and could recover himself only by giving the sharp order, March! and he almost drove his men before him, and soon a turn in the path shut out Livingstone's form forever. Yes, forever, so far as the living, speaking man is concerned, but shut out never from Stanley's life. That one man fixed his destiny for this world, and who knows but for the eternal ages? No wonder that he said, long after, "My eyes grow dim at the remembrance of that parting. For four months and four days I lived with him in the same house, or in the same boat, or in the same tent, and I never found a fault in him. I am a man of a quick temper, and often without sufficient cause, I dare say, have broken ties of friendship; but with Livingstone I never had cause of resentment, but each day's life with him added to my admiration of him."

The caravan marched wearily back, meeting with nothing

eventful till it entered the Ugogo territory, where, owing to a misunderstanding on the part of the natives, who got it into their heads that Stanley meant to pass them without paying the accustomed tribute, a fight seemed inevitable. Had it occurred, it is doubtful whether he or Livingstone's papers would ever have been heard of again. But Stanley had seemed from his infancy a child of destiny, and escaped here, as everywhere, by the skin of his teeth. It was a constant succession of toilsome, painful marches, even when the natives were friendly, while there was often a scarcity of provisions. To secure these he, at last, when on the borders of the wilderness of Marenga Mkali, dispatched three men to Zanzibar, with a request to the consul there to send them back with provisions. These messengers were told not to halt for anything—rain, rivers or inundations—but push right on. "Then," says Stanley, "with a loud, vigorous hurrah, we plunged into the depths of the wilderness which, with its eternal silence and solitude, was far preferable to the jarring, inharmonious discord of the villages of the Wagogo. For nine hours we held on our way, starting with noisy shouts the fierce rhinoceros, the timid quagga and the herds of antelopes, which crowd the jungles of this broad Salina. On the 7th, amid a pelting rain, we entered Mpwapwa, where my Scotch assistant, Farquhar, had died."

In twenty-nine days they had marched three hundred and thirty-eight miles. Twelve miles a day, including stoppages and delays, was in such a country rapid marching—nay, almost unparalleled; but Stanley had turned his face homeward and could stand no African dilly-dallying on the way. We cannot go into the details of this homeward march,—to-day startled by a thousand warriors, streaming along the war-path,—to-morrow on the brink of a collision with the natives, the end of which no one could foresee, but the caravan pressed on until they came to the neighborhood of the terrible Makata swamps, that Stanley had occasion so well to remember. Heavy rains had set in, swelling all the streams and inundating the plains, so that the marching was floundering through interminable stretches of water. Now swimming turbulent rivers—now camping in the midst of pestiferous swamps, and all the time drenched by the rain, that fell in torrents—they struggled on until, at last, they came to the dreaded Makata swamp itself. The sight that met them here was appalling, but there was no retreat, and for long hours they toiled slowly through, sometimes up to their necks in water, sometimes swimming, and where it was shallow sinking in deep mire. They thus fought their way on, and at last, weary, worn and half-starved, came to the Makata River. But no sooner were they over this, than a lake six miles wide stretched before them. The natives warned him against attempting to cross it; but nothing could stop him now, and they all plunged in.

He says: "We were soon up to our armpits, then the water shallowed to the knee, then we stepped up to the neck and waded on tiptoe, until we were halted on the edge of the Little Makata, which raced along at the rate of eight knots an hour." Fierce and rapid as it was, there was no course left but to swim it, and swim it they did. For a whole week they had been wading and swimming and floundering through water, till it seemed impossible that any one could survive such exposure, but, at last they came to dry ground and to the famous walled city of the Sultana Limbamwanni, which we described in his upward journey. But the heavy rains that had inundated the whole country, had so swollen the river, near the banks on which it was situated, that the water had carried away the entire front wall of the town, and some fifty houses with it. The sultana had fled and her stronghold had disappeared. All along the route was seen the devastating power of the flood as it swept over the country, carrying away a hundred villages in its course. The fields were covered with débris of sand and mud, and what was a paradise when he went in was now a desert. With the subsidence of the water the atmosphere became impregnated with miasma, and the whole land seemed filled with snakes, scorpions, iguanas and ants, while clouds of mosquitoes darkened the air till life became almost intolerable. At last, on May 2d, after forty-seven days of incessant marching, and almost continual suffering, they reached Rosako, where, a few minutes after, the three men he had sent forward arrived, bringing with them a few boxes of jam, two of Boston crackers, and some bottles of champagne; and most welcome they were after the terrible journey through the Makata Valley. The last great obstacle (a ferry of four miles across a watery plain) being surmounted, the caravan approached Bagomayo, and in their jubilant excitement announced its arrival by the firing of guns and blowing of horns, and with shouting hurrahs till they were hoarse. The sun was just sinking behind the distant forests, from which they had emerged and which were filled with such terrible associations, when they entered the town, and sniffed with delight the fresh sea-breeze that came softly stealing inland. The putrid air of the swamps, the poisonous miasma that enveloped the entire country, were left far behind with want and famine, and no wonder the heart was elated and their bounding joy found expression in exultant shouts.

Happy in having once more reached civilization; happy in the thought of his triumphant success; and still more happy in the joy that he believed the good news he brought would give to others,

Stanley's heart was overflowing with kindness to all, and the world seemed bright to him. But, in a moment it was all dashed on opening the papers at Zanzibar. Scarcely one had a kind word for him; on the contrary, he found nothing but suspicion, jealousy and detraction, and even charges of fabricating the whole story of having found Livingstone. He was stunned at this undeserved cruel reception of his declaration, and the faith in the goodness of human nature, with which Livingstone had inspired him, seemed about to give way before this evidence of its meanness and littleness. He could not comprehend how his simple, truthful, unostentatious story could awaken such unkind feelings, such baseless slanders. It was a cruel blow to receive, after all that he had endured and suffered. No wonder he wrote bitter words of the kid-glove geographers, who criticized him, and the press that jeered at him. But he has had his revenge, for he has triumphed over them all.

He immediately set to work to organize a caravan to send off to Livingstone the things he had promised, and then started for home.

CHAPTER X

STANLEY'S MAIN EXPEDITION

Stanley, after he had found Livingstone, naturally thought much of the latter's explorations. Africa had become to him an absorbing subject, and he began to imbibe the spirit of Livingstone. This was natural, for Stanley had already won fame there, and why should he not win still greater laurels in the same field? This feeling was much increased after the death of the great explorer, leaving his work unfinished, which Stanley longed to complete. True, Cameron was on the ground to accomplish this very object, but Stanley knew the difficulties one would have to contend with without a boat of his own. The matter was talked over a good deal, and finally the proprietors of the New York Herald and London Telegraph determined to send Stanley once more into Africa.

The vast lake region, embracing some six degrees of longitude, and extending from the equator to fifteen degrees south latitude, had become a region of the greatest interest to explorers.

On this vast water-shed lived a mighty population, and these lakes, with the rivers running into and out of them, must furnish the roads to commerce and be the means by which Africa should be lifted out of its barbarism into the light of civilization.

The large lakes Nyassa and Tanganika had been more or less explored, but the one possessing the greatest interest, the Victoria Nyanza—on account of the general impression that it was the head of the Nile—was almost wholly unknown. The persistence with which the Nile had mocked all previous attempts to find its source, had imparted a mystery to it and caused efforts to be made to unlock the secret, which were wholly disproportioned to its seeming value or real importance. This lake, therefore, was to be Stanley's first objective point. Livingstone, Speke and Burton, and others had seen it—he would sail around it in a boat which he would take with him. This he had made in sections, so that it could be carried the nearly one thousand miles through the jungles of Africa to its destination.

Everything being completed he started on his route, and in the latter part of 1874 found himself once more at Zanzibar, after an absence of four years. Here, in organizing his expedition, he discovered that the builder had made his boat, which he had christened the Lady Alice, a great deal heavier than he had ordered; but he luckily found a man in Zanzibar who was able to reduce its weight so that it could be transported by the carriers. His force consisted in all, of a little over three hundred men, and he took with him several powerful dogs.

The interest of this great expedition begins where he struck off from the regular route of the caravans going west, and entered an entirely new country and encountered a new race of people. Instead of moving directly westward, he turned off to the north, and at length reached the western frontier of Ugogo, on the last day of the year 1874. The country at this point stretched before him in one vast plain, which some of the natives said extended clear to Nyanza. He found that his course led him along the extremity of Whumba, which he was glad to know, as he thought his march would now be unmolested. Two days' march brought them to the borders of Usandawa, a country abounding in elephants. Here he turned to the north-west and entered Ukimbu or Uyonzi on its eastern extremity. The guides he had hired in Ugogo to take him as far as Iramba here deserted him. Hiring fresh ones, he continued two days in the same direction, when these deserted him also, and Stanley found himself one morning on the edge of a vast wilderness without a guide.

The day before, the guides had told him that three days' march would bring him to Urimi. Relying on the truth of this statement, he had purchased only two days' provisions. Thinking, therefore, that they would be there by the evening of the next day, he thought little of the desertion and moved off with confidence. But the next morning, the track, which was narrow and indistinct at the best, became so inextricably mixed up with the paths made by elephants and rhinoceros, that they were wholly at a loss what course to take. Halting, Stanley sent out men to seek the lost trail, but they returned unable to find it. They then, of course, could do nothing but march by compass, which they did.

As might be expected, it brought them, after a few hours' march, into a dense jungle of acacias and euphorbias, through which they could make their way only by crawling, scrambling and cutting the entangling vines. Now pushing aside an obstructing branch—now cutting a narrow lane through the matted mass, and now taking advantage of a slight opening, this little band of three hundred struggled painfully forward toward what they thought was open country, and an African village with plenty of provisions.

In this protracted struggle the third night overtook them in the wilderness, and there they pitched their lonely, starving camp. To make it more gloomy, one of the men died and was buried; his shallow grave seeming to be a sad foreboding of what awaited them in the future. The want of provisions now began to tell terribly on the men, but there was nothing to do but go forward, trusting to some break in this apparently interminable wilderness. But human endurance has its limit, and although Stanley kept his little force marching all day, they made but fourteen miles. It was a continual jungle, with not a drop of water on the route. The poor carriers, hungry and thirsty, sank under their loads and lagged behind the main force for many miles, until it became a straggling, weary, despondent crowd, moving without order and without care through the wilderness. The strong endeavored to help the weak, and did relieve them of their burdens and encourage them to hold on, so that most of them were able to reach the camp at night. But in despite of all effort five sick, despairing men, strayed from the path, which was only a blind trail made by those in advance.

After the camp for the night was pitched, Stanley sent back scouts to find the wanderers. They explored the woods for a mile each side of the track, but only one man was found, and he fully a mile from the trail and dead. The other four had wandered off beyond reach and were never heard of more. This was getting to be fearful marching—five men in one day was a death-roll that could not be kept up long, and Stanley began to cast about anxiously to determine what step he should next take. There was but one course left open to him, to attempt to retrace his steps was certain death by famine, to advance could not be worse, while it might bring relief, so "push on," was the order, and they did push on, weary, thirsty, starving, and on the fifth day they came to a little village recently established, and which consisted of only four huts, occupied by four men with their wives and children. These had scarcely provisions enough to keep themselves, and hence could give nothing to Stanley's starving men. It was useless to attempt further marching without food, for the men staggered into camp exhausted, and would rather die there than attempt to move again.

Stanley's experience had taught him how far he could urge on these African carriers and soldiers, and he saw they had now become desperate and would not budge another inch until they had something to eat. He, therefore, ordered a halt, and selecting twenty of his strongest men, sent them off in search of food. They were to press on to a village called Suna, about thirty miles distant, of which the natives told him, and where they said food was in abundance. As soon as they had disappeared in the forest, Stanley took his gun and strolled out in search of game. But, filled as the country seemed with it, he could find nothing to shoot. One of his men, however, came across a lion's den, in which were two cubs, which he brought to Stanley. The latter skinned them and took them back to camp. As he entered it, the pinched and worn faces of his faithful men, as they sat hungry and despairing, moved him so deeply that he would have wept, but for fear of adding to their despondency. The two cubs would go but a little way toward feeding some two hundred and twenty men, if cooked as ordinary meat, so he resolved to make a soup of them, which would go much farther. But the question was where to get a kettle large enough to make a soup for such a large body of men.

Luckily, he bethought himself of a sheet-iron trunk which he had among his baggage, and which was water-tight. He quickly dumped out of it its contents, and filling it with water, set it over a fire which he had ordered to be made. He then broke open his medical stores, and taking out five pounds of Scotch oatmeal and three one-pound tins of Revalenta Arabica, he made with it and the two young lions a huge trunk full of gruel, that would give even two hundred and twenty men a good bowl apiece. He said it was a rare sight to see those hungry, famished men gather around that Torquay dress-trunk and pile on the fuel, and in every way assist to make the contents boil, while with greedy eyes, with gourds in their hands full of water, they stood ready to pour it in the moment it threatened to boil over and waste the precious contents. "But," he adds, "it was a rarer sight still to watch the famished wretches, as, with these same gourds full of the precious broth, they drank it down as only starving men swallow food. The weak and sick got a larger portion, and another tin of oatmeal being opened for their supper and breakfast, they awaited patiently the return of those who had gone in quest of food."

Stanley's position now became painfully trying. He was five days' march from where he could obtain food, if he attempted to go back. This march, in the present condition of his men, they could never make, and if any did survive, it would be on the terrible condition of the living eating the dead.

The only hope lay in reaching supplies in advance. But what if those twenty strong men he had sent on to find them never returned, having been ambushed and killed on the way, or what if they, at the end of several days, returned and reported nothing but an unbroken wilderness and impassable jungle or swamps in front, and themselves famished, ready to die? These were questions that Stanley anxiously put to himself and dared not contemplate the answer. The hours of painful anxiety and suspense, the maddening thoughts and wild possibilities that fire the brain and oppress the heart in such crises as these cannot be imagined, they can be known only by him who suffers the pangs they inflict. This is a portion of the history of the expedition that Stanley can never write, though it is written on his heart in lines that will never be effaced.

The empty trunk lay on one side, and the night came down and the stars burned bright and tranquilly above, and all was silent in the wide solitude as Stanley sat and listened for the return of his men. But they came not, and the morning broke and the sun rode the tropical heavens once more in his splendor, but no musket-shot from the forest told of the returning scouts. The weary hours wore on and the emaciated men lay around in silent suffering. To Stanley those hours seemed days. Night again darkened the forest and still no sign of the returning party. Would they ever return? was the terrible question Stanley was perpetually putting to himself, and if not, what desperate movement should he attempt?

The third morning broke as calm and peaceful as the rest; he was beginning to despair, when, suddenly, a musket-shot broke over the forest, and then another and another, sending sudden life and activity throughout the despairing camp. The men, as they emerged into view laden with food, were greeted with a loud shout, and the hungry wretches fell on the provisions they brought like ravening wolves. The report of abundance ahead so excited the men that they forgot their feebleness and clamored to be led on that very afternoon. Stanley was quite willing to get away from the jungle, filled with such painful associations, and cheerfully ordered the march, but before they could get away two men breathed their last in the camp and were left to sleep alone in the wilderness.

That night they encamped at the base of a rocky hill, from which stretched away a broad plain. The hill, lifting itself into the clear air, and the open plain, seemed like civilization compared with the gloomy jungle in which they had been starving for the last two days, and where they had left two of their number. They awoke next morning cheerful and refreshed. Starting off with the prospect of abundant provisions ahead, they made a steady march of twenty miles and reached the district of Suna in Urimi.

Stanley was surprised, on entering the rude village, to see a new type of African life. Men and women of great beauty and fine physical proportions met his astonished sight. They stood before him in all their naked beauty, unabashed: the women bearing children alone wearing a covering of goat skins, designed evidently as a protection against external injury, and not caused by any notions of modesty. Their fine appearance seemed to indicate a greater mental development than any other tribes which they had met. Whether this were so or not, it would be difficult to tell, for they were the most suspicious, reserved people Stanley had ever met, being greatly disinclined to barter provisions, of which they had more than they wanted, for cloth and beads, of which they apparently had none.

They had no chief, but seemed to be governed in their actions by the old men. With these Stanley therefore treated for permission to pass through their land. It required great tact to secure this, and still more to obtain the required food. Stanley bore this silent hostility patiently, for though he could have taken all he wanted by force, he wished to avoid all violence. While lingering here, two more of his exhausted company gave out and died, while his sick list swelled up to thirty. Among the latter was Edward Pocoke, whom, with his brother, Stanley had engaged in England to accompany him as attendants. This compelled him to halt for four days, but finding that the hostile feeling of the natives increased the longer he stayed, he determined, dangerous as it was to the sick, especially to Pocoke, to leave. Dysentery and diarrhœa were prevailing to an alarming extent, and rest was especially necessary for these, if they hoped to recover; but he was afraid matters would become dangerously complicated if he remained, and he turned his soldiers into carriers and slung the sick into hammocks. Encouraging them with the prospect of plenty and comfort ahead, he gave the order to march, and they passed out and entered upon a clear, open and well cultivated country. Reaching a village at 10 o'clock they halted, and here, to the great grief of all, young Pocoke breathed his last. In speaking of this sad event, which cast a gloom over the camp, Stanley says: "We had finished the four hundredth mile of our march from the sea and had reached the base of the water-shed, where the trickling streams and infant waters began to flow Nileward, when this noble young man died." They buried him at night under a tree, with the stars shining down on the shallow-made grave; Stanley reading the burial service of the Church of England over the body. Far from home and friends in that distant lonely land he sleeps to-day, a simple wooden cross marking his burial place. Stanley sent the following letter home to the young man's father, describing his sickness and death:

"Kagehyi, on the Victoria Nyanza,
"March 4th, 1875.

"Dear Sir: A most unpleasant, because sad, task devolves upon me, for I have the misfortune to have to report to you the death of your son Edward, of typhoid fever. His service with me was brief, but it was long enough for me to know the greatness of your loss, for I doubt that few fathers can boast of such sons as yours. Both Frank and Ted proved themselves sterling men, noble and brave hearts and faithful servants. Ted had endeared himself to the members of the expedition by his amiable nature, his cheerfulness, and by various qualifications which brought him into high favor with the native soldiers of this force.

"Before daybreak we were accustomed to hear the cheery notes of his bugle, which woke us to a fresh day's labor; at night, around the camp-fires, we were charmed with his sweet, simple songs, of which he had an inexhaustible répertoire. When tired also with marching, it was his task to announce to the tired people the arrival of the vanguard at camp, so that he had become quite a treasure to us all; and I must say, I have never known men who could bear what your sons have borne on this expedition so patiently and uncomplainingly. I never heard one grumble either from Frank or Ted; have never heard them utter an illiberal remark, or express any wish that the expedition had never set foot in Africa, as many men would have done in their situation, so that you may well imagine, that if the loss of one of your sons causes grief to your paternal heart, it has been no less a grief to us, as we were all, as it were, one family, surrounded as we are by so much that is dark and forbidding.

"On arriving at Suna, in Urimi, Ted came to me, after a very long march, complaining of pain in his limbs and loins. I did not think it was serious at all, nor anything uncommon after walking twenty miles, but told him to go and lie down, that he

87

would be better on the morrow, as it was very likely fatigue. The next morning I visited him, and he again complained of pains in the knees and back, which I ascribed to rheumatism, and treated him accordingly. The third day he complained of pain in the chest, difficulty of breathing and sleeplessness, from which I perceived he was suffering from some other malady than rheumatism, but what it could be I could not divine. He was a little feverish, so I applied a mustard-plaster and gave him some aperient medicine. Toward night he began to wander in his head, and on examining his tongue I found it was almost black and coated with dark gray fur. At these symptoms I thought he had a severe attack of remittent fever, from which I suffered in Ujiji, in 1871, and therefore I watched for an opportunity to administer quinine—that is, when the fever should abate a little.

"On the fourth day, the patient still wandering in his mind, I suggested to Frank that he should sponge him with cold water and change his clothing, during which operation I noticed that the chest of the patient was covered with spots like pimples or small-pox pustules, which perplexed me greatly. He could not have caught the small-pox, and what the disease was I could not imagine; but, turning to my medical books, I saw that your son was suffering from typhoid, the description of which was too clear to be longer mistaken, and both Frank and I devoted our attention to him. He was nourished with arrow-root and brandy, and everything that was in our power to do was done; but it was very evident that the case was serious, though I hoped that his constitution would brave it out.

"On the fifth day we were compelled to resume our journey, after a rest of four days. Ted was put in a hammock and carried on the shoulders of four men. At 10 o'clock on the 17th of January, we halted at Chiwyn, and the minute he was laid down in the camp he breathed his last. Our companion was dead.

"We buried him that night under a tree, on which his brother Frank had cut a deep cross, and we read the beautiful service of the Church of England over him as we laid the poor worn-out body in its final resting-place so far from his own home and friends.

"Peace be to his ashes. Poor Ted deserved a better fate than dying in Africa, but it was impossible that he could have died easier. I wish that my end may be as peaceful and painless as his. He was spared the stormy scenes we went through afterwards in our war with the Waturn: and who knows how much he has been saved from? But I know that he would have rejoiced to be with us at this hour of our triumph, gazing on the laughing waters of the vast fountain of the old Nile. None of us would have been more

elated at the prospect before us than he, for he was a true sailor,
and loved the sight of water. Yet again I say peace be to his ashes;
be consoled, for Frank still lives, and, from present appearances, is
likely to come home to you with honor and glory, such as he and
you may well be proud of. Believe me, dear sir, with true sincerity,
your well-wisher,

"Henry M. Stanley."

Stanley still traveled in a northwest direction, and the farther he advanced the more he was convinced that the rivulets he encountered flowed into the Nile, and he became elated with the hope that he should soon stand on the shores of the great lake that served as the head reservoir of the mighty river.

Two days' march now brought them to Mongafa, where one of his men who had accompanied him on his former expedition was murdered. He was suffering from the asthma, and Stanley permitted him to follow the party slowly. Straggling thus behind alone, he was waylaid by the natives and murdered. It was impossible to ascertain who committed the deed, and so Stanley could not avenge the crime.

Keeping on they at length entered Itwru, a district of Northern Urimi. The village where they camped was called Vinyata, containing some two thousand to three thousand souls, and was situated in a broad and populous valley, through which flowed a stream twenty feet wide. The people here received him in a surly manner, but Stanley was very anxious to avoid trouble and used every exertion to conciliate them. He seemed at last to succeed, for at evening they brought him milk, eggs and chickens, taking cloth in exchange. This reached the ears of the great man of the valley, a magic doctor, who, there being no king over the people, is treated with the highest respect and honor by them. The next day he brought Stanley a fat ox, for which the latter paid him twice what it was worth in cloth and beads, besides making a rich present to his brother and son. To all this man's requests Stanley cheerfully consented in his anxiety to conciliate him and the natives.

That day, taking advantage of the bright sun to dry the bales and goods, he exposed his rich stores, an imprudence which he very quickly deeply regretted, for he saw that the display awoke all the greedy feelings of the natives, as was evinced by their eager looks. But the day passed quietly, and on the third morning the great man made his appearance again and begged for more beads, which were given him and he departed apparently very much pleased, and Stanley congratulated himself that he would be allowed to depart in peace.

CHAPTER XI

PRESSING TOWARDS THE INTERIOR

For a half an hour after the magic doctor left, Stanley sat quietly in his camp, his anxieties now thoroughly dissipated, thinking over his speedy departure for the Nyanza. The camp was situated on the margin of a vast wilderness, which stretched he knew not how far westward, while away to the north, south and east extended a wide, open plain, dotted over, as far as the eye could see, with villages. There were nearly two hundred of them, looking is the distance like clusters of beehives. Everything was peaceful, and not a sound disturbed the Sabbath-like stillness of the scene, when there suddenly broke on his ears the shrill war-cry, which was taken up by village after village till the whole valley resounded with it. It was one loud "he-hu, he-hu," the last syllable prolonged and uttered in a high, piercing note that made the blood shiver. Still Stanley felt no alarm, supposing that some war expedition was about to be set on foot, or some enemy was reported to be near, and listened to the barbaric cry simply with curiosity. The men in the camp kept about their usual avocations—some fetching water from a neighboring pool, while others were starting off after wood—when suddenly a hundred warriors appeared close to camp in full war costume. Feathers of the eagle and other birds waved above their heads, "the mane of the zebra and giraffe encircled their foreheads, their left hand held the bow and arrows, while the right grasped the spear." Stanley arose, and telling the men not to leave camp nor do anything to provoke a hostile act, waited to see what this sudden warlike attitude meant.

In the meantime the throng increased till the entire camp was surrounded. A slight bush fence had been built around it, which, though it concealed those within, was too slight to be of use in case of an attack. Seeing that this hostile demonstration was against him, Stanley sent out a young man who spoke their language, to inquire what they wanted. Six or seven warriors advanced to meet him, when a lively conversation followed. The messenger soon returned and reported that they accused one of the party of having stolen some milk and butter from a small village, and they must be paid for it in cloth. He at once sent the messenger back, directing him to tell the warriors that he did not come into their country to rob or steal, and if anything had been taken from them they had but to name the price they asked for it and it should be paid at once. The messenger brought back word that they demanded four yards of sheeting; although this was worth four times as much as the articles were which they alleged had been stolen, he was very glad to settle the matter so easily, and it was measured and sent to them. The elders declared that they were perfectly satisfied, and they all withdrew. But Stanley could not at once shake off the suspicion this unexpected show of hostile feeling had excited, and he watched narrowly the villages in the distance. He soon saw that the warriors were not pacified if the elders were, for he could see them hurrying together from all parts of the plain and gesticulating wildly.

Still he hoped the elders would keep them from any overt act of hostility. While he was watching them, he saw about two hundred men separate themselves from the main body, and taking a sweep, make for the woods west of the camp. They had hardly entered when one of Stanley's men rushed forth from the same vicinity into camp bleeding profusely from his face and arms. He said that Suleiman (a youth) and he were gathering wood when the savages came suddenly upon them. He was struck with a stick that broke his nose, and his arm was pierced with a spear, while Suleiman fell pierced with a dozen spears. His story and bloody appearance so excited the soldiers that Stanley could with difficulty restrain them from rushing out at once and attacking the murderers. He did not yet despair of preventing an outbreak, but took care to open the ammunition and be prepared for the worst. He saw at once that an immensely large force could be brought against him, and he must fortify himself or he would be overwhelmed by numbers, and so ordered the men immediately to commence strengthening the fence. They had not been long employed at it when the savages made a dash at the camp, and sent a shower of arrows into it. Stanley immediately ordered sixty soldiers to deploy fifty yards in front. At the word of command they rushed out, and the battle commenced.

The enemy soon turned in flight and the soldiers pursued them. Every man was now ordered to work on the defenses; some cut down thorn-trees and threw together rapidly a high fence all around the camp, while others were ordered to build platforms within for the sharp-shooters. All this time Stanley could hear the fire of the soldiers growing more and more indistinct in the distance. When the fence was completed he directed the sections of the Lady Alice to be placed so as to form a sort of central camp, to which they could retire in the last extremity. As soon as everything was finished he ordered the bugle to sound the retreat, and soon the skirmishers came in sight. They reported fifteen of the enemy killed. All had fought bravely, even a bull-dog had seized a savage and was

91

tearing him to pieces, when a bullet put the poor wretch out of his misery.

They were not molested again that day, which gave them time to make their position still stronger. The night passed quietly, and they were allowed to breakfast in peace. But about 9 o'clock the savages in great numbers advanced upon the camp. All hopes of peace were now at an end, and since he was forced to fight, Stanley determined to inflict no half-way punishment, but sweep that fair valley with the besom of destruction. He therefore selected four reliable men, placed them at the head of four detachments, assigning to each a fleet runner, whose duty it was, not to fight, but to report any disaster that threatened or befell the detachment to which the man belonged. He then ordered them to move out and attack the savages. As the route of the enemy was certain, he directed them to pursue them separately, yet keep before them as the place of final rendezvous, some high rocks five miles distant down the valley. The detachments poured forth from the camp, and the deadly fire-arms so appalled those savage warriors, armed only with the bow and spear, that they at once turned and fled. The detachments followed in hot pursuit, and what promised to be a fight, became a regular stampede. But one detachment having pursued a large force of the enemy into the open plain, the latter turned at bay.

The leader of the detachment, excited by the pursuit, and believing, in his contempt for the savages, that the mere sight of his little band would send them scurrying away in deadly fear, charged boldly on them. Quick as thought they closed around him in overwhelming numbers. The runner alone escaped and bore the sad tidings to Stanley. The appointment of these runners shows his wonderful prevision—that foresight which on many occasions alone saved him. He at once sent assistance to the detachment that the courier had reported surrounded. Alas, before it arrived every man had been massacred. The aid, though it came too late to save the brave detachment, arrived just in time to save the second, which was just falling into the same snare, for the large force that had annihilated the first had now turned on this, and its fate seemed sealed. The reinforcements hurried off by Stanley found it completely hemmed in by the savages. Two soldiers had already been killed, the captain was wounded, and in a few minutes more they would have shared the fate of the first detachment.

It was at this critical moment they arrived, and suddenly pouring a deadly volley into the rear of the assailants, sent them to the right about with astonishing quickness. The two detachments now wheeled and poured a concentrated volley into the savages, which sent them flying wildly over the plain. A swift pursuit was commenced, but the fleet enemy could not be overtaken, and the march up the valley was scarcely resisted. Stanley, in camp, carefully watched the progress of the fight, which could be distinguished at first by the volleys of his soldiers, and when, receding in the distance, these could be no longer heard, by the puffs of smoke which showed where the pursuit led.

But at length clouds of smoke of a different character began to ascend from the quiet valley. To the right and left the dark columns obscured the noonday sun, and far as the eye could reach, the plain, with its hundreds of villages of thatched huts, presented one wide conflagration, till the murky mass of cloudy vapor, as it rolled heavenward, made it appear like a second Sodom, suffering the vengeance of heaven. To the distance of eight miles, Stanley could see jets of smoke that told of burning villages. He had delayed to the last moment hostile action, but having once commenced it he meant to leave behind him no power of retaliation.

It was a victorious but sad day, and the return of the detachments was anything but a triumphal march, for they bore back twenty-one dead men, besides the wounded, while they could report but thirty-five of the enemy killed. So little difference in the number of the slain, when one was the pursued and the other the pursuing party, and when the former was armed only with spears and bows, and the latter with the deadly rifle, seems at first sight unaccountable, but it must be remembered that the unfortunate detachment that was surrounded and massacred to a man, furnished almost the entire list of the killed.

The camp was at peace that night, but it was a sad peace. A few more such victories as this and Stanley would be left without an expedition.

This unfortunate experience with these people showed the danger of his undertaking a new route. His object was not to travel among new people, but to reach the lake region with his boat and settle great geographical problems and establish certain facts having an intimate bearing on the future of Africa. Yet by his chosen course he really obtained no new and valuable information but imperiled and well-nigh ruined the expedition fitted out with so much expense and care.

His was the nearest course to the lake, yet the long one by which Speke reached it was the safest. He had been in a perilous position, and it was clearly his own foresight that saved him. The appointment of a courier or swift runner to each detachment to act as a telegraph, would probably have occurred to few, yet this certainly saved one detachment from destruction and how much more no one can tell.

But he was not satisfied with the vengeance he had taken and the devastation he had wrought. He had resolved to teach those savage negroes a lesson on the danger of treachery to strangers, and he meant, now he had commenced it, to make it thorough and complete, and so next morning he sent off sixty men to proceed to the farthest end of the valley, some eight miles away, and destroy what yet remained; passing on through the ruins of the villages, they came to a large village in the extreme northeast. A very slight resistance was made here, and they entered it and applied the torch, and soon it shared the fate of all the rest. Before they destroyed it, however, they loaded themselves with grain. Provisions were now plenty, for the frightened negroes had left everything behind them in their flight. There was no longer any need of purchasing food, the valley was depopulated, and all the accumulated provisions of the inhabitants was at the mercy of the victors. Finding he had enough to last the expedition six days, Stanley next morning started westward before daybreak, and was soon far away from this valley of destruction, leaving the thoroughly humbled natives to crawl back to the ashes of their ruined homes. Without further trouble, in three days, he reached Iramba. Here he halted and took a calm survey of his condition and prospects. He found that out of the more than three hundred men with which he had left the coast, but one hundred and ninety-four remained.

Sickness, desertion and battle had reduced his number over a third before he had reached the point where his actual labors were to commence. It was not a pleasant look-out, for, although two hundred men, well armed with rifles, made a formidable force in a country where only arrows and spears were used, still this heavy ratio of loss must stop, or the expedition itself must fail. He was not in a country where he could recruit soldiers, and each one lost was a dead loss, and thousands of miles of exploration lay before him, in prosecuting which, he knew not how many battles would be fought, nor how much sickness would have to be encountered. It would not seem a difficult piece of arithmetical calculation to determine how long three hundred men would last if one-third disappeared in three months, or how many men it would require to prosecute his labors three years. But Stanley never seemed to act as though he thought defeat possible. Whether his faith was in God, himself, or his star, it was nevertheless a strong and controlling faith. Still, now and then it is very evident that he was perfectly conscious of the desperate nature of his condition, and felt disease, which carried off his friends and retainers, or the spear, might end, at any moment, his explorations and his life.

Though out of Urimi at last, yet Stanley found the natives of Iramba a very little improvement on those of the former district. Mirambo was their terror, and hence they were suspicious of all strangers. Again and again he was mistaken for this terrible chieftain, and narrowly escaped being attacked. In fact, this formidable warrior was fighting at one time within a day's march of him.

Urukuma was the next district he entered after Iramba, and he found it thickly peopled and rich in cattle. It consisted for the most part of rolling plains, with scattered chains of jagged hills. He was on the slope that led to the Nyanza, and the descent was so gradual, that he expected to find the lake, whose exploration he designed to make thorough and complete, comparatively shallow, although it covered a vast area. At last he reached a little village, not a hundred yards from the shore, and encamped. At this point he describes the topography of the new country he had passed over. He says:

"As far as Western Ugogo I may pass over without attempting to describe the country, as readers may obtain a detailed account of it from 'How I Found Livingstone.' Thence north is a new country to all, and a brief description of it may be interesting to students of African geography.

"North of Mizanza a level plain extends as far as the frontier of Urandawi, a distance of thirty-five miles (English). At Mukondoku the altitude, as indicated by two first-rate aneroids, was two thousand, eight hundred feet. At Mtiwi, twenty miles north, the altitude was two thousand eight hundred and twenty-five feet. Diverging west and north-west, we ascend the slope of a lengthy mountain-wall, apparently, but which, upon arriving at the summit, we ascertain to be a wide plateau covered with forests. This plateau has an altitude of three thousand eight hundred feet at its eastern extremity; but, as it extends westward it rises to a height of four thousand five hundred feet. It embraces all Uyanzi, Unyanyembe, Usukuma, Urimi and Iramba—in short, all that part of Central Africa lying between the valley of the Rufiji south and the Victoria Nyanza north, and the mean altitude of this broad upland cannot exceed four thousand five hundred feet. From Mizanza to the Nyanza is a distance of nearly three hundred geographical miles; yet, at no part of this long journey did the aneroids indicate a higher altitude than five thousand one hundred feet above the sea.

"As far as Urimi, from the eastern edge of the plateau, the land is covered with a dense jungle of acacias, which, by its density, strangles all other species of vegetation. Here and there, only in the cleft of a rock, a giant euphorbia may be seen, sole lord of its sterile domain. The soil is shallow, and consists of vegetable mould, mixed largely with sand and detritus of the bare rocks, which crown each knoll and ridge, and which testify too plainly to the violence of the periodical rains.

"In the basin of Matongo, in Southern Urimi, we were instructed by the ruins and ridges, relics of a loftier upland, of what has been effected by nature in the course of long ages. No learned geological savant need ever expound to the traveler who views these rocky ruins, the geological history of this country. From a distance we viewed the glistening naked and riven rocks as a singular scene; but when we stood among them, and noted the appearance of the rocky fragments of granite, gneiss and porphyry peeled as it were rind after rind, or leaf after leaf, like an artichoke, until the rock was wasted away, it seemed as if Dame Nature has left these relics, these hilly skeletons, to demonstrate her laws and career. It seemed to me as if she said, 'Lo, and behold this broad basin of Matongo, with its teeming villages and herds of cattle and fields of corn, surrounded by these bare rocks—in primeval time this land was covered with water, it was the bed of a vast sea. The waters were dried, leaving a wide expanse of level land, upon which I caused heavy rains to fall five months out of each year during all the ages that have elapsed since first the hot sunshine fell upon the soil. The rains washed away the loose sand and made deep furrows in course of time, until in certain places the rocky kernel under the soil began to appear. The furrows became enlarged, the waters frittered away their banks and conveyed the earth away to lower levels, through which it wore away a channel, first through the soil and lastly through the rock itself, which you may see if you but walk to the bottom of that basin. You will there behold a channel worn through the solid rock some fifty feet in depth; and as you look on that you will have some idea of the power and force of the tropical rains. It is through that channel that the soil robbed from these rocks has been carried away toward the Nyanza to fill its depths and in time make dry land of it. Now you may ask how came these once solid rocks, which are now but skeletons of hills and stony heaps, to be thus split into so many fragments? Have you never seen the effect of water thrown upon lime? The solid rocks have been broken or peeled in an almost similar manner. The tropic sun heated the face of these rocks to an intense heat, and the cold rain falling upon the heated surface caused them to split and peel as you see them.'

"This is really the geological history of this region simply told. Ridge after ridge, basin after basin, from Western Ugogo to the

Nyanza, tells the same tale; but it is not until we enter Central Urimi, that we begin to marvel at the violence of the process by which nature has transformed the face of the land. For here the perennial springs and rivulets begin to unite and form rivers, after collecting and absorbing the moisture from the water-shed; and these rivers, though but gentle streams during the dry season, become formidable during the rains. It is in Central Urimi that the Nile first begins to levy tribute upon Equatorial Africa, and if you look upon the map and draw a line east from the latitude of Ujiji to longitude thirty-five degrees you will strike upon the sources of the Leewumbu, which is the extreme southern feeder of the Victoria Nyanza.

"In Iramba, between Mgongo Tembo and Mombiti, we came upon what must have been in former times an arm of the Victoria Nyanza. It is called the Lumamberri Plain, after a river of that name, and is about forty miles in width. Its altitude is three thousand seven hundred and seventy-five feet above the sea and but a few feet above Victoria Nyanza. We were fortunate in crossing the broad, shallow stream in the dry season, for during the masika or rainy season the plain is converted into a wide lake.

"The Leewumbu River, after a course of a hundred and seventy-five miles, becomes known as the Monaugh River, in Usukuma. After another run of a hundred miles, it is converted into Shimeeyu, under which name it enters the Victoria east of this port of Kagehyi. Roughly the Shimeeyu may be said to have a length of three hundred and fifty miles."

CHAPTER XII

EXPLORATION OF THE VICTORIA NYANZA

Stanley felt, as he stood and looked off on the broad expanse of water, like one who had achieved a great victory, and he said that the wealth of the universe could not then bribe him to turn back from his work. The boat of a white man had never been launched on its surface, and he longed to see the Lady Alice afloat, that he might change the guesses of Livingstone, Speke and others, into certainty. He had started to complete Livingstone's unfinished work, and now he was in a fair way to do it. How much Cameron, who was somewhere in the interior on the same mission, had accomplished, he did not know, he only knew that with no boat at his command, like the Lady Alice, that he had transported through so many hundreds of miles of jungle, his movements would be very much crippled.

He now mustered his entire force, to see what he had to rely on before setting out, and found it to consist of three white men and one hundred and six Wanguana soldiers, twenty-eight having died since leaving Itwru thirty days before, or at an average of nearly one a day. This was a gloomy prospect. Before beginning his real work one-half of his entire expedition had disappeared. Dysentery had been the great scourge that had thinned their ranks so fearfully. Stanley in the first place was not a physician, while even those remedies which ordinarily might have proved efficacious were rendered well-nigh useless by the necessity of constant marching. Rest alone would have cured a great many, but he felt compelled to march. Whether the necessity for marching with the rapidity he did, was sufficiently urgent to justify him in sacrificing so many lives, he doubtless is the best judge. These poor men were not accustomed to travel at the rate he kept them moving. Had they marched as leisurely as an Arab caravan, they would have been nine months or a year in making the distance which Stanley had accomplished in the short space of one hundred and three days.

He was at last on the lake that Baker hoped to reach with his steam vessels, and here he expected to meet Gordon, his successor, but he evidently had not yet arrived, for the natives told him that no boats had been seen on the water. They related strange tales, however, of the people inhabiting the shores. One told him of a race of dwarfs, another of a tribe of giants, another still of a people who kept a breed of dogs so large that even Stanley's mastiffs were small in comparison. How much or little of this was true, he, of course, could not tell, still it excited his curiosity, and increased his desire to explore the country.

He reached the lake on the 28th of February, and in eight days had everything ready, and launched his boat. He selected ten good oarsmen, who, with the steersman and himself, composed the boat's crew, and the whole force with which he was to overcome all the difficulties that he might encounter.

The camp was left in charge of Frank Pocoke and young Barker. Naming the large body of water, into which the Shimeeyu and Ruano Rivers flowed, Speke Bay, in honor of the distinguished explorer, he sailed east along the irregular coast. To-day passing a district thinly populated, to-morrow a rugged hill country, through which the elephants wandered in immense droves, and of course, thronged with elephant hunters, he passed various tribes, until he came to the mouth of the Ruano River, discharging a large volume of water into Speke Bay, but nothing in comparison with the Shimeeyu and the Kagera, the two great river supplies of the lake. The former is the largest of all, and at its mouth a mile wide. Its length is three hundred and seventy miles and is, he says, the extreme southern source of the Nile.

The water he named Speke Bay is on the northeastern side, and where he crossed it about twelve miles wide. Sterile plains succeeded barren mountains, thin lines of vegetation along the borders of the lake alone giving space for cultivation, came and went until they reached the great island of Ukerewe, divided from the mainland only by a narrow channel. This was a true oasis, for it was covered with herds of cattle, and verdue, and fruits, and rich in ivory. He found the king an amiable man, and his subjects a peaceful, commercial people. Although this was a large island, more than forty miles long, the king owned several of the neighboring islands. Nothing of importance occurred on this voyage, as day after day they wound in and out along the deeply corrugated coast or sailed by islands, the people on shore all being friendly. They at length came in sight of the high table-land of Majita, which Speke thought to be an island, but which Stanley demonstrated, by actual survey, to be only a promontory. It rises some three thousand feet above the level of the lake, and is surrounded by low brown plains, which, to the distant observer, resemble water.

Stanley continued his course along the eastern shore of the lake, proceeding northerly, and at last reached the coast of the Uriri country, a district of pastoral land dotted over with fine cattle. Bordering on this is Ugegeya, a land of fables and wonders, the "El Dorado" of slave hunters and traders in ivory. It is the natural home of the elephant, which is found here in great numbers. In crossing a broad bay he first got sight of it, rising in a series of tall mountains before him. From their base the country rolls away to the east in one vast plain twenty-five miles wide, over which roam great herds of cattle, getting their own living and furnishing plenty of meat to the indolent inhabitants. Stanley constantly inquired of the natives concerning the country inland, its character and people, and was told many wonderful stories, in which it was impossible to say how much fable was mixed. Among other things, they reported that about fifteen days' march from this place, were mountains that spouted forth fire at times and smoke.

Keeping north, he says: "We pass between the Island Ugingo and the gigantic mountains of Ugegeya, at whose base the Lady

Alice seems to crawl like a mite in a huge cheese, while we on board admire the stupendous height, and wonder at the deathly silence which prevails in this solitude, where the boisterous winds are hushed and the turbulent waves are as tranquil as a summer dream. The natives, as they pass, regard this spot with superstition, as well they might, for the silent majesty of these dumb, tall mounts awes the very storms to peace. Let the tempests bluster as they may on the spacious main beyond the cape, in this nook, sheltered by tall Ugingo isle and lofty Goshi in the mainland, they inspire no fear. It is this refuge which Goshi promises the distressed canoemen that causes them to sing praises of Goshi, and to cheer one another when wearied and benighted, that Goshi is near to protect them."

Sailing in and out among the clustering islands, they see two low isolated islands in the distance, and make toward them to camp there for the night. "There," says Stanley, "under the overspreading branches of a mangrove tree we dream of unquiet waters, and angry surfs, and threatening rocks, to find ourselves next morning tied to an island, which, from its peculiarity, I called Bridge Island. While seeking a road to ascend the island, to take bearings, I discovered a natural bridge of basalt, about twenty feet in length and twelve in breadth, under which one might repose comfortably, and from one side see the waves lashed to fury and spend their strength on the stubborn rocks, which form the foundation of the arch, while from the other we could see the boat, secure under the lee of the island, resting on a serene and placid surface, and shaded by mangrove branches from the hot sun of the equator. Its neighborhood is remarkable only for a small cave, the haunt of fishermen." After taking a survey of the neighboring mainland, he hoisted sail and scudded along the coast before a freshening breeze. At noon he found himself, by observation, to be under the equator. Seeing an opening in the lake that looked like the mouth of a river, he sailed into it to find it was only a deep bay. Coming in sight of a village, he anchored near it and tried to make friends with some wild-looking fishermen on the shore, but the naked savages only "stared at them from under penthouses of hair, and hastily stole away to tell their families of the strange apparition they had seen."

This sail of one hundred miles alone the coast of this vast lake, though somewhat monotonous and tame in its details to the reader, furnished one of the most interesting episodes in Stanley's life—not because the scenery was new and beautiful, but because he, with his white sail, and fire-arms, and strange dress, was as strange and wonderful to these natives as was Columbus, with his ship, and cannon, and cavaliers to the inhabitants of the New World. Though often differing in appearance, and language, and manner, they were almost uniformly friendly, and in the few cases where they proved hostile, they were drunk, which makes civilized men, as well as savages, quarrelsome. It was frequently very difficult to win their confidence, and often Stanley would spend hours in endeavoring to remove their suspicions. In this wild, remote home, their lives pass on without change, each generation treading in the footsteps of the preceding one—no progress, no looking forward to increased knowledge or new developments. There were no new discoveries to arouse their mental faculties, no aspirations for a better condition, and they were as changeless as their tropical climate. Hence, to them the sudden appearance of this strange phenomenon on their beautiful lake could not be accounted for. It had seemingly dropped from the clouds, and at the first discharge of a pistol they were startled and filled with amazement.

Stanley, whether rowing or sailing, kept close to the shore, that nothing worthy of note should escape him, frequently landing to ascertain the name of the district he was in, the bays he crossed, the mountains he saw, and the rivers that emptied into the lake. In short, he omitted nothing which was necessary to a complete survey and knowledge of this hitherto unknown body of water.

After leaving this bay, they came in a short time to a river which was full of hippopotami. Two huge fellows swam so near the boat that Stanley was afraid they would attack it, and ordered the men to pull away from them. Although hunting these huge beasts might be very exciting sport, and a tolerably safe one in boats properly built, to expose the Lady Alice, with her slender cedar sides, to their tusks would have been a piece of folly close akin to madness. Her safety was of more consequence than all the hippopotami in Africa. He was an explorer, not a hunter; and to risk all the future of the former to gratify the pleasure of the latter would have shown him unfit to command so important an expedition as this. Like the boat that carried Cæsar and his fortunes, the Lady Alice bore in her frail sides destines greater than the imagination can conceive. So hoisting sail they caught the freshening breeze and flew along the ever-changing shore lined with villages, out of which swarmed a vast crowd of people, showing a much more densely populated district than they had yet seen. He found the name of it to be Mahita; and wishing to learn the names of some of the villages he saw, the boat was turned toward shore and anchored within fifty yards of it, but with a cable long enough to let them drift to within a few feet of it. Some half a dozen men wearing small shells above their elbows and a circle round their heads came down to the beach, opening a conversation with them. Stanley learned the name of the country, but they refused to tell him anything more till he landed.

While getting ready to do so, he noticed the numbers on the shore increased with astonishing rapidity, and seemed to be greatly excited. This aroused his suspicions, and he ordered the rowers to pull off again. It was lucky he did, for he had scarcely put three lengths between him and the shore, when suddenly out of the bushes on each side of the spot where he was to land arose a forest of spears.

Stanley did not intend to go away entirely, but lie off till they became less excited, but this evidence of treachery caused him to change his mind, and he ordered the sail to be hoisted, and moved away toward a point at the mouth of the cove, which, with the wind as it was blowing, they could but little more than clear. The negroes seeing this, sent up a loud shout, and hurried off to reach it before the boat did. Stanley penetrating their design, ordered the sail to be lowered and the rowers to pull dead to windward. The discomfited savages looked on in amazement to see the prize slip through their fingers so easily. It was a narrow escape, for had Stanley landed, he would doubtless have been overpowered and killed before he could use his weapons.

It was now late in the afternoon, and the savages made no attempt to follow them, and at dusk, coming to a small island, they tied up and camped for the night, lulled to sleep by the murmur of the waves on the beach.

The next day continuing their course, they at last sailed into the bay, which forms the northeastern extremity of the Victoria Nyanza. The eastern side of this bay is lined with bold hills and ridges, but at the extreme end where the Tagama River comes in, the country is flat. The expedition now began to move westward in its slow circumnavigation of the lake, and came at length to Muiwanda. Here they found the savages friendly, and they landed and obtained from them, at fair prices, such provisions and vegetables as they desired. They also gave Stanley all the information they could of the neighboring country. They told him that the name of the bay in which they rode, and which was the extreme northern limit of the lake, was Baringo. They had evidently not been great travelers or much visited by any tribes living away from their own coast, for they said that they had never heard of any other lake, great or small, except that one—the Nyanza. Considering that this whole central region of Africa is dotted with lakes, and that the Tanganika, an inland sea, is not three hundred miles distant, it is evident they must live very much isolated from any but their own people. Stanley had now surveyed the southern, eastern and northeastern shores of the lake, and had taken thirty-seven observations and entered almost every nook and cove of this vast body of water. He had corrected the map of Speke, made on the report of the natives—proved that he was wrong in his latitude of the lake, and taken such ample notes that he could make out an accurate chart of that portion he had thus traversed. He makes the extreme eastern point of the lake end in 34° 35' east longitude, and 33' 43" north latitude.

After he had finished his exploration thus far, Stanley went over his route, to gain a general knowledge of the country, the location and approximate size of the various districts, and general character of the inhabitants. The north shore he found indented with deep bays, and so completely land-locked, that they might easily be mistaken for separate lakes, while the islands clustered so thickly and closely to the shore that unless thoroughly examined, would be taken for portions of the mainland. But Stanley has traced it out so plainly, that the outline of the shore is as distinct as that of Lake Ontario.

CHAPTER XIII

EXPLORATION OF THE VICTORIA NYANZA

The voyage continued along the northern and then along the western shore of the lake, revealing at almost every turn new features of scenery and some new formation of land or new characteristic of the people, till the journey was like an ever-shifting kaleidoscope. A tribe friendly and trusting would be succeeded by one suspicious or treacherous, so that it was impossible to be governed by any general rule, and Stanley was compelled to be constantly on the alert, watching the motions of each tribe without reference to the actions of the last, and laying his plans accordingly. He continued his course down the western shore toward his camp from which he started, finding this side more densely populated than the others, and the tribes that occupied it of a more independent, fearless character, and more inclined to hostilities.

At Uvuma, an independent country and the largest on the Victoria Nyanza, the hostility took a more determined form. The natives made signs of friendship to induce Stanley's party to come near the shore. They did so, sailing up to within a few yards of it. At that point a large number of natives were hid behind the trees, who suddenly emerged and hurled a shower of huge stones at the boat in order to sink it. Stanley instantly ordered the helm to be put hard up, and the boat was quickly steered away from the dangerous spot, but not before Stanley, enraged at this act of treachery, leveled his revolver at the wretches and dropped one of them.

Going on some miles farther, they entered a channel between some islands and the shore, where they discovered a fleet of canoes, thirteen in number, with over one hundred warriors in them, armed with shells, and spears, and slings. The foremost one had some sweet potatoes aboard, which one of the natives held up as though he wished to trade. Stanley ordered the crew to cease rowing, but as the breeze was light the sail was kept up, and the progress was so slow that this canoe soon came up. While he was bargaining for the potatoes, the other boats approached and completely surrounded the Lady Alice and began to reach over and seize everything they could lay hands on. Stanley warned them away with his gun, when they jeered at him and immediately seized their spears, while one man held up a string of beads he had stolen and dared Stanley to catch him. With that promptness which has many a time saved his life, the latter drew his revolver and shot the villain dead. Spears instantly flashed in the air, but Stanley seizing his repeating rifle poured shot after shot into them, knocking over three of them in as many seconds, when the amazed warriors turned in flight. He then seized his elephant rifle and began to pour its heavy shot into their canoes, throwing them into the wildest confusion. As they now continued on their way, an occasional shot from the big gun waked the echoes of the shore to announce beforehand what treatment treachery would receive.

As they kept on to the northward, they felt the current drawing them on, and soon they came to the Ripon Falls, their foam and thunder contrasting strangely with the quietness of the lake a short time before, and the silence and tranquility of the scene. It was the Nile starting on its long journey to the Mediterranean, fertilizing Egypt in its course. Coasting westerly, they came to the island of Krina, where they obtained guides to conduct them to King Mtesa, the most renowned king of the whole region. Sending messengers to announce to the king his arrival, Stanley continued to coast along Uganda, everywhere treated with kindness, so far as words went, but very niggardly in fact.

He here observed a curious phenomenon. He discovered an inlet in which there was a perceptible tide, the water flowing north for two hours and then south for the same length of time. On asking the guides if this was usual, they said yes, and it was common to all the inlets on the coast of Uganda. At Beya they were welcomed by a fleet of canoes sent to conduct them to the king.

On the 4th of April, Stanley landed, amid the waving of flags, volleys of musketry and shouts of two thousand people, assembled to receive him. The chief officer then conducted him to comfortable quarters, where, soon after, sixteen goats, ten oxen, with bananas, sweet potatoes, plantains, chickens, rice, milk, butter, etc., etc., in profuse quantities were sent him.

In the afternoon, the king sent word to his guest, that he was ready to receive him. Issuing from his quarters, Stanley found himself in a street eighty feet broad and half a mile long, lined with the personal guards, officers, attendants and retinue of the king, to the number of three thousand. At the farther end of this avenue was the king's residence, and as Stanley advanced he could dimly see the form of the king in the entrance, sitting in a chair. At every step volleys of musketry were fired and flags waved, while sixteen drums beaten together kept up a horrible din. As he approached the house, the king, a tall, slender figure, dressed in Arab costume, arose and advancing held out his hand in silence, while the drums kept up their loud tattoo. They looked on each other in silence. Stanley was greatly embarrassed by the novelty of the situation, but soon the king, taking a seat, asked him to be seated also, while a hundred of his captains followed their example.

Lifting his eyes to the king, Stanley saw a tall and slender man, but with broad, powerful shoulders. His eyes were large, his face intelligent and amiable, while his mouth and nose were a great improvement on those of the ordinary negro, being more like those of a Persian Arab. As soon as he began to speak, Stanley was captivated by his courteous, affable manner. He says that he was infinitely superior to the sultan of Zanzibar, and impressed you as a colored gentleman who had learned his manners by contact with civilized, cultivated men, instead of being, as he was, a native of Central Africa, who had seen but three white men before in his life. Stanley was astonished at his innate polish and he felt he had found a friend in this great king of this part of the country, where the tribal territories are usually so small. His kingdom extends through three degrees of longitude and almost as many of latitude. He professes Islamism now, and no cruelties are practised in his kingdom. He has a guard of two hundred men, renegades from Baker's expedition, defalcators from Zanzibar, and the élite of his own kingdom.

Behind his throne or arm-chair, stood his gun-bearers, shield-bearers and lance-bearers, and on either side were arranged his chief courtiers, governors of provinces, etc., while outside streamed away the long line of his warriors, beginning with the drummers and goma-beaters. Mtesa asked many intelligent questions, and Stanley found that this was not his home, but that he had come there with that immense throng of warriors to shoot birds. In two or three days, he proposed to return to his capital at Ulagala or Uragara (it is difficult to tell which is right). The first day, for Stanley's entertainment, the king gave a grand naval review with eighty canoes, which made quite an imposing display, which the king with his three hundred wives and Stanley viewed from shore. The crews consisted of two thousand five hundred men or more. The second day, the king led his fleet in person to show his prowess in shooting birds. The third day, the troops were exercised in general military movements and at target practice, and on the fourth, the march was taken up for the capital.

In Mtesa Stanley sees the hope of Central Africa. He is a natural born king and tries to imitate the manners, as he understands them, of European monarchs. He has constructed broad roads which will be ready for vehicles whenever they are introduced. The road they traveled increased from twenty to one hundred and fifty feet as they approached the capital, which crowned a commanding eminence overlooking a beautiful country covered with tropical fruit and trees. Huts are not very imposing, but a tall flagstaff and an immense flag gave some dignity to the surroundings.

The capital is composed of a vast collection of huts on an eminence crowned by the royal quarters, around which run five several palisades and circular courts, between which and the city runs a circular road from one hundred to two hundred feet in width, from whence radiate six or seven magnificent avenues lined with gardens and huts.

The next day, Stanley was introduced into the palace in state. The guards were clothed in white cotton dresses, while the chiefs were attired in rich Arab costumes. This palace was a large, lofty structure built of grass and cane, while tall trunks of trees upheld the roof—covered inside with cloth sheeting. On the fourth day, the exciting news was received that another white man was approaching the capital. It proved to be Colonel Lerant de Bellfonds of the Egyptian service, who had been dispatched by Colonel Gordon to make a treaty of commerce with the king and the khedive of Egypt.

This Mtesa, we said, was a Mohammedan, having been converted by Khamis Ben Abdullah some four or five years before. This Arab, from Muscat, was a man of magnificent presence, of noble descent, and very rich, and dressed in splendid Oriental costume. Mtesa became fascinated with him, and the latter stayed

106

with the king over a year, giving him royal presents and dressing him in gorgeous attire.

No wonder this brilliant stranger became to such a heathen a true missionary. But Stanley, in a conversation with the king, soon upset his new faith, and he agreed at once to observe the Christian as well as the Moslem Sabbath, to which his captains also agreed. He, moreover, caused the Ten Commandments, the Lord's Prayer, and the Golden Rule, "Thou shalt love thy neighbor as thyself," to be written on a board for his daily perusal. In stating this remarkable fact, Stanley says; "Though I am no missionary, I shall begin to think I may become one if such success is so feasible;" and exclaims, "Oh, that some pious, practical missionary would come here. What a field and harvest, ripe for the sickle of the Gospel. Mtesa would give him everything he desired—houses, cattle, lands, ivory, etc. He might call a province his own in one day." But he says he must not be a theological one, nor a missionary of creeds, but a practical Christian, tied to no church or sect, but simply profess God and His Son, and live a blameless life and be able to instruct the people in building houses, cultivating land, and in all those things that make up human civilization. Such a man, Stanley says, would become the temporal saviour of Africa. Mtesa begged Stanley to tell such men to come, and he would give them all they wanted.

The subjects of this heathen king number not far from two millions, and Stanley affirms that one good missionary among them would accomplish more toward the regeneration of Africa in one year than all other missionaries on the continent put together. He suggests that the mission should bring to Mtesa several suits of military clothes, heavily embroidered, pistols, swords, dinner-service, etc., etc. This sounds rather strange to the modern missionary, and seems like trusting too much to "carnal weapons," but it is eminently practical. Anything to give the missionary a firm footing on which to begin his labors is desirable, if not wrong in itself or leading to wrong. For its own use the mission should, he says, bring also hammers, saws, augers, drills for blasting, and blacksmith and carpenter-tools, etc., etc. In short, the missionary should not attempt to convert the black man to his religious views simply by preaching Christ, but that civilization, the hand-maiden of religion, should move side by side with it in equal step. The practical effect of the missionary work, in order to influence the natives, must not be merely a moral change, which causes the convert to abjure the rites and follies of Paganism, but to lift the entire people, whether converted or not to Christianity, to a higher plane of civilization. We know there are different theories on this subject, but we think that Stanley's mode might safely be tried. It was tried, after a fashion, almost immediately, but the station has been broken up and the missionaries murdered.

Perhaps it is as good a place here as anywhere to correct a wrong statement that has been going the rounds of the papers, which puts Stanley in a false light. It was not pretended that King Mtesa had anything to do with this outrage, but that a tribe with which Stanley had had a fight, killing some of its number, committed it in revenge for what he did. The truth is, the mission was established by enthusiasts, and some three or four started with false views and hopes entirely. Only two of them reached the ground, one of them not being a minister. They were, however, well received, and allowed to go to work. The king, or chief of a neighboring tribe, had a daughter with whom a native fell in love. This man was repugnant to the father, and he refused to let him have his daughter for a wife. The consequence was they eloped and fled to the island on which the missionaries were stationed, and placed themselves under their protection and remained with them. The enraged savage heard of this, and doubtless believing that the missionaries had connived at the elopement—certainly harbored the fugitives against his wish—attacked the station and murdered the missionaries. How much or how little they were to blame, or, if not guilty of any wrong, how unwisely they acted, they unfortunately do not live to tell us. But Stanley's conduct in that region had nothing to do with the tragedy. It was an act of wild justice by an enraged and savage chieftain, and militates in no way against carrying out the project of Stanley.

CHAPTER XIV

EXPLORATION OF THE VICTORIA NYANZA

Though this royal hospitality was very grateful after his long toils, and though intercourse with a white man in that remote land was refreshing, and though he longed to rest, yet Stanley felt he must be about his work. To finish this would require much time, and he had now been long absent from his men, who might prove intractable while he was away, and he was anxious to get back, for the exploration of this lake was only the beginning of what he proposed to do.

With two canoes belonging to his friend, King Mtesa, accompanying him as an escort until the grand admiral of his sable majesty, Magassa, who, with thirty canoes, had been detached for his service, should overtake him, he set sail from the river, and camped that night on a smooth, sandy beach, at a point called Kagya. The natives who lived there received them in a friendly, and for African negroes, hospitable manner. Stanley took this as a good augury of the reception he should meet with along the coast of Usongora, which he designed to explore.

In the morning he again set sail, and sweeping leisurely along, came in the afternoon to the village of Makongo. As the Lady Alice approached the shore, he saw a crowd of naked savages squatted on the ground, sucking the everlasting pombé, or beer, through a straw, just as white men suck punch or a sherry cobbler. As the boat reached the shore, the chief, with the vacant stare of a drunkard, arose and reeled toward him and welcomed him in a friendly, though maudlin manner. The natives also appeared good-natured and quite content with their arrival. After they had satisfied their curiosity by examining him and his boat, they went away, leaving him to arrange his camp for the night and prepare his supper.

The sun went down in glory beyond the purple mountains—a slight ripple dimpled the surface of the lake, while slender columns of smoke ascended here and there along the shore from the huts of the natives; and all was calm and peaceful, though wild and lonely. As night came down, and the stars, one by one, came out in the tropical sky, Stanley and his companions stretched themselves on their mats, and, unsuspicious of danger, fell asleep. About 10 o'clock he was suddenly awakened by a loud and hurried beating of drums, with ever and anon a chorus of shrieks and yells that rung through the clear, still air with a distinctness and sharpness that made the blood shiver. Stanley immediately aroused his men, and they listened, wondering what it foreboded. The lake was still below, and the heavens calm and serene above, but all around it seemed as if demons of the infernal regions were out on their orgies. Stanley thought it was the forerunner of an attack on the camp, but Mtesa's men, the Waganda, told him that the drumming and yelling were the wild welcome of the natives to a stranger. He doubted it, for he had seen too many savage tribes, and knew their customs too well to believe this blood-curdling, discordant din was a welcome to him.

It is strange that he did not at once quietly launch his boat and lie off the rest of the night a little way from the shore till morning, and see what it all meant. It would seem that ordinary prudence would have prompted this. His neglect to do so, very nearly cost him his life, and ended there his explorations. For some reason or other, which he does not give, he determined to remain where he was, contenting himself with the precaution of placing his weapons close beside him, and directing his eleven men to load their guns and put them under their mats. He lay down again, but not to sleep, for all night long the furious beat of drums and unearthly yells rang out over the lake keeping him not only awake, but anxious.

At daybreak he arose, and as he stepped out of his tent, he started as if he had seen an apparition, for in the gray light of morning, he saw five hundred naked, motionless forms, with bows, shields and spears, standing in a semicircle around him, and completely cutting him off from his boat and the lake. It was a fearful moment, and to his inquiry what it meant, no answer was given. There was no shouting or yelling, none of the frantic gesticulations so common to the African savage. On the contrary, they wore a calm and composed, though stern and determined aspect. Shoulder to shoulder like a regiment of soldiers they stood, the forest of spears above them glittering in the early light. There was nothing to be done—Stanley was entrapped, and with the first attempt to escape or seize his rifle would be transfixed by a hundred spears. It was too late to repent the folly of not heeding the warning of the night before, and so he calmly stood and faced the crowd of stern, malignant faces. For some minutes this solitary white man met glance for glance, when the drunken chief of the day before stalked into the semicircle, and with a stick which he held in his hand forced back the savages by flourishing it in their faces. He then advanced, and striking the boat a furious blow, shouted "be off," and to facilitate matters, took hold and helped launch it. Stanley was only too glad to obey him, and his heart bounded within him as he felt the keel gliding into deep water, and soon a hundred rods were between him and the savages that lined the shore. The Waganda were still on the beach, and Stanley prepared to sweep it with a murderous fire the moment they were attacked. So dense was the crowd of natives, that had he fired at that close range, he would have mowed them down with fearful slaughter. But although there was much loud wrangling and altercation, they were, at length, allowed to embark, and followed him as he sailed away toward the isle of Musua. He had learned a lesson that he did not soon forget.

The whole had been a strange proceeding, and why he was not killed, when so completely in their power, can be accounted for only on the ground that they were in Mtesa's dominions, and feared he would take terrible revenge for the murder. Later in the day this drunken chief came to visit him on the island, and demanded why he had come and what he wanted. Being told, he went away, and sent three branches of bananas, and left him and his party to their fate. They rested here quietly till afternoon, when they saw Magassa's fleet coming slowly down the lake, steering for a neighboring island. The canoes were beached and the men disembarked and began to prepare their camp for the night. Stanley was getting impatient at these delays, and thinking he would quicken Magassa's movements by hastening forward, he set sail for Alice Island, thirty-five miles distant. The two chiefs, with the escorting canoes, accompanied him for about a mile and a half, but, getting alarmed at the aspect of the weather, turned back, shouting, as they did so, that as soon as it moderated they would follow. Bowling along before a spanking breeze, the little craft danced gayly over the cresting waves, and when night came down and darkness fell on the lonely lake, kept steadily on and, finally, at midnight reached the island, where they luckily struck upon a sheltered cove and came to anchor. When morning dawned they found they were almost against the base of a beetling cliff, with overhanging rocks all around them, dotted with the fires of the natives. These came down to the shore holding green wisps of grass in their hands as tokens of friendliness. Stanley and his men were hungry, and now rejoiced in the prospect of a good breakfast. But these friendly natives, seeing their need, became so extortionate in their demands that they would not trade with them, and Stanley determined to steer for Bumbirch Island, twenty five miles distant, and there obtain food.

The breeze was light and they made slow headway, and it was evidently going to be a long sail to the island. As the sun went down, huge black clouds began to roll up the sky, traversed by lightning, while the low growl of thunder foretold a coming storm. As the clouds rose higher and higher the lightning became more vivid, and the thunder broke with startling peals along the water, and soon the rain came down in torrents, drenching them to the skin. The waves began to rise while darkness, black as midnight, settled down on the lake. The little craft tossed wildly on the water, and the prospect before them looked gloomy enough. Fortunately, about midnight, they came upon Pocoke Island, and anchored under its lee amid thunder and lightning, and rain, and the angry roar of the surf on every side. All night long the flashes lit up the angry scene, while the heavy, tropical thunder shook the bosom of the lake. The haven they had reached was so poor a protection that all hands were kept bailing, to prevent the overstrained boat from foundering at her anchor.

We have a very faint idea in our northern latitudes of what a thunderstorm is in the tropics, and the slight affair that Stanley made of it is one of those apparently insignificant, and yet most striking illustrations of his character. Storms on the water—starvation on land—deadly perils of all kinds are spoken of by him as one would speak of the ordinary incidents of travel. He has no time, and apparently no taste, for sensational writing; or perhaps it would be nearer the truth to say—in his cool courage, calm self-reliance and apparent contempt of death he does not see the dramatic side of the scenes in which he performs so important a part. The most tragic events—the most perilous crises are treated by him as ordinary events. An escape so narrow that one's heart stops beating as he contemplates it, he narrates with as much coolness and apparent indifference as he would his deliverance from a disagreeable companion.

In the morning, Stanley, as he looked around him and saw the surf breaking on every side, ordered the anchor up and the sail hoisted, for this was too dangerous a place for the Lady Alice. The thunder-storm had passed, and a stiff northeast breeze had sprung up, before which he bowled swiftly along, and in three hours reached the mouth of a quiet cove near the village of Kajuri, at the southeastern extremity of Bumbirch Island. After the storm and peril of the last forty-eight hours, it was a welcome sight that greeted them. The green slopes of this gem set in the sparkling waters were laden with fruits and covered with cattle. Groves of bananas, herds of cattle lazily feeding, and flocks of goats promised an abundance of food; and Stanley and his men, as they drew near the lovely, inviting shore, revelled in anticipation of the rest and good cheer awaiting them. Filled with the most peaceful intentions themselves—their hearts made glad at the sight of the bountiful provisions before them—they did not dream of any hostility, when suddenly they heard a wild, shrill war-cry from the plateau above the huts of the village near the shore, on which were gathered a crowd of excited men. Stanley was surprised at this unexpected hostile demonstration, and halted just as the boat was about to ground, to ascertain what it meant. The savages in the meantime were rushing wildly toward the shore in front of where the boat lay rocking on the water. As they approached, they suddenly changed their warlike attitude, and, ceasing their loud yells, assumed a friendly manner, and invited them to land in tones and gestures so kind and affable that Stanley's first suspicions were at once disarmed, and he ordered the rowers to send the boat ashore. But the moment the keel grated on the pebbly beach, all this friendliness of manner changed, and the naked savages rushed into the water, and, seizing the boat, lifted it up bodily and, with all on board, carried it high and dry on the bank.

Stanley was terribly aroused at this sudden treachery, and reckless of consequences, determined to avenge it, and twice he raised his revolver to shoot down the audacious wretches, but his crew begged him to desist, declaring earnestly that these people were friends, and that if he would wait a few minutes, he would see that all was right. He accordingly sat down in the stern sheets and waited to see the end. In the meantime, the savages came leaping from the hill-sides, tossing their naked limbs in the air, and uttering loud yells, till a wild, frantic multitude completely surrounded the boat in which Stanley still sat unmoved and calm. The wretches seemed crazed with passion, and poised their spears as if about to strike him, and drew their arrows to the head, one discharge of which would have riddled Stanley, struck the boat by his side with their spear handles, gnashed their teeth, foamed at the mouth, and yelled till their eyes seemed bursting from their sockets. Stanley, however, never moved nor uttered a word. His life did not seem worth a thought in that frenzied, demoniacal crowd. But resistance and expostulation were alike useless, and he could do nothing but wait the final assault, and then sell his life dearly as possible.

For some strange, unaccountable reason, their chief, Thekha, kept them from the last act of violence, and at last so quieted them that Stanley calmly asked him how much he demanded to let him go. The most curious part of this whole affair is, that the chief condescended to enter into negotiations with Stanley. Everything the latter had was in the boat, and he had only to give the word, and in five minutes all was his. But instead of doing this, he struck up a bargain with Stanley, and agreed to let him off for four cloths and ten necklaces of large beads. Stanley at once took them from his packages and gave them to him. But no sooner had he received them, than he gave a quick order to his men to seize the oars of the boat. In a twinkling, before Stanley had time to think what they were about, the oars were caught up and carried away. The natives seeing through the treacherous trick, enjoyed it thoroughly, and their loud laughing jeers roused all the devil in Stanley's nature, but he still said nothing. Having got possession of the oars, they thought he was helpless as a tortoise on his back, and became quiet, seemingly enjoying the white man's helplessness. Having no fear of his escape, they at noon leisurely walked to their huts to get their noonday meal, and to discuss what the next move should be. Stanley says he was not idle, he wished to impose on the savages by his indifferent manner, but he was all the while planning how to escape and the best mode of meeting the attack when it came.

While the savages were at their dinner, a negress came near them and told them to eat honey with Thekha, as it was the only way to save their lives, for he had determined to kill them and take everything they had. Stanley permitted his coxswain to go to Thekha and make the proposition to eat honey. The wily chief told him to be at ease, no harm was intended them and next day he would eat honey with them. The coxswain returned delighted, and reported the good news. But Stanley checked the confidence of the men, and told them that nothing but their own wit and courage could save their lives. This, he said, was all a trick, the next move would be to seize their guns as they had the oars, when they would be helpless, and by no means to leave the boat, but be prepared to act at any moment when he should give the word. The men saw at once the force of Stanley's suspicions, and kept close by him.

Thus nearly three long hours passed away, neither he nor his crew doing or attempting to do anything. But about three o'clock, the war-drums began again their horrid din, and soon the loping, naked savages were seen running from every quarter, and in half an hour five hundred warriors had gathered around the chief within thirty paces of the boat. He was sitting down, and when the warriors were all assembled, he made them an address. As soon as he had finished, about fifty of them dashed up to Stanley's men, and seizing his drum, bore it back in triumph. From some cause or other, this last and apparently most harmless act of all aroused Stanley's suspicions to a point that made him act promptly and decisively.

Perhaps it was their scornful, insulting language as they walked off, bidding him get his guns ready, as they were coming back soon to cut his throat. At all events, the moment he saw them approach the chief with the drum, he shouted to his men to push the boat into the water. The eleven men sprang to its sides, and lifting it as if it had been a toy, carried it, with Stanley in it, to the water's edge and shot it, with one desperate effort, far out into the lake and beyond their depth, and where they had to swim for it. Quickly as it was done, the savages instantly detected the movement, and before the boat had lost its headway, were crowding the very edge of the water, to which they had rushed like a whirlwind, shouting and yelling like madmen. Seizing his elephant rifle, Stanley sent two large conical balls into the dense mass with frightful effect. Then pulling one of the men in the boat, and bidding him help the others in, he seized his double-barreled gun, loaded with buck-shot, and fired right and left into the close-packed, naked crowd. It was like firing with small shot into a flock of pigeons, and a clean swath was cut through the naked mass, which was so stunned at the horrible

114

effect, that they ran back up the slope without hurling a spear or shooting an arrow.

With the oars gone, the great struggle would be to get out into the open lake, where they could hoist sail; for, this once accomplished, they could bid defiance to their enemies. Stanley knew the first move of the savages would be to man their canoes, which lined the shore, and surround his helpless vessel and overwhelm him. He therefore watched the first movement to launch a canoe, and as soon as a desperate-looking savage made the attempt, he dropped him with a bullet through his body. A second, following his example, fell on the beach, when they paused at the certain death that seemed to await the man who dared to touch a boat. Just then Stanley caught sight of the sub-chief, who commanded the party that took the drum, and taking a cool, deliberate aim at him with his elephant rifle, he sent one of its great conical balls tearing through his body, killing at the same time his wife and infant, behind him. This terrified them, for there seemed something supernatural about this deadly work, and they ceased their efforts to launch the boats, and hastened to get out of the reach of such fatal firing. In the meantime, the men were slowly working the boat toward the mouth of the cove. But, just as they were feeling safe, Stanley saw two canoes, loaded heavily with warriors, push out of a little bay and pull toward him. Putting two explosive shells into his elephant rifle, he waited till they came within the distance where they would be most destructive, and then commenced firing. He fired rapidly, but being a dead-shot, with great accuracy, and the shells, as they struck inside the canoes, burst with terrible effect. Four shots killed five men and sunk both the canoes, leaving the warriors to swim ashore. This ended the fight, and the enraged and baffled crowd vented their fury by shouting out, "Go and die in the Nyanza."

Stanley's rapid deadly firing killed fourteen, and wounded with buck-shot eight, which, he coolly remarks, "I consider to be very dear payment for the robbery of eight ash oars and a drum, though barely equivalent, in our estimation, to the intended massacre of ourselves." This cool-blooded treachery and narrow escape roused Stanley's whole nature, and terrible as had been the punishment he had inflicted, he resolved that he would make it more terrible still before he had done with them.

During the perils of the next night that followed, he had plenty of time to nurse his wrath. Having got clear of the land, he hoisted sail, and favored by a light breeze, by night was eight miles from the treacherous Bumbireh. A little after dark the breeze died away, and he set the men to paddling. But, their oars being gone, they made slow headway. At sunrise they were only twenty miles from the island, but near noon, a strong breeze springing up from the northwest, they bowled along at the rate of five miles an hour, and soon saw it sink in the distant horizon. At sunset they saw an island named Sousa, toward which they steered, hoping to reach it by midnight and find a safe haven. But about eight o'clock the breeze began to increase till it rose to a fierce gale, and the sail had to be taken in.

Being without oars, they could not keep the light boat before the wind, and she was whirled away by it like a feather, and wallowed amid the waves that kept increasing, till it seemed impossible to keep much longer afloat. The men strove desperately with their boards for paddles to reach the island, and get to the leeward of it, till the storm should break, but it was of no avail. They were swept by it like a piece of drift-wood, and the lightning, as it lit up its green sides, seemed to mock their despair. The terrific crash of the thunder, the roar of the tempest, and the wild waste of the wrathful water as it was incessantly lit up by the blinding flashes, made it the most terrific night Stanley had ever passed in all his wide wanderings. Between the dashing of the waves over the gunwale and the downfalling deluge of rain, the helpless boat rapidly filled, and it required constant and rapid bailing to keep it from going to the bottom.

The imagination cannot conceive the terrors that surrounded that little boat with its helpless crew on that storm-swept lake during that long, wild night. Above them, rushed the angry clouds, pierced incessantly by the lightning; the heavy thunder shook the very heavens, while all around them were islands and rocks, and a few miles ahead, the main-land peopled by hostile savages. Yet, amid all their terror, the men worn out with their long fasting and exhausting labors, would drop asleep, till awakened by the stern order to bail. The men of Bumbireh had shouted after them, "go and die in the Nyanza," and they now seemed to be prophetic words. Stanley remembered them, and he lived to make the murderous savages remember them, too. At daybreak the tempest broke, and the waves not having the heavy roll of the ocean, quickly subsided, and they saw they had drifted eight miles off the isle of Susa, which they had made such desperate efforts to reach the night before, while other islands rose in the distance. There was not a morsel of food in the boat, and it was now forty-eight hours since they had tasted any, yet the men took to their paddles cheerfully. Soon a gentle breeze set in from the westward, and hoisting sail, they steered for an unknown island, which Stanley named Refuge Island. It was small and uninhabited, but on exploring it, they discovered that the natives had once occupied and cultivated it. To their great joy, they found green bananas, and a small fruit resembling cherries, but tasting like dates. Stanley succeeded, also, in shooting two fat ducks. The men soon stripped these of their feathers and had them in the pot, with which, and the fruit, they made what seemed to them in their famished condition, a right royal repast. The camp was pitched close by the sandy beach, and when night closed sweetly in on the wanderers, "there were few people in the world," says Stanley, "blessed God more devoutly than we did." And well they might, for their double deliverance from the savages on shore and the tempest on the water, was almost miraculous.

They rested here all the next day recruiting, and then set sail, and coming to friendly natives, laid in a supply of provisions. While at anchor, some of the men plucked the poultry they had bought, and they feasted till they were thoroughly satisfied.

At midnight, a favorable wind rising, they set sail for Usukuma. About three in the morning they were in the middle of the Speke Gulf, from which they had started nearly two months before, and bound for their camp. The wind had died away, and the water lay calm and unruffled beneath the tropical sky. But this calm was only the prelude to a fearful storm. Clouds, black as ink, began to roll up the heavens, their edges corrugated and torn by the contending forces that urged them on, while out from their foldings the lightning leaped in blinding flashes, and the thunder, instead of rolling in angry peals, came down in great crashes as if the very frame-work of nature was rending, and then the hail, in stones big as filberts, beat down on their uncovered heads. The waves rose to an astonishing height, and tore like wild horses over the lake. The boat became unmanageable, and was whirled along at the mercy of the wind and waves. But the staunch little craft outrode the fury of the gale, with a buoyancy that surprised Stanley.

Next morning, although almost under the equator, they saw the day dawn gray, and cheerless, and raw. On taken his observations, Stanley found that he was only about twenty miles northwest of his camp. The news sent new life into the crew. They hoisted sail, and, though at first the wind was unfavorable, yet, as if good luck had come at last, it shifted astern, and, with a full sail, they steered straight for camp—every heart bounding with joy.

The men in camp discovered the boat when miles away, and hurrying to the shore sent up shout after shout, and tossed their arms joyfully in the air. As the boat drove swiftly on, the shouts were changed to volleys of musketry and waving of flags, while "the land seemed alive with leaping forms of glad-hearted men." Rumors of their destruction had reached camp, and his long absence seemed to confirm them, and they had made up their minds, that, with their leader lost, they must turn back. As the boat grated on the pebbly shore, fifty men leaped into the water and seizing Stanley lifted him bodily out, and, running up the bank, placed him on their shoulders, and danced around the camp like madmen. They seemed unable to contain their joy. It showed how strong was the hold Stanley had on their affections. Stern in enforcing discipline and relentless in punishing crime, he was always careful of their welfare, attentive to their wants, just in all his dealings, and generous in his reward for good behavior and faithful service, and by this course he had bound these simple children of nature to him with cords of iron.

CHAPTER XV

AN INTERVAL OF REST

The next morning, as Stanley looked out of his tent-door upon the broad and beautiful lake, it was with that intense feeling of satisfaction with which one contemplates a great and perilous undertaking, which, after being well-nigh abandoned, is at last successfully accomplished. The waters, glittering in the morning sun, had but a short time before seemed to him an angry foe, but now they wore a friendly aspect. They seemed to belong to him. Livingstone, and Speke, and Burton, and others had looked on that lake, and sighed in vain to solve the mystery that enveloped it, while he had not only followed its winding shores their entire length, but had sounded its depths and fixed its geographical position forever. His toils were over, and the victory won in this his first great enterprise, and he could well look forward with hope to the great work still before him. His escapes had been wonderful, and he might take them as good omens for the future.

It seemed as if fate delighted to place him in positions of danger, from which there appeared to be no escape, in order to show her power to save him under any and all circumstances. Even now, when contemplating so satisfactorily his success, he was startled by the narrowness of his escape from a danger of which he had never before dreamed. That trouble, disorder and desertion might befall his camp during his absence he had often feared, but now he was told by the men he had left in charge of it, that in a few hours more the expedition would have broken up and disappeared forever.

This was Frank Pocoke's report. He said that a rumor had reached camp that Stanley and his crew had been taken prisoners soon after leaving, and he at once sent off fifty soldiers to effect his release, who found the report false. They had also heard of his fight with the Wamma, and that he was killed. In the meantime a conspiracy had been formed by three neighboring tribes to capture the camp and seize all the goods. It was discovered, and everything put in the best state possible to defeat it, when the whole fell through on account of the sudden death of one of the conspirators and the disaffection of another.

With the report of Stanley's death uncontradicted—nay, corroborated by his long absence—and in view of the dangers surrounding them, the soldiers and men held a meeting to determine what course they should take. He had then been gone nearly a month and a half, and it should not have taken more than half that time to have circumnavigated the lake with a boat that, in a fair breeze, could go five or six miles an hour.

Something must have happened to him; that was certain; and it mattered little whether it was death or captivity. It was finally decided to wait fifteen days longer, or till the new moon, when, if he did not appear, they would strike camp and march back to Unyanyembe. The fifteen days would have expired the next day after Stanley's arrival. If, therefore, he had been delayed forty-eight hours longer, instead of being received with the waving of flags, shouts and volleys of musketry, and wild demonstrations of delight, there would have been no welcome, but a silent, deserted camp. This would have been a terrible blow, and would have dashed with the bitterest disappointment all the joy at his task successfully accomplished. But he had been saved all this; still one calamity had befallen him for which there was no remedy; young Barker had died only a few days before his arrival, and six of his strong men had fallen victims to dysentery and fever. Thus while in all the danger through which he had passed on the lake he had not lost a man, seven had died while lying idly in a healthy camp. The death of Barker he felt keenly, for of the three white men who had started with him, two had already fallen, and now only one was left.

In writing to his mother, announcing his death, and expressing his sympathy with her in her affliction, he thus speaks of the manner in which it occurred: "I was absent on an exploring expedition on Lake Victoria, having left Francis Pocoke and Frederick Barker in charge of my camp. Altogether I was absent fifty-eight days. When I returned, hoping that I would find that all had gone well, I was struck with the grievous news that your son had died twelve days before, of an intermittent fever. What little I have been able to learn of your son's death, amounts to this: On April 22d, he went out on the lake with Pocoke to shoot hippopotami, and all day enjoyed himself. On the morning of the 23d he went out for a little walk, had his tea and some pancakes, washed himself, and then suddenly said he felt ill, and lay down in bed. He called for a hot stone to be put to his feet; brandy was given him, blankets were heaped on him, but he felt such cold in his extremities that nothing availed to restore heat in his body. His blood seems to have become congealed. At eight o'clock, an hour after he lay down, he was dead. Such is what I have been able to glean from Pocoke of the manner of his death. But by our next letter-carrier, Pocoke shall send you a complete account." He then goes on to speak of his excellent qualities and promising future, and his own great loss.

One of the curious things that struck Stanley as he looked on his party, was the strange contrast between Pocoke's face and his own. The former being most of the time in camp, had bleached to his old English whiteness, while, under the reflection of the fierce rays of an equatorial sun, he had been burned till his face was the color of a lobster—in fact, the natives had come to call him, not the pale, but the red-faced man, to which his blood-shot eyes gave a still more sanguinary appearance.

Now followed a season of rest and of sweet repose; and how deep and sweet it was, may be gathered from his own language. He says: "Sweet is the Sabbath day to the toil-worn laborer, happy is the long sea-tossed mariner on his arrival in port, and sweet were the days of calm rest we enjoyed after our troublous exploration of the Nyanza. The brusque storms, the continued rains, the cheerless gray clouds, the wild waves, the loneliness of the islands, the inhospitality of the natives that were like mere phases of a dream, were now but the reminiscences of the memory, so little did we heed what was past while enjoying the luxury of a rest from our toils. Still it added to our pleasure to be able to conjure up in the mind the varied incidents of the long lake journey; they served to enliven and employ the mind while the body enjoyed repose, like condiments quickening digestion. It was a pleasure to be able to map at will, in the mind, so many countries newly discovered, such a noble extent of fresh water explored for the first time. As the memory flew over the lengthy track of exploration, how fondly it dwelt on the many picturesque bays, margined by water-lilies and lotus plants, or by the green walls of the slender reed-like papyrus, inclosing an area of water, whose face was as calm as a mirror, because lofty mountain ridges almost surround it. With what kindly recognition it roved over the little green island in whose snug haven our boat had lain securely at anchor, when the rude tempest without churned the face of the Nyanza into a foaming sheet." The lofty rocks once more rose before him in imagination, while the distant hills were outlined against the fervid horizon, and the rich grain fields of some of the districts smiled in the sun. But his memory dwelt with fondest recollection on Uganda and its hospitable King Mtesa, for there, it not only recalled the present, but pictured a glorious future, in which smiling villages took the places of rude huts, from the midst of which church spires rose, and the clear tones of the bell called the dusky inhabitants to the place of worship. As he thus lay dreaming, close by the equatorial circle, he saw the land smiling in affluence and plenty; its bays crowded with the dark hulls of trading vessels, heard the sound of craftsmen at their work, the roar of manufactories and foundries, and the ever-buzzing noise of industry.

With these bright anticipations of the future, the happy result of his endeavors, would mingle his desperate encounters with the savages, his narrow escapes, his nights of danger on the tempestuous lake, his wonderful success so near a failure at last—of all these marvelous experiences and events crowded on him as he lay and rested, and dreamed on the shores of the lake that he felt to be his own. If half that he anticipated, as he lay and rested and dreamed, turns out true, his name will be linked with changes that will sink all his great discoveries into nothingness—moral changes and achievements as much above mere material success as mind is above matter—civilization above barbarism—Christianity above Paganism.

This successful voyage and safe return inspired the members of the expedition with renewed confidence in their leader, and Stanley soon set about prosecuting the great work to which he had devoted himself, and which, with all its toils and dangers and great sacrifice of life, had only just begun.

The Grand Admiral Magassa had not yet joined him. There was no reason he had not done so, except that the fight at Bumbireh and subsequent storm on the lake had sent them wide apart. But he had two of Stanley's best men with him, who would direct him to the camp in Speke Bay, toward which he knew Stanley was working, and where he should have been before this time. The latter waited nine days in camp for him, and then concluding that he did not intend to come at all, resolved to march back overland with his party (as he had no canoes to carry them by water) to Uganda. Just as they were ready to start, there came into camp a negro embassy from Ruoma, which lay between him and Ugondo on the land route, with the following message: "Ruoma sends salaams to the white man. He does not want the white man's cloth, beads or wire, but the white man must not pass through his country. Ruoma does not want to see him or any other man with long red hair down to his shoulders, white face and big red eyes. Ruoma is not afraid of him, but if the white man will come near his country, Ruoma and Mirambo will fight him."

"Here, indeed," as Stanley says, "was a dilemma." Mtesa's admiral had proved false to the instructions given him by the king, and no boats had arrived to convey his party to Uganda by water, and now the ruler of the district through which he must pass to reach it by land forbade him to cross it. To force a passage was impossible; for Ruoma, besides having a hundred and fifty muskets and several thousand spearmen and bowmen, had the dreaded Mirambo, with his fierce warriors, within a day's march of him and ready to aid him. Even if he could fight his way across the country, it would be at a sacrifice of life that he could not afford, and which the results he hoped to secure would not justify. Still, he could not give up Uganda, with its half-civilized king, for it was not only the most interesting country that bordered on the lake, but it comprised the unknown region lying between it and Tanganika. If he could only get canoes from some other quarter, he could take his party to Uganda by water; and once there, his friend Mtesa would give him all the aid he wanted. He therefore set on foot inquiries respecting the various tribes bordering on the gulf on which he was encamped, to ascertain the number of canoes each possessed. He found that the king of Ukerewe, the large island lying at the mouth of the gulf, was the most likely person to have the canoes he wanted, and he applied to him. But he was unable to negotiate for them in person, as he was taken suddenly and seriously ill—the result of his long exposure on the lake under an equatorial sun—so he sent Pocoke, with Prince Kaduma, to make proposals for them. These, taking a handsome present for the king, departed. In twelve days they returned with fifty canoes and some three hundred natives under the command of the king's brother; but to convey him and his party to the king, not to Uganda.

Stanley's joy at the sight of the canoes was dampened by this request, and he told the king's brother that even if the king would give all his land and cattle, he would not let the expedition go to Ukerewe, but that he himself would go, and the messenger himself might return as soon as he pleased. As soon as he was well enough he set out, and on the second day he reached the island. Knowing how much was at stake, he put on his court costume, which meant the best clothes in his wardrobe, and equipped himself with his best arms, while his attendants bore valuable presents.

The next day after his arrival was fixed for the great audience. When the hour arrived Stanley mustered the crew of the Lady Alice, who had been dressed for the occasion, and the bugle sounded the order to march. In ten minutes they came to a level stretch of ground, in the centre of which was a knoll, where the king was seated in state, surrounded by hundreds of bowmen and spearmen. He was a young man, with a color tending more to the mulatto than the negro—possessing an amiable countenance, and altogether he made a favorable impression on Stanley. He was quite a conspicuous object sitting on that knoll in the midst of warriors, for he was wrapped in a robe of red and yellow silk damask cloth. His reception of Stanley consisted in a long, steady stare, but being informed that the latter wished to state the object of his visit to him and a few of his chiefs alone, he stepped aside a short distance to a pile of stones, and invited them to join him. Stanley then stated what he wanted, how far he wished the canoes to go, what he would pay for them, etc., etc. The king listened attentively, and replied in a kind and affable manner; but he said his canoes were many of them rotten and unfit for a long voyage, and he was afraid they would give out, and then he would be blamed and accused of being the cause of the loss of his property. Stanley replied that he might blame the canoes, but not him. At the close of the conference, the king said he should have as many canoes as he wanted, but he must remain a few days and partake of his hospitality. This was given in no stinted measure, for beeves, and goats, and chickens, and milk, and eggs, and bananas, and plantains were furnished in prodigal quantities, together with native beer for the crew. They luxuriated in abundance, and on the fifteenth day the king came to Stanley's tent with his chief counselor, and gave him his secret instructions and advice. He said he had ordered fifty canoes to carry him as far as Usukuma, Stanley's camp, but his people would not be willing to go to Uganda. He, therefore, had resorted to stratagem, and caused it to be reported that Stanley was going to come and live among them. He said that the latter must encourage this report, and when he got to Usukuma, and the canoes were drawn up on shore he must seize them and secure the paddles. Having thus rendered it impossible for them to return, he was to inform them what he intended to do.

Stanley having promised to obey his instructions implicitly, the king sent with him his prime minister and two favorites, and he departed, after leaving behind him a handsome present as an earnest of what he would do in the future. The natives bent to their paddles cheerfully, and at length reached Stanley's camp; but instead of fifty, he found there but twenty-three canoes. Though disappointed, he was compelled to be content with these.

He accordingly whispered his orders to the captains of his expedition to muster their men and seize the canoes and paddles. This was done, and the canoes were drawn up far on land. The astonished natives inquired the meaning of this, and when told, flew into a furious passion, and being about equal in number to Stanley's party, showed fight. The latter saw at a glance that any attempt to mollify them by talk would be fruitless, and that energetic, prompt measures alone would answer, and he immediately ordered the bugle to sound the rally. The soldiers stepped quickly into line, when he ordered a charge with the muzzles of their guns, and the astonished, duped creatures were driven out of camp and away from the shore. Stanley then held a parley with them and proposed to send them back, and did, or at least a portion of them, in four canoes, which could return and take off the rest. The other canoes he kept, and on the third day started for Uganda with a portion of the expedition, and at the end of five days arrived at Refuge Island. Remembering when he was there before, that the inhabitants of the mainland, which was not more than six miles off, were not kindly disposed toward him, he built a strong camp among the rocks, locating it so that each high rock could furnish a position for sharp-shooters, and in every way he could, rendered it impregnable, in case it should be attacked during his absence.

As he had not been able to embark all his expedition and baggage, he now returned for them, reaching his old camp again after an absence of fifteen days. He learned on his arrival that two neighboring chiefs were planning to seize him and make him pay a heavy ransom. He, however, said nothing; spoke pleasantly every day to one of them—Prince Kaduma, and made presents to his pretty wife, and went on loading his canoes. When the day of embarkation arrived, the two chiefs, with a strong force came to the water's edge and looked on moodily. Stanley appeared not to notice it, but laughed and talked pleasantly, and proceeding leisurely to the Lady Alice, ordered the boats crew to shove her off. When a short distance was reached, he halted, and swinging broadside on shore, showed a row of deadly guns in point-blank range of the shore. Taken completely aback by this sudden movement, and not daring to make a hostile demonstration with those guns covering them, the treacherous chiefs let the process of embarkation go on without molestation, and soon the last canoe was afloat and a final good-bye given to the camp, a scornful farewell waved to the disappointed natives on shore, and the little fleet steered for Refuge Island.

Rough weather followed, and the rotten canoes gave out one after another, so that he had only fifteen when he reached the island. He found the camp had not been disturbed in his absence. On the contrary, the neighboring kings and chiefs, seeing that his camp was impregnable, had proffered their friendship and supplied the soldiers with provisions. They also provided him with a guide and sold him three canoes.

CHAPTER XVI

PREPARATIONS FOR FURTHER EXPLORATIONS

Stanley now rested a few days on this island before beginning his explorations. It was associated in his mind with bitter memories, and, as he wandered over it, he remembered the insults he had received, and his almost miraculous escape from death near it. The treacherous Bumbireh was almost in sight, and it awakened in him a strong desire for revenge, and he determined to visit the island again, and demand reparation for the wrongs he had received, and if it was not given, to make war on them and teach them a lesson on good behavior. So at the end of three days he set sail and camped on Mahyiga Island, five miles distant, and sent a message to the natives saying, that if they would deliver their king and two principal chiefs into his hands, he would make peace with them, otherwise he would make war. This was a cool request, and Stanley himself, suspecting it would be refused, sent a party to invite the king of Iroba, an island only a mile from Bumbireh, to visit him, who, dreading the vengeance of the white man, came, bringing with him three chiefs. On what principle of morals Stanley will justify his course we cannot say, but the moment the king arrived, he had him and his chiefs put in chains; the conditions of their release being that his people should deliver the king of Bumbireh, and two of his principal chiefs into his hands.

Although the people of Bumbireh had treated his message with contempt, the subjects of Iroba seized their king and delivered him into the hands of Stanley. The peril of their own king had stimulated them to effort, and Stanley at once released him, while he loaded his new royal captive heavily with chains. He also sent a message to king Antari, on the mainland, to whom Bumbireh was tributary, requesting him to redeem his land from war. In reply, the latter sent his son and two chiefs to him to make peace, who brought a quantity of bananas as a promise of what the king would do in the future. Stanley, in conversing with them, detected them in so many falsehoods, and thinking he saw treachery in their faces, or perhaps it would be more in accordance with truth to say, that having got them in his power, he thought it better to keep them as hostages for the appearance of the two chiefs of Bumbireh, who had not been brought with the king, and he, therefore, did so. In the meantime, seven large canoes of Mtesa came up, which were out on an expedition of the king's. The chief commanding them told Stanley that Magassa had recovered the oars captured at Bumbireh, and that on his returning and reporting Stanley dead, he had been put in chains by Mtesa, but subsequently he had been released and dispatched in search of him. Stanley persuaded this chief, with his canoes, to remain and assist in the attack on Bumbireh, if his followers refused the terms of peace.

Two days after, this chief sent some of his men to Bumbireh for food, but they were not allowed to land. On the contrary, they were attacked, and one man was killed and eight were wounded. This gave Stanley another strong reason for making war at once without further negotiations, to which Mtesa's chief gladly consented. Accordingly, next morning, he mustered two hundred and eighty men with fifty muskets, and two hundred spearmen, and placed them in eighteen canoes and set out for Bumbireh, eight miles distant, and reached the island at two o'clock in the afternoon.

The natives of Bumbireh were evidently expecting trouble, for they felt sure the attack on the friends of Stanley the day before would be quickly avenged. As the latter, therefore, drew near the shore, he saw lookouts on every eminence. Looking through his field-glass, he soon discovered messengers running to a plantain grove which stood on a low hill that commanded a clear, open view of a little port on the southern point of the island, from which he concluded that the main force of the enemy was assembled there. He then called the canoes together, and told them to follow him and steer just as he steered, and by no means to attempt to land, as he did not mean that one of Mtesa's men should be killed, or, indeed, any of his own soldiers—he intended to punish Bumbireh without any damage to himself. He then ordered his crew to row straight for the port—the other canoes following in close order behind. He managed to keep out of sight of the lookouts; and skirting close to the land, at the end of a little more than a mile, rounded a cape and shot into a fine bay, right in the rear and in full view of the enemy. They were gathered in such large numbers that Stanley saw it would not do to attack them in such a cover, and so steered for the opposite side of the bay, as though he intended to land there, where the sloping hill-sides were bare of everything but low grass. The savages, perceiving this, broke cover and ran yelling toward the threatened point. This was exactly what Stanley wanted, and he ordered the rowers to pull slowly, so as to give them time to reach the spot toward which he was moving. Very soon they were all assembled on the naked hill-side, brandishing their weapons fiercely in the air. Stanley kept slowly on till within a hundred yards of the beach, when he anchored broadside on the shore—the English and American flags waving above him. The other seventeen canoes followed his example. Seeing a group of about fifty standing close together, he ordered a volley to be fired into it. Fifty muskets and his own trusty rifle spoke at once, and with such terrible effect that nearly the whole number was killed or wounded. The natives, astounded at this murderous work, now separated and came down to the water's edge singly, and began to yell and sling stones and shoot arrows. Stanley then ordered the anchors up, and gave directions to move the canoes to within fifty yards of the shore, and each soldier to select his man and fire as though he was shooting birds. The savages dropped right and left before this target practice, but the survivors stood their ground firmly, for they knew if Stanley effected a landing he would burn everything on the island.

For an hour they endured the deadly fire, and then, unable longer to stand it, moved up the hill, but still not out of range, especially of Stanley's unerring rifle. Though every now and then a man would drop, they refused to move farther away, for they knew that if they were not near enough to make a dash the moment the boats touched the shore, all would be lost. Another hour was therefore passed in this long-range firing, when Stanley ordered the canoes to advance all together, as if about to make a sudden landing. The savages, seeing this, rushed down the hill-side like a torrent, and massed themselves by the hundreds at the point toward which the canoes were moving, some even entering the water with their spears poised ready to strike. When they were packed densely together, Stanley ordered the bugle to sound a halt, and, as the crews rested on their oars, directed a volley to be fired into them, which mowed them down so terribly that they turned and fled like deer over the hill. Stanley's men had now got their blood up and urged him to let them land and make a complete end of this treacherous people, but he refused, saying that he came to punish, not destroy.

They had fired in all about seven hundred cartridges, and as the savages were completely exposed, and in the afternoon, with the sun directly behind the boats, and shining full in their faces, the mortality was great. Over forty were left dead on the field, while the number of the wounded could not be counted, though more than a hundred were seen to limp or to be led away. It was a great victory, and Stanley's dusky allies were in a state of high excitement, and made the air ring with their shouts and laughter, as they bent to their paddles. It was dark when they got back to the island, where they were received with wild songs of triumph. Stanley was a great hero to these untutored children of nature.

The next morning more canoes arrived from Uganda, and Stanley prepared to depart. He had now thirty-two canoes, all well loaded with men, which made quite an imposing little fleet as they moved into order on the lake, and constituted a strong force. They sailed close to Bumbireh, and Stanley looked to see what had been the effect of the severe thrashing he had given them the day before. He found their audacity gone, and their proud, insulting spirit completely quelled. There were no shouts of defiance, no hostile demonstrations. Seeing a hundred or more gathered in a group, he fired a bullet over their heads, which scattered them in every direction. The day before they had breasted bravely volley after volley, but now the war spirit was thoroughly cowed. In another place some natives came down to the shore and begged them to go away and not hurt them any more. This gave Stanley an opportunity to preach them a sermon on treachery, and exhort them hereafter to treat strangers who came to them peaceably with kindness. The dead in almost every hut was, however, the most effectual sermon of the two.

They camped that evening on the mainland, in the territory of King Kattawa, who treated them in a magnificent style for a savage, to show his gratitude for the punishment they had inflicted on Bumbireh, who had a short time before killed one of his chiefs. They stayed here a day, and then steered for the island of Muzina, where he had last seen Magassa and his fleet. The people were not friendly to him, but they had heard of the terrible punishment he had inflicted on the Bumbireh, and hastened to supply him with provisions. They brought him five cattle, four goats, and a hundred bunches of bananas, besides honey, milk and eggs.

The king of Ugoro, near by, also sent him word that he had given his people orders to supply him with whatever food he wanted. Stanley replied that he wanted no food, but if he would lend him ten canoes to carry his people to Uganda, he would consider him as his friend. They were promptly furnished. Mtesa's chief urged him to attack the king, as he had murdered many of Mtesa's people, but Stanley refused, saying he did not come to make war on black people, he only wished to defend his rights and avenge acts of treachery. Five days after he landed at Duomo Uganda, half-way between the Kagera and Katonga rivers, and pitched his camp. He selected this spot as the best place from which to start for the Albert Nyanza, which he designed next to explore. He wanted to see Mtesa, and get his advice as to which was the best route to take, because between these two lakes were several powerful tribes, who were continually at war with the king of Uganda.

In summing up his losses during this journey of two hundred and twenty miles by water, he found he had lost six men drowned, five guns and one case of ammunition, besides ten canoes wrecked and three riding asses dead, leaving him but one. He had been gone fifty-six days, and though the distance was but two hundred and twenty miles, a large portion of it had been traversed three times, so that he had really travelled by water over seven hundred and twenty miles. He had bought scarcely any provisions, the expedition subsisting on the corn he bought at the start with one bale of cloth, but considerable quantities of food had been given them.

He now resolved, after he had settled his camp, to visit Mtesa again, and consult with him about the aid he could give him to reach Albert Nyanza. This lake was the source of the White Nile, up which Baker was forcing his way, the very year Stanley started on his expedition. Baker hoped to launch steamers upon it, but he failed even to reach it, though he saw its waters, twenty miles distant. Between it and the Victoria Nyanza is an unknown region. The distance from one to the other in a straight line is probably not two hundred miles, though by any travelled route it is, of course, much farther. Nothing is definitely known of its size or shape. Colonel Mason made a partial exploration of it last year, but it still remains a new field for some future explorer, for Stanley failed to reach it if Mason's map is correct. The Victoria Nyanza he computed to contain twenty-one thousand five hundred square miles, and to be nine thousand one hundred and sixty-eight feet above the sea level.

There is a large lake almost directly west of the Nyanza called Muta Nzienge, which Stanley conjectures may be connected with the Albert Nyanza. The region around the latter is wholly unknown, except that fierce cannibals occupy its western shore. We say that Stanley did not reach the Albert Nyanza at all, though if it and the Muta Nzienge are one, he did. He inserts in his journal that he reached the shore of the lake, yet by his map he did not. This discrepancy is owing probably to the fact that he thought, when he wrote, that the lake he saw was the Albert Nyanza, and though

129

Colonel Mason explored it partially last year, and makes it an entirely distinct lake, yet Stanley's opinion may still be unchanged. At all events, his map and journal should agree, but they do not, which confuses things badly. His route, as he has marked it down, does not go near this lake. On the other hand, if the Albert and the Muta Nzienge are one, it rivals in length the great Tanganika, which no one, however, thinks it to do.

Stanley found Mtesa at war with the Wavuma, who refused to pay their annual tribute. According to his account this monarch had an army with him which, with its camp followers, amounted to a quarter of a million of souls. He remained with Mtesa several weeks, as the war dragged slowly along, and, in the meantime, translated, with the help of a young, educated Arab, a part of the Bible for him, and apparently sent him forward a great way toward Christianity. He at length, after he had witnessed various naval battles that did not seem to bring the war any nearer to a termination, built for the king a huge naval structure, wholly inclosed, which, when it moved against the brave islanders, filled them with consternation, and they made peace.

At this point, Stanley makes a break in his journal and devotes nearly a hundred pages to a narrative of Uganda and its king, Mtesa. He gives its traditions, mingled with much fable; a description of its land, fruits, customs of the people—in short, a thorough history, as far as the natives know anything about it. This possesses more or less interest, though the information it conveys is of very little consequence, while it is destitute of any incident connected with his journey.

It was now October, and he turned his attention directly to the next scene of his labors—the exploration of the Albert Nyanza. The great difficulty here was to get through the warlike tribes that lay between the lakes and around the latter, of which Abba Rega was one of the most hostile chiefs. This king, it will be remembered, was the great foe of Baker, whom the latter drove out of the country, after burning his capital, and put Rionga in his place. He said then, that this treacherous king had gone to the shores of the Albert Nyanza. By the way, Baker's statement and Stanley's journal, placed together, seem to make it certain that the Muta Nzienge, which the latter reached, and the Albert Nyanza are the same; for, in the first place, it will be remembered, Baker's last journey was to Unyoro, where he saw the Albert Nyanza. Now Stanley, it will be seen hereafter, traverses this same district to reach the lake he called Muta Nzienge. Again, Baker says that Abba Rega fled to the Albert Nyanza, and yet Stanley found him on Lake Muta Nzienge. If Stanley's attention had been called to this, we hardly think he would have made two lakes on his map, when, from these corroborating statements, there could have been but one. The fact that these separate statements, made two years apart, are purely incidental, makes the fact they go to prove the more certain to be true. It seems impossible that Baker and Stanley should reach through the same tribe two large and entirely separate lakes.

Knowing not only of the hostility, but also the power of some of the tribes between Uganda and Lake Albert, Stanley asked Mtesa for fifty or sixty thousand men—a mighty army. With such a force he thought he could not only overcome all opposition on the way, but hold the camp he wished to establish, while he spent two months in exploring the lake. But Mtesa told him two thousand would be ample, which he would cheerfully furnish. He said that he need not fear Abba Rega, for he would not dare to lift a spear against his troops, for he had seated him on the throne of Kameazi. Though Stanley was not convinced of the truth of Mtesa's statements, he would not urge him further and accepted, with many expressions of thanks, the two thousand soldiers, commanded by General Lamboozi as an escort.

CHAPTER XVII

THE EXPEDITION TO ALBERT NYANZA

Stanley's expedition consisted of one hundred and eighty men, which, with the troops Mtesa gave him, made a total of two thousand two hundred and ninety men. To this little army were attached some five hundred women and children, making a sum total of two thousand eight hundred. With this force, all ordinary opposition could be overcome, and as it moved off with the sound of drums and horns, and the waving of the English and American flags, conspicuous amid those of the negro army, it presented a very animated appearance. But Stanley was destined to find out what others have learned before him, that a small force under one's own immediate command is better than a large, undisciplined one, that is subject to the orders of another.

General Lamboozi had no heart in this expedition, and soon showed it. But they moved off gayly over the swelling pasture-lands

131

of Uganda, striking northwest toward the lake, which Stanley hoped to explore, as he had the Victoria Nyanza. The march through Uganda was a pleasant one and they at length reached the frontier of Unyoro and prepared for war.

On the 5th of January they entered Abba Rega's territory, whom, two years before, Baker had driven from his throne, and who naturally felt peculiarly hostile to all white men. But no resistance was offered—the people, as if remembering the past, fleeing before them, leaving their provisions and everything behind them, of which the army made free use. Three days after they came to the base of a mighty mountain, called Kabrogo, rising five thousand five hundred feet into the air, presenting, in its naked, rugged outline, a sublime appearance. They encamped that night on a low ridge, in sight of the Katonga River, flowing east in its course to the Victoria Nyanza, bringing up many associations to Stanley's mind—while to the west the Ruanga filled the night air with its thunderous sound, as it tumbled over cataracts toward the Albert Nyanza. From an eminence near by could be seen in the distance the colossal form of Gambaragara Mountain looming up from the wilderness—a second Mont Blanc, rising some three miles into the cloudless heavens. Though under the equator, snow is often seen on its summit. But what gives it peculiar interest is, that on its cold and lonely top dwell a people of an entirely distinct race, being white, like Europeans. The king of Uzigo once spoke to Stanley and Livingstone of this singular people, and now the latter saw half a dozen of them. Their hair, he says, is "kinky," and inclined to brown in color; their features regular; lips thin, and noses well shaped. Altogether, they are a handsome race—the women, many of them possessing great beauty. Some of their descendants are scattered through the tribes living near the base of the mountain, but the main body occupy its lofty summit. The queen of one of the islands in the Victoria Nyanza is a descendent of them. The history of this singular people is wrapped in mystery.

There is a tradition that the first king of Unyoro gave them the land at its base, and the approach of a powerful enemy first drove them to the top for safety. They have become so acclimated that they can stand the cold, while the dwellers of the plain are compelled to flee before it. Mtesa once dispatched his greatest general with an army of a hundred thousand men to capture them. They succeeded in making their way to a great height, but finally had to withdraw—the cold became so intense.

The retreat of this pale-faced tribe is said to be inaccessible. The top is supposed to be the crater of an extinct volcano; for on it there is a lake nearly a third of a mile long, from the centre of which rises a huge rock to a great height. Around the top of this runs a rim of rock, making a natural wall, in which are several villages, where the principal "medicine-man" and his mysterious people reside in their peculiar separateness.

This account, if true, does not touch the origin of this peculiar race of people, nor in any way explain the fact of their existence here in tropical Africa. Two men belonging to this tribe joined Stanley's expedition in this march to the Albert Lake, yet he seems to have obtained no information from them of the history of their tribe. Whether they had any traditions or not we are not informed—we only know that Stanley found them extremely uncommunicative. It is possible they had nothing to tell, for a vast majority of the negro tribes of Africa have no past; they care neither for the past or future, so far as external life is concerned, living only in the present. These two men occupied a high position, for some cause, in the army under Lamboozi, and were the only ones who were allowed more than two milch cows on the route. Various stories about these people were told Stanley, and it is difficult to come at the truth. About the only thing that seems established is that this white race exists, of whose origin nothing definite has as yet been obtained. Stanley says that he heard they were of Arab origin, but there are plenty of Arabs in Africa—in fact, all the soldiers attached to the expedition were Arabs, and colonies of them had long existed in Central Africa; but they are not white men.

It seems impossible that Livingstone, years before, should have heard of this singular people, and Stanley seen specimens of them, if no such tribe really existed. It seems almost equally strange that they should be able for centuries to keep so isolated that their very home is a myth. The truth is, that Africa is a land of fables and traditions, that partake of the wonderful and often of the miraculous. Mr. Stanley was told of other tribes of white people living in a remote unknown region, possessing great ferocious dogs, and also of dwarfs of singular habits and customs. These traditions or reports, that are invariably vague in their character, usually have more or less foundation in truth. Mixed with the wonderful, that always holds an important place in savage literature, there will generally be found at least a grain of truth; and the traditions of white races among a people who had never seen white men, could hardly arise if no such tribes existed.

The diet of this strange race consists of milk and bananas. Stanley says the first specimen he saw of the tribe was a young man, whom he first took for a young Arab from Cairo, who for some reason had wandered off to Uganda, and taken up his residence with King Mtesa. The two attached to his expedition would easily have been mistaken for Greeks in white shirts. Stanley, after seeing these white Africans, the stories concerning whose existence he had regarded as one of the fables of the ignorant, superstitious natives, says that he is ready to believe there is a modicum of truth in all the strange stories that he has been accustomed to listen to as he would to a fairy tale. Four years previous, while exploring the Tanganika with Livingstone, they both smiled at the story told them of a white people living north of Uzigo, but now he had seen them, and if it were not that their hair resembles somewhat that of the negro, he should take them for Europeans. He heard afterwards that the first king of Kisbakka, a country to the southwest, was an Arab, whose scimiter is still preserved by the natives, and infers that these people may be his descendants. He also heard of a tribe that wore armor and used a breed of fierce and powerful dogs in battle.

From this point the expedition moved on toward the Albert Nyanza, along the southern bank of the Rusango River, a rapid, turbulent stream, winding in and out among the mountains, and rushing onward in fierce, rapid and headlong cataracts to the peaceful bosom of the lake. For ten hours they marched swiftly through an uninhabited country, and then emerged into a thickly populated district. Their sudden appearance, with drums beating and colors flying, filled the people, who had no intimation of their coming, with such consternation, that they took to the woods, leaving everything behind them, even the porridge on the fire and the great pots of milk standing ready for the evening meal. Fields and houses were alike deserted in a twinkling, and the army marched in and took possession. Thus far they had met with no opposition whatever, and the warlike tribe Stanley had feared so much, and had taken such a large force to overcome, seemed to have no existence. In fact, the days had passed by monotonously; for the most part the scenery was tame, and the march of the troops from day to day was without incident or interest, and now at this village they were within a few miles of the lake, to reach which was the sole object of all this display of force. Instead of fighting their way, they found themselves in undisputed possession of a large and populous district, with not a soul to give them any information.

We confess there is something about this journey from the Victoria Nyanza to the Albert that we do not understand. By the route on the map it must have been nearly two hundred miles, and yet the expedition started on January 5th, and on the evening of the 9th was within three miles of the latter, which would make the marching about fifty miles a day—an impossibility.

Now, fifty miles a day for four days would be terrible marching for veteran troops. Hence, we say, the map or journal is wrong. If he took the route he has marked down and completed it in the time he says he did, one instead of two parallels of longitude should indicate the distance between the two lakes. In fact, this whole expedition was such a miserable failure, that anywhere but in Africa it would be looked upon as a farce. It shows how utterly futile it is to rely on the native Africans in any great enterprise. The Arabs are bad enough, but they are fidelity itself compared to these black savages.

Here was an expedition numbering nearly three thousand souls, organized to secure a safe march to a lake not five days distant. It met with no obstacles of any moment, reached the lake, and there, on the mere rumor that hostilities were intended, practically broke up and returned. Stanley had, with about three hundred men, traversed an unknown country for months, fought battles, and at the end of a thousand miles reached the lake he was seeking, pitched his camp, and with a crew of eleven men explored the lake in its entire circuit, and returned in safety. Here, with a small army, after a four days' march, he reaches the Albert Nyanza, yet does nothing but turn round and march back again. It would seem, at first sight, strange that if he could march a thousand miles from the sea to the Victoria Nyanza and then explore it, he could not now with the same men explore this lake without the aid of Lamboozi and his two thousand or more soldiers. Doubtless he could but for this very army. Its disaffection and declaration that they were not strong enough to resist the force about to be brought against them, created a panic among Stanley's men. If two thousand fled, it would be madness for one hundred and eighty to stay. The simple truth is, the more such men one has with him, unless he is the supreme head and his will is law, even to life and death, the worse he is off. Stanley, planning, controlling and directing every movement, is a power; Stanley under the direction of a swaggering, braggart African negro general, is nobody.

Lamboozi did, next morning after their approach to the lake, send out two hundred scouts to capture some natives, by whom they could get a message to the king of the district, saying that they had no hostile intentions, and if permitted to encamp on the shores of the lake for two months, would pay in beads, cloth and wire for whatever provisions they consumed. Five were captured and sent to the king with this proposition, but he did not deign an answer. On the 11th, they moved the camp to within a mile of the lake, on a plateau that rose a thousand feet above its surface. A place was selected for a camp and men sent out to capture all the canoes they could find. In three hours they returned with only five, and those too small for their purpose. But they brought back word that the whole country was aroused, and that a large body of strange warriors had arrived on the coast to aid the king in making war on the newcomers.

General Lamboozi now became thoroughly alarmed, and stubbornly refused to grant Stanley's request to move to the edge of the lake and intrench. It seemed probable that the natives meant to give battle, but with what numbers or prospect of success, Lamboozi took no measure to ascertain. Next day he resolved to march back. Entreaties and threats were alike in vain, and there was nothing left for Stanley to do but march back with him. He was greatly disappointed and thoroughly disgusted, but there was no help for it. That Unyoro and Abba Rega would be hostile, Stanley knew before he started, and on that account took so large a force with him. Yet he says, after this miserable failure, that it was a foolhardy attempt at the outset. Looking at it calmly, he pronounces it a great folly, redeemed from absurdity only by "the success of having penetrated through Unyoro and reached the Albert." It is difficult to see wherein lies the greatness of this success; for, according to his own account, it was one of the most peaceful marches he ever performed, with hardly enough incident in it to make it interesting. It matters little, however; all that can be said is, they marched up to the lake and then marched back again.

On the morning of the 13th, they began their return in order of battle—five hundred spearmen in front, five hundred as a rear guard, and the expedition in the centre—but no enemy attacked them or attempted to do anything but pick up some stragglers. The next day the expedition formed the rear guard, and once some natives rushed out of the woods to attack them, but were quickly dispersed by a few shots.

This is all that happened to this army in terrible Unyoro, and presents a striking contrast to Baker's gallant march through it with his little band, fighting every day for nearly a week. Four days after, without any further molestation, they re-entered Uganda, where Lamboozi turned off to his home. Stanley had heard no news of Gordon or of the steamers he was to place on the lake according to the plan of Baker; and though at first he thought that he would seek some other way to reach it and make his explorations, he finally resolved to start for Tanganika, which he would reach in about four months, and explore it. Hence, while Lamboozi turned eastward toward Lake Victoria, he with his little band, turned southward. He sent a letter, however, to Mtesa, informing him of Lamboozi's cowardice and refusal to build a camp at Lake Albert, and telling him also that this redoubtable general had robbed him. He had intrusted to his care three porter's loads of goods to relieve his own carriers, and these he had appropriated as his own.

When the letter reached the emperor he was thrown into a towering passion, and immediately dispatched a body of troops to seize the general, with orders to strip him of his wives, slaves, cattle and everything he possessed, and bring him bound to his presence. He also sent letter after letter to Stanley, begging him to return, and he would give him ninety thousand men, with brave generals to command them, who would take him to Lake Albert, and protect him there till he had finished his explorations. Stanley was very much moved by this generous offer and the anxiety of the king to make amends for Lamboozi's poltroonery and thieving conduct. The noble savage felt it keenly that he, who valued so highly the esteem of Stanley, should be disgraced in his sight, and it was hard for the latter to refuse his urgent request to be allowed to redeem his character and his pledge. But Stanley had had enough of Waganda troops, and felt that whatever was accomplished hereafter must be by his own well-trained, compact, brave little band. He kept on his way, and never saw Mtesa again.

He had been able to add considerably to the geography of the country bordering on Lake Albert. Usongora, a promontory running thirty miles into the lake southward, he ascertained to be the great salt field, from whence all the surrounding countries obtain their salt. From all he could hear, it was truly a land of wonders, but he says the man who should attempt to explore it would need a thousand muskets, for the natives cannot be enticed into peace by cloth and beads. They care for nothing but milk and goat skins. "Among the wonders credited to it," he says, "are a mountain emitting fire and stones, a salt lake of considerable extent, several hills of rock-salt, a large plain encrusted thickly with salt and alkali, a breed of very large dogs of extraordinary ferocity, and a race of such long-legged natives, that ordinary mortals regard them with surprise and awe." They do not allow members of their tribe to intermarry with strangers, and their food, like that of the dwellers in the Himalaya Mountains, consists chiefly of milk. Mtesa once invaded their territory with one hundred thousand men, to capture cows, of which the natives have an immense number, and in watching which consists their sole occupation. The army returned with twenty thousand, but they were obtained at such a fearful sacrifice of life, that the raid will not be repeated.

Stanley rested a few days after Lamboozi left him, before proceeding northward. He then continued his march leisurely through the country, inquiring on the way the character of the tribes westward toward that part of Lake Albert which extended south from where he struck it, but one and all were reported hostile to the passage of any strangers through their territory.

Arriving on the Kagera River, in Karagwe, he found the King Rumanika, a mild, pleasant-spoken man and very friendly, but he told him that none of the neighboring tribes would let him enter their lands. Stanley being a little suspicious of the motives that prompted this bad report of the surrounding tribes, to test him, asked him if he had any objections to his exploring his country. He said no, and cheerfully promised to furnish him guides and an escort, and his party should be supplied with food free of charge. Stanley, surprised at this generosity, at once got ready to start. He first went south to Lake Windermere, a small body of water so named by Captain Speke, because of its fancied resemblance to the lake of that name in England. The Lady Alice was taken there, screwed together, and launched on the peaceful waters. Accompanied by six native canoes, he sailed round it and then entered Kagera River, called by Speke the Kitangule. Suddenly it flashed on Stanley's mind that he had discovered the true parent of the Victoria Nile. It fed and drained this little lake some nine miles long. Moreover, he found that there was a depth of fifty-two feet of water and a breadth of one hundred and fifty feet. He therefore pushed up it some three days, and came to another lake nine miles long and six miles wide. Working up through the papyrus that covered the stream, he came to another lake or pond a mile and a half long. Ascending an eminence, he discovered that this whole portion of the river was a lake, large tracts of which were covered with papyrus, or that vegetation which we have seen Baker had to contend with in ascending the Nile. It seemed solid ground, while in fact it was a large body of water covered over, with here and there an opening, making a separate lake, of which Windermere was the largest. This apparently underground lake was some eighty miles in length and fourteen in width.

Following the river as it flowed eastward into the Victoria Nyanza, he found he entered another lake, thirteen miles long and some eight miles broad. This was, of course, the continuation of the lake, covered at intervals with this tropical vegetation, which gave to it the appearance of land. There were in all, seventeen of these lakes. This river now broadening as the formation of the land causes it to expand, now narrowing till its channel is forty feet deep, it at last tumbles over cataracts and rushes through rapids into the Victoria Nyanza. All this seems of little account, except, as Stanley says, he has found in it the true source of the Victoria Nile.

The great and persistent efforts to find out the source of the Nile have led explorers to push their theories to an absurd extent.

Because Herodotus made the Nile to rise in some large springs, they seem to think they must find something back and beyond a great lake as its source. Now, when a river flows right on through one lake after another, making lakes as the formation of the ground allows, it of course maintains its integrity and oneness.

In this case there is but one main stream and as long as the lakes are the mere spreading out of that stream on low, flat lands, it must remain the same. But when you come to great reservoirs like the Albert and Victoria Nyanza and the Tanganika—into which a hundred streams, and perhaps twice that number of springs, flow—to go beyond such reservoirs to find the head of the stream is bringing geography down to a fine point. The outlet is plain—you have traced the river up till you see it roaring from its great feeder. This is very satisfactory, and should end all research after the source of the stream. But to insist on taking measurements of a dozen different rivers that flow into a lake a thousand miles in circumference, to find which is a mile longest or ten feet deepest, and thus determine the source of the outlet, is preposterous. A lake covering twenty-two thousand square miles, fed by a hundred rivers, is a reservoir of itself, and not an expansion of any one river. One might as well try to prove which is the greatest source or feeder of the Atlantic Ocean—the Amazon, Mississippi or Congo.

Thus we find Stanley, when he struck the Shimeeyu in Speke Gulf, declaring he had found the extreme southern source of the Nile; and now, when exploring another river of a larger volume on another side of the lake, he changes his mind and thinks he has made a great discovery in ascertaining at last the true source of the river. He found it over fifty feet deep, which showed what a volume of water it poured into the Victoria Nyanza. Descending it again, he entered another lake some thirteen miles long by eight wide. Exploring this, he was driven back by the natives when he attempted to land, who hailed him with shrill shouts and wild war-cries. The Kagera, through its entire length, maintains almost the same depth and volume.

Returning to his generous host, he asked for guides to take him to the hot springs of Mtagata, the healing properties of which he had heard of far and wide from the natives. These were cheerfully given, and after a march of two days he reached them. Here he was met by an astonishing growth of vegetation. Plants of an almost infinite variety, covered the ground, growing so thick and crowding each other so closely, that they became a matted mass—the smaller ones stifled by the larger—and out of which trees shot up an arrow's-flight into the air, with "globes of radiant green foliage upon their stem-like crowns." He found a crowd of diseased persons here, trying the effect of the water. Naked men and women were lying promiscuously around in the steaming water, half-asleep and half-cooked, for the water showed a temperature of one hundred and twenty-nine degrees. The springs were, however, of different temperature. The hottest one issued from the base of a rocky hill, while four others, twenty degrees cooler, came bubbling up out of black mud, and were the favorites of the invalids. Stanley camped here three days, and bathed in the water and drank it, but could perceive no effect whatever on his system. Returning to his friend Rumaniki, he prepared to start on his journey south to Lake Tanganika, and finish its explorations.

Having discovered that the Kagera River formed a lake eighty miles long, and was a powerful stream a long distance from its mouth, he resolved, as it flowed from the south, to follow it up and try to find its source. A broad wilderness lay before him, the extent of which he did not accurately know, and he packed ten days' provisions on the shoulders of each man of the expedition, and bidding the soft-voiced pagan king, by whom he had been treated so kindly, a warm good-bye, he entered the forest and kept along the right bank of the stream. This was the 27th of March, and for six days he marched through an uninhabited wilderness, with nothing to break the monotony of the journey. At the end of that time he came to the borders of Karagwe and to the point where the Akanyaru River entered the Kagera. He dared not explore this river, for the natives that inhabit both banks are wild and fierce, having a deadly hatred of all strangers. They are like the long-legged race of Bumbireh, and he did not care to come in collision with them. They possess many cattle, and if one sickens or dies, they do not attribute it to accident, but believe it has been bewitched, and search the country through to find the stranger who has done it, and if he is found, he dies.

All the natives of the region are passionately fond of their cows, and will part with anything sooner than with milk. Stanley says that his friend Rumaniki, with all his generosity, never offered him a teaspoonful of milk, and if he had given him a can of it, he believes his people would have torn him limb from limb. He thinks that half of their hostility arises from the fear of the evil effect that the presence of strangers will have on their cattle. Hence they keep a strict quarantine on their frontiers. It is not strange that they should cherish this stock carefully, for it is their sole means of subsistence.

This long journey through various tribes is singularly barren of incident. On the route he lost his last dog, Bull, who had bravely held out in all their long wanderings, but at last he gave up and laid down and died, with his eyes fixed on the retiring expedition. He also met the redoubtable Mirambo, and found him not the blood-thirsty monster he had been represented to be, but a polite, pleasant-mannered gentleman, and generous to a fault. They made blood brotherhood together, and became fast friends. At length, in the latter part of May, he reached Ujiji, where he formerly found Livingstone. The following extract from a private letter of Stanley's, written to a friend while at Lake Victoria, gives a domestic picture that is quite charming, he says that "Kagehyi is a straggling village of cane huts, twenty or thirty in number, which are built somewhat in the form of a circle, hedged around by a fence of thorns twisted between upright stakes. Sketch such a village in your imagination, and let the centre of it be dotted here and there with the forms of kidlings who prank it with the vivacity of kidlings under a hot, glowing sun. Let a couple of warriors and a few round-bellied children be seen among them and near a tall hut which is a chief's, plant a taller tree, under whose shade sit a few elders in council with their chief; so much for the village.

"Now outside the village, yet, touching the fence, begin to draw the form of a square camp, about fifty yards square, each side flanked with low, square huts, under the eaves of which, plant as many figures of men as you please, for we have many, and you have the camp of the exploring expedition, commanded by your friend and humble servant. From the centre of the camp you may see Lake Victoria, or that portion of it I have called Speke Gulf, and twenty-five miles distant you may see table-topped Magita, the large island of Ukerewe, and toward the northwest a clear horizon, with nothing between water and sky to mar its level. The surface of the lake which approaches to within a few yards of the camp is much ruffled just at present with a northwest breeze, and though the sun is growing hot, under the shade it is agreeable enough, so that nobody perspires or is troubled with the heat. You must understand there is a vast difference between New York and Central African heat. Yours is a sweltering heat, begetting languor and thirst—ours is a dry heat, permitting activity and action without thirst or perspiration. If we exposed ourselves to the sun, we should feel quite as though we were being baked. Come with me to my lodgings, now. I lodge in a hut little inferior in size to the chief's. In it is stored the luggage of the expedition, which fills one-half. It is about six tons in weight, and consists of cloth, beads, wire, shells, ammunition, powder, barrels, portmanteaus, iron trunks, photographic apparatus, scientific instruments, pontoons, sections of boat, etc., etc. The other half of the hut is my sleeping, dining and hall-room. It is dark as pitch within, for light cannot penetrate the mud with which the wood-work is liberally daubed. The floor is of dried mud, thickly covered with dust, which breeds fleas and other vermin to be a plague to me and my poor dogs.

"I have four youthful Mercuries, of ebon color, attending me, who, on the march, carry my personal weapons of defense. I do not need so many persons to wait on me, but such is their pleasure. They find their reward in the liberal leavings of the table. If I have a goat killed for European men, half of it suffices for two days for us. When it becomes slightly tainted, my Mercuries will beg for it, and devour it at a single sitting. Just outside of the door of my hut are about two dozen of my men sitting, squatted in a circle and stringing beads. A necklace of beads is each man's daily sum wherewith to buy food. I have now a little over one hundred and sixty men. Imagine one hundred and sixty necklaces given each day for the last three months—in the aggregate the sum amounts to fourteen thousand necklaces—in a year to fifty-eight thousand four hundred. A necklace of ordinary beads is cheap enough in the States, but the expense of carriage makes a necklace here equal to about twenty-five cents in value. For a necklace I can buy a chicken, or a peck of sweet potatoes, or half a peck of grain.

"I left the coast with about forty thousand yards of cloth, which, in the States, would be worth about twelve and a half cents a yard, or altogether about five thousand dollars—the expense of portage, as far as this lake, makes each yard worth about fifty cents. Two yards of cloth will purchase a goat or sheep; thirty will purchase an ox; fifteen yards are enough to purchase rations for the entire caravan."

Why these naked savages put such a high value on cloth, none of these African explorers informs us. We can understand why they should like beads, brass wire, shells and trinkets of all sorts. They certainly use very little cloth on their persons.

He adds: "These are a few of the particulars of our domestic affairs. The expedition is divided into eight squads of twenty men each, with an experienced man over each squad. They are all armed with Snider's percussion-lock muskets. A dozen or so of the most faithful have a brace of revolvers in addition to other arms."

He then goes on to speak of the battles he has fought, and it is but just to him to give his feelings as he describes them in confidential private correspondence, on being compelled to kill the savages. He says: "As God is my judge, I would prefer paying tribute, and making these savages friends rather than enemies. But some of these people are cursed with such delirious ferocity that we are compelled to defend ourselves. They attack in such numbers and so sudden, that our repeating rifles and Sniders have to be handled with such nervous rapidity as will force them back before we are forced to death; for if we allow them to come within forty yards, their spears are as fatal as bullets; their spears make fearful wounds, while their contemptible-looking arrows are as deadly weapons. * * * Since I left Zanzibar, I have traveled seven hundred and twenty miles by land and a thousand miles by water. This is a good six months' work."

CHAPTER XVIII

EXPLORATIONS OF LAKE TANGANIKA

It was with strange feelings that Stanley caught from the last ridge the sparkling waters of Tanganika. Sweet associations were awakened at the sight, as he remembered with what a thrilling heart he first saw it gleam in the landscape. Then it was the end of a long, wasting and perilous journey—the goal of his ambition, the realization of his fondest hopes; for on its shores he believed the object for which he had toiled so long was resting. No more welcome sight ever dawned on mortal eye than its waters as they spread away on the horizon; and though he should see it a hundred times, it will never appear to him like any other sheet of water. He has formed for it an attachment that will last forever; and whenever in imagination it rises before him, it will appear like the face of a friend.

As he now descended to Ujiji, it was with sensations as though he were once more entering civilized life, for there was something almost homelike about this Arab colony. People dressed in civilized garments were moving about the streets, cattle were coming down to the lake to drink, and domestic animals scattered here and there made quite a homelike scene.

At first sight, it seems strange that Stanley should have selected this lake as the next scene of his explorations. He had previously, with Livingstone, explored thoroughly the upper half of it, and passed part way down the western side; Livingstone had been at the foot of it, and to crown all, Stanley had heard, before leaving Zanzibar, that Cameron had explored the entire southern portion, so that really there was nothing for him to do but follow a path which had been already trodden. To employ an expedition fitted out at so great a cost, and spend so much valuable time in going over old ground, seems an utter waste of both time and labor, especially when such vast unexplored fields spread all around him. But there was a mystery about Tanganika, which Stanley probably suspected Cameron had not solved, and which he meant to clear up. Here was a lake over three hundred miles long, with perhaps a hundred streams, great and small, running into it, and yet with no outlet, unless Cameron had found it, which he thinks he did. To find this was the chief object of the expedition Stanley and Livingstone made together to the north end of the lake. They had heard that the Rusizi River at that extremity was the outlet, but they found it instead a tributary. In fact, they proved conclusively that there was no outlet at the northern end. It therefore must be at the southern, and if so, it was the commencement of a river that would become a mighty stream before it reached the ocean. But no such stream was known to exist. The Caspian Sea has large rivers flowing into it, but no outlet, yet it never fills up. Evaporation, it is supposed, accounts for this. But the Caspian is salt, while the Tanganika is fresh water, and such a large body of fresh water as this was never known to exist without an outlet, and if it could be that evaporation was so great as to equal all the water that runs into it, it would not remain so fresh as it is.

We will let Cameron state his own case concerning the solution of this mystery. He started with two canoes and thirty-seven men, and sailed down the eastern shore of the lake, now ravished with the surpassing beauty of the scene composed of water and sky, and smiling shores, and again awed by beetling cliffs; one evening camping on the green banks and watching the sun go down behind the purple peaks, and another drenched with rain, and startled by the vivid lightning and awful thunder crashes of a tropical storm, yet meeting with no incident of any peculiar interest to the reader. The natives were friendly, and he describes the different villages and customs of the people and their superstitions, which do not vary materially from other native tribes. At last, on the 3d of May, he entered the Lukuga Creek, which a chief told him was the outlet of the lake. He says that the entrance was more than a mile wide, "but closed up by a grass sand-bank, with the exception of a channel three or four hundred yards wide. Across this there is a rill where the surf breaks heavily, although there was more than a fathom of water at its most shallow part." The next day he went down it four or five miles, until navigation was rendered impossible, owing to the masses of floating vegetation. Here the depth was eighteen feet, and breadth six hundred yards, and the current a knot and a half an hour. The chief who accompanied him said that it emptied into the Lualaba. He tried in vain to hire men to cut a passage through the vegetation that he might explore the river. This was all the knowledge he obtained by actual observation, the rest of his information being obtained from the natives.

Now, we must say, that this is a sorry exhibit for the outlet to a lake almost twice as long as Lake Ontario. That such an immense body of water should trickle away at this rate seems very extraordinary. Stanley at Ujiji started inquiries respecting this stream, and found Cameron's guide, who stoutly denied that the river flowed south from the lake. Another veteran guide corroborated this statement, while many others declared that before Cameron came, they had never heard of an outflowing river.

These contradictory statements, together with the universal testimony that the lake was continually rising (the truth of which he could not doubt, as he saw palm-trees which stood in the market-place when he was there in 1871, now one hundred feet out in the lake), made him resolve to explore this stream himself. He started on the 11th of June, and three days after landed to take a hunt, and soon came upon a herd of zebras, two of which he bagged, and thus secured a supply of meat.

On the 19th, on approaching a large village, they were astonished to see no people on the shore. Landing, they were still more astonished at the death-silence that reigned around, and advancing cautiously came upon corpses of men and women transfixed with spears or with their heads cut off. Entering into the village they found that there had been a wholesale massacre. A descent had been made upon the place, but by whom no one was left to tell. Its entire population had been put to death.

As Stanley proceeded, he found many evidences of the steady rise of the lake. He continued on his course, finding the same varied scenery that Cameron did, with nothing of peculiar interest occurring, except to the travelers themselves, and at length came to the Lukuga Creek. He found various traditions and accounts here— one native said the water flowed both ways. The spot on which Cameron encamped, some two years before, was now covered with water, another evidence that the lake was rising. Stanley very sensibly says, that the "rill," which Cameron states runs directly across the channel, is conclusive evidence that the Lukuga runs into the lake, not out of it; for it must be formed by the meeting of the inflowing current and the waves. An outpouring stream driven onward by waves would make a deep channel, not a dam of sand. He tried several experiments, by which he proved, to his entire satisfaction, that the stream flowed into the lake instead of being its outlet. Having settled this question he set about finding the other river, which the natives declared flowed out or westward. After traveling some distance inland he did find a place where the water flowed west; it was, however, a mere trickling stream. His account of his explorations here, and of the traditions of the natives, and his description of the formation of the country and of its probable geological changes, is quite lengthy, and possesses but little interest to the general reader.

The result of it all, however, is that he believes the Lukuga was formerly a tributary of the lake, the bed of which at some former time was lifted up to a higher level; that the whole stretch of land here has been sunk lower by some convulsion of nature, taking the Lukuga with it, and thus making a sort of dam of the land at the foot, which accounts for the steady rise of the river year by year; and that in three years the lake will rise above this dam, and, gathering force, will tear like a resistless torrent through all this mud and vegetation, and roaring on, as the Nile does where it leaves the Victoria Nyanza, will sweep through the country till it pours its accumulated waters into the Lualaba, and thus swell the Congo into a still larger Amazon of Africa. This seems to be the only plausible solution of the mystery attached to Tanganika. The only objection to it is, no such convulsion or change of the bed of the Tanganika seems to have occurred during this generation, and what has become, then, for at least seventy years, of all the waters these hundred rivers have been pouring into the lake? We should like the estimate of some engineer of how many feet that lake would rise in fifty years, with all its tributaries pouring incessantly such a flood into it. We are afraid the figures would hardly harmonize with this slow rise of the lake. It may be that there is a gradual filtering of the water through the ooze at the foot, which will account for the slow filling up of the great basin—a leakage that retards the process of accumulation. But if Stanley's explorations and statements can be relied upon, the mystery will soon solve itself, and men will not have to hunt for an outlet long. He makes the length of Tanganika three hundred and twenty-nine geographical miles, and its average breadth twenty-eight miles.

The wonderful influence of Livingstone over all African explorers is nowhere more visible than at Ujiji, on both Cameron and Stanley. Both of these set out with one object—to try to complete the work that the great and good man's death had left unfinished. His feet had pressed the shores of almost every lake they had seen, as well as of others which they had not seen. The man had seemed to be drawn on westward until he reached Nyangwe, where dimly arose before him the Atlantic Ocean, into which the waters flowing past his camp might enter, and did enter, if they were not

146

the Nile. Discouraged, deserted and driven back, he could not embark on the Lualaba and float downward with its current till he should unveil the mystery that wrapped it. Cameron became filled with the same desire, but disappointed, though not driven back, he had pressed on to the ocean, into which he had no doubt the river emptied, though by another route. And now, last of three, comes Stanley, and instead of finishing Livingstone's work around the lakes, he, too, is drawn forward to the same point. It seemed to be the stopping-place of explorations in Africa; and although he knew that Cameron had not returned like Livingstone, and hence might have discovered all that was to be discovered, so making further explorations in that direction useless, still he felt that he must go on and find out for himself. True, there was an interesting district between Ujiji and the Lualaba. There was the beautiful Manyema region, about which Livingstone had talked to him enthusiastically, with its new style of architecture, and beautiful women and simple-minded people. But those did not form the attraction. He must stand on the spot where Livingstone stood, and look off with his yearning desire, and see if he could not do what this good man was willing to risk all to accomplish.

At all events, he must move somewhere at once, and westward seemed the most natural direction to take, for if he stayed in Ujiji much longer the expedition would break up. He found on his return that the small-pox had broken out in camp, filling the Arabs with dismay. He had taken precaution on starting to vaccinate every member of his party, as he supposed, and hence he felt safe from this scourge of Africa. He did not lose a single man with it on his long journey from the sea to the Victoria Nyanza. But it had broken out in Ujiji with such fury that a pall was spread over the place, and it so invaded his camp that in a few days eight of his men died.

This created a panic, and they began to desert in such numbers that he would soon be left alone. Thirty-eight were missing, which made quite a perceptible loss in a force of only one hundred and seventy men. The chiefs of the expedition were thoroughly frightened, but they told him that the desertions would increase if he moved westward, for the men were as much afraid of the cannibals there, as of the small-pox in their midst. They were told horrible stories of these cannibals till their teeth chattered with fear. Besides there were hobgoblins—monsters of every kind in the land beyond the Tanganika. Stanley saw, therefore, that prompt measures must be taken, and he at once clapped thirty-two of the discontented in irons, drove them into canoes, and sent them off to Ukurenga. He with the rest followed after by land to Msehazy Creek, where the crossing of the lake was to be effected. Reaching the other side he proceeded to Uguha, where, on mustering his force, he found but one hundred and twenty-seven out of one hundred and seventy, showing that one-third had disappeared. Among the last to go, and the last Stanley expected would leave him, was young Kalulu, whom he had taken home to the United States with him on his return from his first expedition. He had him placed in school in England for eighteen months, and he seemed devoted to Stanley. A gloom hung over the camp, and desertion was becoming too contagious. If such men as Kalulu could not be trusted, Stanley knew of no one who could be, and with his usual promptness he determined to stop it. He therefore sent back Pocoke and a faithful chief with a squad of men to capture them.

Paddling back to Ujiji, they one night came upon six, who, after a stout fight, were secured and brought over to camp. Afterward young Kalulu was found on an island and brought in. This desertion is a chronic disease among the Arabs. Their superstitious fears are quickly aroused, and they are easily tempted to break their contract and leave in the lurch the man to whom they have hired themselves.

Stanley's march to Manyeme was noticeable only for the curious customs or habits of the people, and on the 5th of October he reached the frontier of this wonderful country. Livingstone had halted here several months, and this was an inducement for Stanley to stop a few days. The weapons of the natives were excellent, and there was one custom that attracted his particular attention—the men wore lumps in various forms of mud and patches of mud on their beard, hair and head, while the women wove their front hair into head-dresses, resembling bonnets, leaving the back hair to wave in ringlets over their shoulders. He, as well as Cameron, was amazed at their villages, which, usually had one or more broad streets running through them, each being from one hundred to one hundred and fifty feet wide, and along which are ranged the square huts, with well-beaten, cleanly-kept clay floors, to which they cheerfully invite strangers.

On the 12th he reached the village on the Luma which he had been following, where both Livingstone and Cameron left it and turned directly west to Nyangwe. He, however, determined to follow it till it reached the Lualaba, and then proceed by this stream to the same place. He found the natives kind but timid, with many curious traditions and customs. The expedition at last reached the Lualaba, and moving majestically through the forest and making rapid marches, it arrived on the next day at Tubunda.

CHAPTER XIX

NYANGWE AND ITS HISTORY

Nyangwe is the farthest point west in Africa ever reached by a white man who came in from the east. It is about three hundred and fifty miles from Ujiji, or a little over the distance across New York State, but the journey is not made in one day—Stanley was forty days in accomplishing it. Here he found that Livingstone, the first white man ever seen there, must have remained from six to twelve months. Livingstone had made a profound impression on the natives of this region. "Did you know him?" asked an old chief, eagerly. Stanley replying in the affirmative, he turned to his sons and brothers, and said: "He knew the good white man. Ah, we shall hear all about him." Then turning to Stanley, he said: "Was he not a very good man?" "Yes," replied the latter, "he was good, my friend; far better than any white man or Arab you will ever see again." "Ah," said the old negro, "you speak true; he was so gentle and patient, and told us such pleasant stories of the wonderful land of the white people—the aged white was a good man indeed."

Livingstone made a strong impression on Stanley also, who, speaking of him says: "What has struck me while tracing Livingstone to his utmost researches—this Arab depôt of Nyangwe,—revived all my grief and pity for him, even more so than his own relation of sorrowful and heavy things, is, that he does not seem to be aware that he was sacrificing himself unnecessarily, nor to be warned of the havoc of age and that his old power had left him. With the weight of years pressing upon him, the shortest march wearying him, compelling him to halt many days to recover his strength, and frequent attacks of illness prostrating him, with neither men nor means to escort him and enable him to make practical progress, Livingstone was at last like a blind and infirm man moving aimlessly about. He was his own worst taskmaker."

Whether Stanley's views of the mental condition of Livingstone—growing out of his sickness and want of money while in Nyangwe—are correct or not, one thing is true: that after the great explorer had seemingly reached the very point when the problem was to be solved as to where the mysterious Lualaba flowed, he waited there till he found a caravan going east, and then returned to Ujiji "a sorely tried and disappointed man." Standing on the last point which this intrepid explorer reached, Stanley is reminded of his own earnest efforts to induce that worn hero to

149

return home and recruit, to which the invariable answer was: "No, no, no; to be knighted, as you say, by the Queen, welcomed by thousands of admirers, yes—but impossible, must not, can not, will not be."

Stanley, on this outmost verge of exploration, remembered the words of Livingstone when speaking of the beauties of the region lying west of the Goma Mountains, and says, "It is a most remarkable region; more remarkable than anything I have seen in Africa. Its woods, or forest, or jungles, or brush—I do not know by what particular term to designate the crowded, tall, straight trees, rising from an impenetrable mass of brush, creepers, thorns, gums, palm, ferns of all sorts, canes and grass—are sublime, even terrible. Indeed, nature here is remarkably or savagely beautiful. From every point the view is enchanting—the outlines eternally varying, yet always beautiful, till the whole panorama seems like a changing vision. Over all, nature has flung a robe of varying green, the hills and ridges are blooming, the valleys and basins exhale perfume, the rocks wear garlands of creepers, the stems of the trees are clothed with moss, a thousand streamlets of cold, pure water stray, now languid, now quick, toward the north and south and west. The whole makes a pleasing, charming illustration of the bounteousness and wild beauty of tropical nature. But, alas! all this is seen at a distance; when you come to travel through this world of beauty, the illusion vanishes—the green grass becomes as difficult to penetrate as an undergrowth, and that lovely sweep of shrubbery a mass of thorns, the gently rolling ridge an inaccessible crag, and the green mosses and vegetation in the low grounds that look so enchanting, impenetrable forest belts."

Stanley once penetrated into one of these great forests and was so overwhelmed by the majesty and solemn stillness of the scene, that he forgot where he was, and his imagination went back to the primeval days when that great, still forest was sown, till the silent trees seemed monuments of past history. But still, this district of Manyema (pronounced in various ways), he does not think so interesting as that of Uregga. In speaking of the Lualaba, after describing the various ways in which it is spelled and pronounced, he says if he could have it his own way he would call it "Livingstone River, or Livingstone's Lualaba," to commemorate his discovery of it and his heroic struggles against adversity to explore it. The letter in which he thus speaks of this region is dated November 1st, 1876. In three days he says he is going to explore this mysterious river to the utmost of his power. Two days previous to this letter, he wrote a long one on the horrors of the slave-trade that casts a pall as black as midnight over all this tropical beauty. He says that from

150

Unyanyembe to Ujiji one sees horrors enough, but in this region they are multiplied tenfold. The traffic in slaves is so profitable and keeps up such a brisk trade with Zanzibar and the interior of Africa, that the native chiefs enter into it on the grandest scale, or rather it is more accurate to say, banditti under the leadership of so-called chiefs enter into it thus, and carry it on with remorseless zeal.

Raids are made on small independent villages, the aged are slain and hung up to terrify other villages into a meek acquiescence in their demands, and young men, young women, and children are marched off to Ujiji, from whence they are taken to Zanzibar, becoming, by their cruel treatment on the route, living skeletons before they reach their destination. Gangs, from one hundred to eight hundred, of naked, half-starved creatures Stanley met in his travels, and he wonders that the civilized world will let insignificant Zanzibar become the mart of such an accursed, cruel traffic.

There are regular hunting-grounds for slaves. When the business is dull, the inhabitants are left to grow and thrive, just like game out of season in a gentleman's park; but when the business begins to look up, the hunt begins, and the smiling villages become arid wastes. The country, long before he reached Nyangwe, was a wilderness, where a few years before dwelt a happy population. Stanley gives extracts from his diary, showing up the horrors of this system, which make the heart sicken as it thinks of what is daily transpiring in this unknown land.

Livingstone saw enough when he was at this place to awaken his deepest indignation, but since that time the Arabs have pushed further inland, and swept, with the besom of destruction, districts that in his time had been but slightly touched.

The trade in ivory is but another name for trade in human beings, and the only real commerce this vast, fruitful region has with Zanzibar is through its captured inhabitants, while the slain equal the number sent into captivity. But, while Mr. Stanley feels keenly the disgrace to humanity of this accursed traffic, he evidently does not see so clearly the way to put a stop to it. He is opposed to filibustering of all kinds, and to the interference of strong powers to coerce weak ones on the ground of humanity or Christianity, because it opens the door too wide to every kind of aggression. In fact, this makes it only necessary to use some philanthropic catch-word, in order to justify the annexation of any feeble territory.

Stanley evidently thinks there is some limit to the Monroe doctrine of non-interference in the affairs of other nations, as the following extract from one of his letters shows, in which, after discussing the whole matter carefully, he says he writes, "hoping he may cause many to reflect upon the fact that there exists one little

151

State on this globe, which is about equal in extent to one English county, with the sole privilege of enriching itself by wholesale murder, and piracy and commerce in human beings, and that a traffic forbidden in all other nations should be permitted, furtively monopolized by the little island of Zanzibar, and by such insignificant people as the subjects of Prince Burghosh." Mr. Stanley is entirely opposed to filibustering and encroachments of strong powers on feeble ones, under the thousand and one false pretences advanced in support of unrighteous conquests, yet he evidently thinks little Zanzibar should be wiped out, or cease to be the source and centre of this cruel traffic in human beings. One has to travel, he says, in the heart of Africa to see all the horrors of this traffic.

The buying and selling of a few slaves on the coast gives no idea of its horrors. At Unyambembe, sometimes a sad sight is seen. At Uganda the trade begins to assume a wholesale character, yet it wears here a rather business aspect; the slaves by this time become hardened to suffering, "they have no more tears to shed," the chords of sympathy have been severed and they seem stolid and indifferent. At Ujiji, one sees a regular slave-market established. There are "slave-folds and pens," like the stock-yards of railroads for cattle into which the naked wretches are driven by hundreds, to wallow on the ground and be half-starved on food not fit for hogs. By the time they reach here they are mere "ebony skeletons," attenuated, haggard, gaunt human frames. Their very voices have sunk to a mere hoarse whisper, which comes with an unearthly sound from out their parched, withered lips. Low moans, like those that escape from the dying, fill the air, and they reel and stagger when they attempt to stand upright, so wasted are they by the havoc of hunger. They look like a vast herd of black skeletons, and as one looks at them in their horrible sufferings he cannot but exclaim, "how can an all-merciful Father permit such things?" No matter whether on the slow and famishing march or crowded like strayed pigs in the overloaded canoes, it is the same unvarying scene of hunger and horror, on which the cruel slave-trader looks without remorse or pity.

It may be asked how are these slaves obtained. The answer is, by a systematic war waged in the populous country of Marungu by banditti, supported by Arabs. These exchange guns and powder for the slaves the former capture, which enables them to keep up the war. These Arabs, who sell the slaves on the coast, furnish the only market for the native banditti of the interior. These latter are mostly natives of Unyamwege who band together to capture all the inhabitants of villages too weak to resist them. Marungu is the great productive field of their Satanic labors. Here almost every small village is independent, recognizing no ruler but its own petty chief. These are often at variance with each other, and instead of banding together to resist a common foe, they look on quietly while one after another is swept by the raiders. In crossing a river, Stanley met two hundred of these wretches chained together, and, on inquiry, found they belonged to the governor of Unyambembe, a former patron of Speke and Burton, and had been captured by an officer of the prince of Zanzibar. This prince had made a treaty with England to put a stop to this horrible traffic, and yet here was one of his officers engaged in it, taking his captives to Zanzibar, and this was his third batch during the year.

There are two or three entries in Stanley's journal which throw much light on the way this hunt for slaves is carried on.

"October 17th. Arabs organized to-day from three districts, to avenge the murder and eating of one man and ten women by a tribe half-way between Kassessa and Nyangwe. After six days' slaughter, the Arabs returned with three hundred slaves, fifteen hundred goats, besides spears, etc."

"October 24th. The natives of Kabonga, near Nyangwe, were sorely troubled two or three days ago by a visit paid them by Uanaamwee in the employ of Mohommed el Said. Their insolence was so intolerable that the natives at last said, 'we will stand this no longer. They will force our wives and daughters before our eyes if we hesitate any longer to kill them, and before the Arabs come we will be off.' Unfortunately, only one was killed, the others took fright and disappeared to arouse the Arabs with a new grievance. To-day, an Arab chief set out for the scene of action with murderous celerity, and besides capturing ten slaves, killed thirty natives and set fire to eight villages—'a small prize,' the Arabs said."

"October 17th. The same man made an attack on some fishermen on the left bank of the Lualaba. He left at night and returned at noon with fifty or sixty captives, besides some children."

"Are raids of this kind frequent?" asked Stanley.

"Frequent!" was the reply, "sometimes six or ten times a month."

One of these captives said to Stanley, on the march from Mana to Manibo, "Master, all the plain lying between Mana, Manibo and Nyangwe, when I first came here eight years ago, was populated so thickly that we traveled through gardens, villages and fields every quarter of an hour. There were flocks of goats and black pigs around every village. You can see what it now is." He saw that it was an uninhabited wilderness. At that time, Livingstone saw how the country was becoming depopulated before the slave-traders, but says Stanley, "Were it possible for him to rise from the dead and take a glance at the districts now depopulated, it is probable that he would be more than ever filled with sorrow at the misdoings of these traders."

He thinks there is but one way of putting a perpetual end to this infernal traffic, and that is by stopping it in the interior. English and American cruisers on the coast can have but partial success. The suggestion of the Khedive of Egypt is the right one. Annex the interior of Africa to some strong power and establish stations on the great highways over which these traders are compelled to transport their human chattels, where they will be pounced upon and made to give up their captives, and the trade will soon cease from its being too hazardous and unprofitable.

Portugal has no right to the west coast, which it claims. Let England, or England and America together, claim and exercise sovereignty over it, and it will need no cruisers on the coast to stop the trade in slaves. At any rate, it is high time the Christian nations of the world put a stop to this disgrace and blot upon humanity.

CHAPTER XX

ORGANIZING A NEW EXPEDITION

Arriving near Nyangwe, one of the first to meet Stanley was the Arab, Tipo-tipo, or Tipo-tib, or Tippu-tib (which is the proper spelling neither Cameron nor Stanley seems to know), who had once conducted Cameron as far as Utotera or the Kasongo country. He was a splendid specimen of a man physically, and just the one to give Stanley all the information he wanted respecting Cameron's movements. He told him that the latter wanted to follow the river to the sea, but that his men were unwilling to go; besides, no canoes could be obtained for the purpose. He also told him that after staying a long time at Kasongo, he had joined a company of Portuguese traders and proceeded south.

One thing was clear: Cameron had not settled the great problem that Livingstone wished of all things to solve—this great unfinished work had been left for Stanley to complete, or to leave for some future, more daring or more successful explorer. Could he get canoes—could he surmount difficulties that neither Livingstone nor Cameron were able to overcome? were the grave questions he asked himself. He had long dialogues with Tipo-tipo and other Arab chiefs, all of whom dissuaded him from attempting to follow the Lualaba by land, or trying to get canoes. They told him frightful stories of the cannibals below—of dwarfs striped like Zebras and ferocious as demons, with poisoned arrows, living on the backs of elephants, of anacondas, of impenetrable forests—in short, they conjured up a country and a people that no stranger who placed any value on his life would dare to encounter.

The fact that the Lualaba flowed north to a distance beyond the knowledge of the natives was doubtless one, and perhaps the chief, reason why Livingstone suspected it emptied into the Nile. Stanley now knew better. How far north it might flow before it turned he could not say, yet he felt certain that turn west it would, sooner or later, and empty into the Atlantic Ocean, and the possibility of his tracing it had a powerful fascination for him. Its course he knew lay through the largest half of Africa, which was a total blank. Here, by the way, it is rather singular that Stanley, following Livingstone who alone had explored Lake Bembe and made it the source of the Lualaba, adopts his statement, while Cameron, on mere hearsay, should assert that its source was in marshes. The river, after leaving the lake, flows two hundred miles and empties into Lake Mweru, a body of water containing about one thousand eight hundred square miles. Issuing from this, it takes the name of Lualaba, which it holds and loses by turns as it moves on its mighty course for one thousand one hundred miles, till it rolls, ten miles wide at its mouth, into the broad Atlantic as the Congo.

Stanley, from first to last, seemed to have a wonderful power, not only over the Arabs that composed his expedition as we have before mentioned, but over all those with whom he came in contact in his explorations. Notwithstanding all the horrors depicted as awaiting any attempt to advance beyond Nyangwe, this Tipo-tipo agreed, for $5,000, to accompany him with a strong escort a distance of sixty camps, on certain conditions. That he would do it on any conditions was extraordinary, considering the fact, if it was a fact, that the last attempt to penetrate this hostile territory resulted in the loss of five hundred men. The conditions were, that the march should commence from Nyangwe—not occupy more than three months—and that if Stanley should conclude, at the end of the sixty marches, that he could not get through, he would return to Nyangwe; or if he met Portuguese traders and chose to go to the coast in the direction they were moving, he should detail two-thirds of his force to accompany said Tipo back to Nyangwe for his protection.

155

To all these Stanley agreed, except the one promising, if he concluded to go on at the end of the sixty marches, to give him two-thirds of the men of the expedition to see him safely back. On this article of agreement there was a hitch, and Stanley showed his Yankee education, if not Yankee birth, by putting in a last article, by which, if Tipo-tipo through cowardice should fail to complete his sixty marches, he should forfeit his $5,000, and have no escort for his return. Stanley then gave him time to think of it, while he went to see young Pocoke and confer with him. They went over the whole ground together, and Stanley told him it was a matter of life and death with both of them; failure would be certain and perhaps horrible death; success would be honor and glory. It was a fearful picture he drew of the possible future, but Frank's ready response was, "go on."

At this point Stanley reveals one of his strongest characteristics, which we mentioned in the sketch of him at the beginning of the book—the Napoleonic quality of relying on himself. Ordinary well-established principles and rules often condemned the action of Bonaparte—results approved them. So ordinary prudence would have turned Stanley back as it did Cameron—the stories told him of the character of the tribes in advance—the obstacles he would have to encounter, all the mystery, perils and uncertainty of the future—the universal warning and fearful prognostications of those who were supposed to know best—his isolated condition in the heart of Africa—all things that could surround a man to deter him in his actions, were gathered there around that lonely man at that outpost of civilized enterprise; yet, falling back on himself, rising superior to all outward influences, gauging all the probabilities and possibilities by his own clear perceptions and indomitable will, he determined to push forward. If he could not get canoes, which he feared he could not any more than Cameron, then he would try to follow the river by land; if that failed, he would make canoes in the African forest; if he could not go peaceably, he would fight his way, and not turn back till deserted by his own men and left alone in the midst of a savage, hostile people. This determination, under the circumstances, shows him to be no ordinary character, and marks him as one who in a revolution would control the stormy elements around him and mount to power or to the scaffold.

There were also minor obstacles attending this desperate effort to trace the Lualaba to the sea. He had thirteen women in his expedition, wives of his chief Arabs, some of them with young children, others in various stages of pregnancy, who would be delivered of children before they reached the Atlantic coast, and under what circumstances the hour of travail might come no one knew. It might be in the hour of battle, or in the desperate race for life, when one hour's delay would be total ruin to the expedition and death to all. It might be in the struggle and fight around a cataract, or in the day of extreme famine. A thousand things had to be taken into consideration before resolving on this desperate movement. But no matter, the obstacles might even be more formidable than represented, the risk tenfold greater, his mind was made up—the secrets of that mysterious river he would unlock, or his last struggles and mysterious fate would add one more to the secrets it held.

At length the contract with Tipo-tipo to escort him sixty marches was made and signed, and then Stanley informed his own men of it, and told them that if at the end of that time they came across a caravan bound for the west coast, part would join it, and the rest might, if they wished, return to Nyangwe. They agreed to stand by the contract and Stanley moved forward into Nyangwe. Here Stanley was received by one of the two Arab chiefs that bear sway in the place, with becoming courtesy. He seemed surprised at the orderly, quiet march of this force, and still more when told that the distance from Tanganika, some three hundred and forty miles, had been made in about forty days.

Stanley describes minutely the place and its political management, but seems, like Livingstone and Cameron, to be particularly struck with its market. This is held every fourth day, and from one to three thousand people assemble to trade; most of the vendors are women, and the animated manner in which trade is carried on amused Livingstone exceedingly. Though he could not understand their language he could interpret their gestures, which were very expressive. This pleasant scene, however, was marred one day by a messenger stalking into the market with ten jawbones of men tied to a string and hanging over his shoulder, he boasting of having killed and eaten these men and describing with his knife how he cut them up.

Early in the morning of the market-day the river, as far as its course can be seen, presents a lively appearance. It is covered with canoes loaded to their gunwales with natives and articles for the market piled on each other, and they all press toward one point. Amid the laughter and jargon of the natives, may be heard the crowing of cocks, and squealing of pigs and the bleating of goats. Having reached the landing-place, the men quietly shoulder their paddles and walk up the bank, leaving the women to carry the articles up to the market-place. These are placed in large baskets and slung on their backs by a strap across their foreheads. When this great crowd of two or three thousand are assembled the babel begins. But the talking and chaffering are done by the women; the men move about paying but little attention to the bartering, unless something important, as the sale of a slave, is going on. The women do not walk about, but having selected a spot where they propose to do business, they let down the basket, and spreading the articles on the ground so as to appear to the best advantage, they squat themselves in the basket, where they look like some huge shell-fish.

The vendors being thus stationary, the buyers also become so, and hence it is always a close, jammed mass of human beings, screaming, sweating and sending forth no pleasant odor, for three or four hours. They do not break up gradually, but on the movement of some important person a general scramble will commence, and in twenty minutes the whole two thousand or more will be scattered in every direction. The markets of this region are held on neutral ground by the various tribes, and their feuds are laid aside for that day. Except at Nyangwe, uninhabited spots are selected. The neighboring chiefs are always present, and can be seen lounging lazily about. Stanley counted fifty-seven different articles for sale, ranging from sweet potatoes to beautiful girls, while the currency was shells, beads, copper and brass wire and palm cloth.

There are two foreign chiefs at the place, who are very jealous of each other, as each wished to be regarded by the natives as the most powerful. Sheikh Abed, a tall, thin old man with a white beard, occupies the southern section of the town, and Muini Dugumbi the other. It has not long been an Arab trading post, for Dugumbi is the first Arab that came here, and that was no later than 1868, and pitched his quarters, and now the huts of his friends, with their families and slaves, number some three hundred. He is an Arab trader from the east coast, and soon after his arrival he established a harem, composed of more than three hundred slave women. Though a rollicking, joking man himself, his followers are a reckless, freebooting set. The original inhabitants of Nyangwe were driven out by Muini Dugumbi, and now occupy portions of both sides of the river, and live by fishing, and are said to be a singular tribe. Stanley estimated there must have been forty-two thousand of them in the region previous to the coming of this Arab chief, who spread desolation on every side. There remain to-day only twenty thousand of this people.

Stanley remained here only about a week, for Tipo-tipo arriving on the 2d of November, he prepared to start on his unknown journey. The expedition, when he mustered it on the morning of the 4th, numbered one hundred and seventy-six, armed with sixty-three muskets and rifles, two double-barreled guns and ten revolvers. Besides these, there were sixty-eight axes, that Stanley, with great forethought, purchased, thinking the time might come when he would need them as much as his guns. Tipo-tipo brought with him seven hundred followers, though only four hundred were to accompany the expedition the sixty marches. Together, they made quite a little army, but many of them were women and children, who always accompany the Arabs in their marches or forays; still, the force, all drawn up, presented an imposing display. A hundred of these were armed with flint-lock muskets, the rest with spears and shields.

CHAPTER XXI

THROUGH THE FORESTS

On the 5th of November, Stanley, at the head of his motley array, turned his back on Nyangwe and his face to the wilderness. It was an eventful morning for him. Eighteen hundred miles of an unknown country stretched before him, wrapped in profound mystery, peopled with races of which the outside world had never heard, and filled with dangers that would appall the bravest heart. He felt, as he turned and gave a last look at Nyangwe, that the die was cast—his fate for good or ill was sealed. What sad misgivings must at times have made a feeling of faintness creep over his heart— what terrible responsibilities must have crowded upon him; aye, what gloomy forebodings, in spite of his courage, would weigh down his spirit. If he had used canoes, the starting would have been more cheerful, but the dense and tangled forest, whose dark line could be traced against the sky, wore a forbidding aspect. They marched but nine miles the first day, and though the country was open, the manner in which the men bore it did not promise well for their endurance when they should enter the jungle. Every pound was carried on men's shoulders, besides their weapons, all the provisions, stores of cloth, and beads, and wire, the arms and ammunition, of which there had to be a large quantity, for they might be two years fighting their way across the continent, and in addition to these burdens, the boat in sections. The next morning, Tipo-tipo's heterogeneous crowd started first, which impeded the

159

march by frequent halts, for the women and children had to be cared for. They soon entered the gloomy forest of Mitamba, where the marching became more difficult, and the halts more frequent, while the dew fell from the trees in great rain-drops, wetting the narrow path they were following, till the soil became a thick mud. The heavy foliage shut out the sky, and the disordered caravan marched on in gloomy twilight, and at last, drenched to the skin, reached a village four miles from camp and waited for the carriers of the boat to arrive. These found the boat a heavy burden, for the foliage grew so thick and low over the path, that the sections had to be pushed by sheer force through it. To make the camp even more gloomy, one of the Arab chiefs who had been in the forest before, said, with great complacency, that what they had endured was nothing to that which was before them. The next day the path was so overgrown and obstructed by fallen trees, that axemen had to go before the carriers of the boat to clear the way for them. On the 10th, having reached Uregga, a village in the very heart of the forest, they halted for a rest. Its isolated inhabitants seemed to be in advance of those whom Stanley had seen elsewhere. The houses were built in blocks, which were square like those of Manyema, and they contained various fancy articles, some of them displaying great taste. Here Stanley saw curiously carved bits of wood, and handsome spoons, and for the first time in Africa, he beheld a cane settee.

The men carrying the boat did not come up for two days, and then quite broken and disheartened. Indeed, here almost at the very outset, everything seemed to point to an early dissolution of the expedition. Not only were his men discontented, but Tipo-tipo, with all his elegance of manner and pompous pretence, began to glower and grumble, not merely at the hardships his people were compelled to encounter, but because sickness had broken out in his camp.

On the 13th, three hundred out of the seven hundred of his men branched off from the expedition. The marching now became not only monotonous but extremely painful, and so slow that it took a whole day's march to make a distance of nine miles—a rate of progress that Stanley saw very clearly would never bring him to the Atlantic Ocean. They had now been seven days on the march and had made but about forty miles, and scarcely one mile west. Thus far their course had been almost due north toward the great desert of Sahara, and not toward the Atlantic Ocean. These five days had been utterly thrown away, so far as progress in the right direction was concerned; not an inch had been gained, and the whole expedition was discouraged. The carriers of the boat begged Stanley

160

to throw it away or go back to Nyangwe, while the Arab chiefs made no attempt to conceal their discontent, but openly expressed their disinclination to proceed any farther. Even the splendid barbarian dandy, Tipo-tipo, who prided himself on his superiority to all other Arabs, began to look moody, while increasing sickness in the camp cast additional gloom over it. Huge serpents crossed their path, while all sorts of wild beasts and vermin peopled the dense forest and swarmed around them.

On the 15th, they made but six miles and a half and yet, short as was the distance, it took the men carrying the boat twenty-four hours to make it, and all were so weary that a halt of an entire day was ordered to let them rest. In addition to this, the forest became ten times more matted than before. Both the heavier timber and the undergrowth grew thicker and thicker, shutting out not only the light of the sun, but every particle of moving air, so that the atmosphere became suffocating and stifling. Panting for breath, the little army crawled and wormed itself through the interlacing branches, and when night came down were utterly disheartened. Even the elegant Tipo-tipo now gave out, and came to Stanley to be released from his engagement. It was in vain that the latter appealed to his honor, his pride and fear of ridicule should he now turn back to Nyangwe. But to everything he could urge, the very sensible answer was returned: "If there is nothing worse than this before us, it will yet take us, at the rate we are going, a year to make the sixty marches and as long a time to return. You are only killing everybody by your obstinacy; such a country was never made for decent men to travel in, it was made for pagans and monkeys."

It is in circumstances like these that those qualities which have made Stanley the most successful explorer of modern times, exhibit themselves. Napoleon said, when speaking of troops, "Even brave soldiers have their 'moment de peur,'" the time when they shrink. But this man seems an exception to this rule. To him the moment of fear never seems to come, for he never feels the contagion of example. He adheres to his resolution to go on, if but a handful stand by him. He seems impervious to the contagion that seizes others, and a panic in battle would sweep by him unmoved. After talking to Tipo-tipo for two hours, he finally got him to agree to accompany him twenty marches farther.

There were two things in this village, shut up in the heart of the forest, that impressed Stanley very much. He found here a primitive forge, in which the natives smelted iron-ore, found in the neighborhood, and a smithy, in which the iron was worked up into instruments of all kinds, from a small knife to a cleaver; hatchets, hammers, even wire and ornaments for the arms and legs were made. How this rude people, to whom even an Arab trader had never come, should have discovered the properties of iron-ore, how to disengage the iron and then work it into every variety of instruments, is inexplicable. The whole must have been the product of the brain of some native genius.

The other remarkable thing was a double row of skulls, running the entire length of the village, set in the ground, leaving the naked, round top glistening in the sun. There were nearly two hundred of them. Amazed, he asked his Arabs what they were, they replied "soko skulls." The soko, Cameron calls a gorilla, and we have no doubt many of the remarkable stories about gorillas refer to this monkey. But Livingstone says it is an animal resembling the gorilla, and his account of their habits shows they are not the fierce, fearless gorilla that is afraid of neither man nor beast. The soko is about four feet ten inches in height, and often walks erect, with his hands resting on his head as if to steady himself. With a yellow face adorned with ugly whiskers, a low forehead and high ears, he looks as if he might be a hideous cross between a man and a beast. His teeth, though dog-like in their size, still slightly resemble those found in the human head. The fingers are almost exactly like the natives. He is cunning and crafty, and will often stalk a man or woman as stealthily as a hunter will a deer. He seldom does much damage, unless driven to bay, when he fights fiercely. He takes great pleasure in nabbing children and carrying them up into a tree and holding them in his arms, but if a bunch of bananas is thrown on the ground he will descend, and leaving the child, will seize it. He seldom uses his teeth, but in conflict with a man he has been known to bite off his opponent's fingers and then let him go. They are hunted and trapped by the natives for their flesh, which is regarded as very good eating.

Stanley, not satisfied with the answer of his men concerning the skulls, sent for the chief and asked him whose they were. He said of the sokos, which they hunt because of the destruction they make of the bananas, and that their meat was good. Stanley offered him a hundred cowries if he would bring one to him alive or dead. The chief went into the woods to hunt them, but at evening returned without success. He, however, gave him a portion of what he affirmed to be the skin of one. Stanley had the curiosity to take two of these skulls home with him, and gave them to Professor Huxley to examine, who reported they were the skulls of a man and a woman. Stanley, therefore, came to the conclusion that they were the skulls of men and women who had been eaten by these cannibals. But we do not believe this conclusion fairly justifiable, from Professor Huxley's report on two skulls. In the first place, the

Arabs would scarcely have made such a mistake as this implies—they had seen too many soko skulls. In the second place, the chief corroborated their statement, and he had no reason for telling a falsehood. If those skulls were placed thus prominently in the streets, it was to boast of them, not to lie about them. It is far more likely that there were a few human skulls mixed in with the sokos, and that when Stanley asked for a couple, the largest and best-shaped were selected for him which proved to belong to human beings. His hunting for one was certainly not to prove he had told Stanley a falsehood. The same peculiarity was noticed here that Baker mentions of the natives of Fatiko—the women go naked, while the men are partly covered with skins. The whole apparel of the women is an apron four inches square.

On the 19th of March, they reached the Lualaba, sweeping majestically through the silent forest. Stanley immediately determined there should be no more tangled forests for him, but that the broad current of the river should bear him to the Atlantic Ocean or to death. The camp was prepared and the breakfast eaten, while Pocoke was getting the Lady Alice screwed together. Soon she was launched on the stream, amid the huzzas of the party. Although the river here was nearly three-quarters of a mile wide, and the opposite shore appeared like an uninhabited forest, yet sharp eyes detected the wonderful apparition that had appeared on the farther shore, and the news spread so rapidly, that when Stanley in the Lady Alice approached it, he saw the woods alive with human beings, and several canoes tied to the shore. He hailed them, and tried to make a bargain with them to transport his party across. They refused point-blank, but afterwards seemed to relent and offered to exchange blood-brotherhood with them, and appointed a place on a neighboring island where the ceremony should be performed. It was, however, discovered that it was a treacherous plot to murder them, and but for precautions taken in view of its possibility, there would have been a fight.

Stanley now determined to cross his men by detachments in his own boat. He took over thirty above the village and told the natives that they had better assist him in carrying over the rest, for which he promised they should be well paid. They finally consented, and the whole expedition was soon landed safely on the left bank of the river.

CHAPTER XXII

FLOATING DOWN THE CONGO

Having been ferried across the river by the natives, Stanley felt quite secure of the friendship of this first tribe he had met on the banks of the Lualaba. But here he resolved to change its name to Livingstone, which ever after he continues to call it. Villages lined the banks, all, he says, adorned with skulls of human beings. But instead of finding the inhabitants of them friendly, there were none to be seen; all had mysteriously disappeared, whether from fright or to arouse the tribes below, it was impossible to determine; it seemed from the former, for notwithstanding they had overcome their first fear so much as to ferry the expedition across the river, they had not taken away their canoes, nor carried with them their provisions. Leaving these untouched, as a sort of promise to the tribes below that their property should be held sacred, the expedition took up its march down the river. Stanley, with thirty-three men, went by water, in the Lady Alice, while Tipo-tipo and young Pocoke with the rest of the party marched along the bank. Village after village was passed; the natives uttering their wild war-cry, and then disappearing in the forest, leaving everything behind them. Whether it was a peaceful village, or a crowded market-place they passed, they inspired the same terror, and huts and market-places were alike deserted. This did not promise well for the future.

In the middle of the afternoon, Stanley, in the Lady Alice, came to a river one hundred yards wide. Knowing that the land party could not cross this without a boat, he halted to wait for its approach in order to ferry it over, and built a strong camp. This was on November 23d, 1876. At sunset it had not arrived, and he became anxious. Next morning it did not make its appearance, and still more anxious, he ascended this river, named the Ruigi, several miles, to see if they had struck it farther up.

Returning, in the afternoon without hearing anything of the expedition, he was startled as he approached the camp, by the rapid firing of guns. Alarmed, he told the rowers to bend to their oars, and sweeping rapidly downward, he soon came to the mouth of the stream and found it blocked with canoes filled with natives. Dashing down upon them with loud shouts, they fled in every direction. One dead man floating in the stream was the only result of the first fight on the Livingstone.

The day wore away and night came down, and silence and

164

solitude rested on the forest stretching along the banks of the Ruigi, where he anxiously waited to hear musket-shots announcing the arrival of the land party. It was a long and painful night, for one of two things was certain; Tipo-tipo and Pocoke had lost their way or had been attacked and overpowered. The bright tropical sun rose over the forest east of the river Ruigi, but its banks were silent and still. Stanley could not endure the suspense any longer, and dispatched Uledi, with five of the boat's crew, to seek the wanderers. This Uledi, hereafter to the close of the march, becomes a prominent figure. Stanley had made him coxswain of the boat Lady Alice, and he had proved to be one of the most trustworthy men of the expedition, and was to show himself in its future desperate fortunes, one of the most cool and daring, worthy, only half-civilized as he was, to stand beside Stanley. The latter gave him strict directions as to his conduct in hunting up the fugitives—especially respecting the villages he might come across. Uledi told Stanley not to be anxious—he would soon find the lost party.

Stanley, of course, could do nothing but wait, though filled with the most anxious thoughts. The river swept by calmly as ever, unconscious of the troubled hearts on its banks; the great forest stood silent and still in the tropical sun, and the day wore away as it ever does, thoughtless of the destinies its hours are settling, and indifferent to the human suffering that crowds them. But at four o'clock a musket-shot rang out of the woods, and soon Uledi appeared leading the lost party. They had gone astray and been attacked by the natives, who killed three of their number. Luckily they captured a prisoner, whom they forced to act as a guide to conduct them back to the river, and, after marching all day, met Uledi in search of them. They were ferried across and allowed to scatter abroad in search of food, which they took wherever found, without any regard to the rights of the natives. Necessity had compelled Stanley to relax his strict rules in this respect.

The next day the march was continued as before, communication being kept up by those on the land and on the water by drum-taps. The villages they passed were deserted—every soul fleeing at their approach. Proceeding down the river, they came across six abandoned canoes more or less injured. Repairing these, they lashed them together as a floating hospital for the sick of the land party, the number of which had greatly increased from the exposures and hardships they were compelled to undergo. In the afternoon they came upon the first rapids they had met. Some boats, attempting their descent, were upset and attacked by the natives, who were, however, soon beaten off. Four Snider rifles were lost, which brought down on Pocoke, who had permitted the Arabs to run this risk, a severe rebuke, and a still severer one on the Arab chief, who had asked the former to let him make the attempt. The chief, enraged at the reproaches heaped upon him, went to Tipo-tipo, and declared that he would not serve Stanley any longer. This, together with the increased hostility of the natives, the alarming sickness, and the dangerous rapids, brought the head chief to Stanley with a solemn appeal to turn back before it was too late. But the latter had reached a point where nothing but absolute fate could turn him back.

The rapids were passed in safety by the canoe—the Lady Alice being carried around them on men's shoulders. Natives were occasionally met, but no open hostility was shown for several days. The river would now be contracted by the bold shores, and rush foaming along and now spread into lake-like beauty, dotted with green islands, the quiet abodes of tropical birds and monkeys, which filled the air with a jargon of sounds.

On the 4th of December they came to a long, straggling town, composed of huts only seven feet long by five wide, standing apart, yet connected by roofs, the intervening spaces covered and common to the inhabitants of both the adjacent huts. It was, however, deserted, like the rest. This persistent desertion was almost as dispiriting as open hostility, and an evil fate seemed to hang over the expedition. The sickness kept increasing, and day after day all that broke the monotony of the weary hours was the tossing over now and then of dead bodies into the river. The land party presented a heart-broken appearance as they crawled, at night, laden with the sick and dying, into camp. At this place Stanley found an old, battered, abandoned canoe, capable of carrying sixty people. This he repaired, and added it to his floating hospital.

On the 8th of December he came to another large town, the inhabitants of which, in spite of all attempts to make peace, were determined to fight. With fourteen canoes they approached the bank on which the land party were encamped, and commenced shooting their arrows. This lasted for some time, when Stanley took the Lady Alice and dashed among them, pouring in at the same time such a close and deadly fire that they turned and fled.

The story of the slow drifting and marching of the expedition down the Livingstone is a very monotonous one to read, but was full of the deepest interest to the travelers, for the forest on either side of the great river seemed filled with horns and war-drums, while out from a creek or from behind an island canoes would dart and threaten an attack. Floating peacefully through those primeval forests on this stately river, bearing them ever on to the unknown, would make the heart heave with emotion, but when danger and death were ever present, the intensest feelings were aroused.

At length they came to a series of villages lining the bank and surrounded with plenty. There was a large population, and the natives, at the approach of Stanley, blew their ivory horns and beat their drums, and soon a whole fleet of canoes, heavily manned, attacked the little party in the boat. By a bold dash Stanley was able to seize and occupy the lower village, where he quickly intrenched himself. The savages came down in immense numbers, filling the air with hideous shouts and rushed on the slender defenses with desperate fury. It was astonishing to see these men, to whom fire-arms were new, show so little fear of them. They were the boldest fighters Stanley had as yet encountered in Africa, and though he punished them severely they kept up the attack, with short intervals between, for nearly two days. At last the appearance of Tipo-tipo along the bank with the land forces made them beat a retreat, which they did with a tremendous noise of horns and loud threats of vengeance. Out of the few with Stanley, four were killed and thirteen wounded, or seventeen out of forty—nearly half of the whole force. This showed desperate fighting, and as the enemy advanced by hundreds their loss must have been fearful.

Stanley, who was equal in stratagem to an American Indian, played them a trick that night which took all their bravado out of them. Waiting till he thought they were asleep, he took the Lady Alice, and Frank Pocoke a canoe, and both with muffled oars, rowed up the river to find their camp. It was a rainy, dark and windy night, and, hence, favorable to the enterprise he had in hand, and his movements were undiscovered. By the light of a fire on the bank he ascertained the location of the camp, and advancing cautiously saw some forty canoes drawn up on shore. Bidding Frank go down stream and lie to, to catch them as they floated down, he quietly cut them all adrift. They were caught by the former, and by midnight were at Stanley's camp. He knew that he now had them in his power, and so in the morning proceeded to their camp and made offers of peace, which they were glad to accept on the condition that their canoes were returned to them. This was agreed to and blood-brotherhood made. Stanley, however, whose great need had been canoes, determined not to let all these slip through his hands, and retained twenty-three, giving back only fifteen.

Tipo-tipo now told Stanley that he would proceed no further, his people were dying rapidly, the difficulties of marching were increasing and he must return. The latter saw he was determined to go, although eight marches remained to be made, and released him. In truth, now he had boats enough to carry his entire expedition,

Tipo-tipo, cumbered with the sick, would be a burden rather than a help, and at the rate they were moving, eight marches, more or less, would not amount to much. Besides, marching by land, Stanley saw must be given up or they would never get to the sea. Thus far they had scarcely made any westing at all, having gone almost due north, and were nearly as far from the Atlantic Ocean as when they left Nyangwe. The only thing he feared was the effect the departure of the escort would have on his men. In announcing to them that on the sixth day they should start down the river, he made them quite a speech, in which he asked them if he had not always taken good care of them and fulfilled all his promises, and said that if they would trust him implicitly he would surely bring them out to the ocean and see them safe back to Zanzibar. "As a father looks after his children," he said, "so will I look after you." A shout greeted him at the close. One of his chiefs followed in an address to the Arabs, while Uledi, the coxswain, spoke for the boatmen in a very satisfactory strain.

Preparations for starting were now set on foot, canoes were mended, provisions gathered and everything that could be thought of provided against future contingencies. Christmas day came, and the poor fugitives had quite a frolic there in the wilderness. The twenty-three boats they had captured were christened by the men, amid much merriment, and then canoe races followed, rowed by both men and women; all wound up with a wild war-dance on the banks of the river.

The next day Tipo-tipo gave a grand dinner. The day after, the camps separated, and all intercourse between them ceased.

On the morning of the 28th, Stanley embarked his men to the sound of drum and trumpet, and Tipo-tipo hearing it in his camp, knew that the parting hour had come, and paraded his men on the bank. As the expedition slowly floated down the stream toward it, there was heard a deep, plaintive chant from the Arabs on the bank, as a hundred melodious voices arose in a farewell song; out from the dim forest, and over the rippling water it floated, in sweet melancholy strains, that touched every heart in that slowly-moving fleet of canoes. Louder and louder swelled the chant, increasing in volume and pathos, as the wanderers drew nearer. As they approached the Arab camp they saw the singers ranged in a row along the bank. Passing slowly by them, they waved a silent adieu, for their hearts were too full to speak. On they floated, and still the chant went on, until, at last, it died away in the distance, and sadness and silence rested on the stream. No one spoke a word, and Stanley cast his own eyes, not wholly dry, over the crowded boats, and was moved with the deepest pity. Nearly all were sitting with their faces hidden in their hands and sobbing. Those they were leaving behind were about to return to their homes—they to enter new dangers, out of which they might never emerge. No wonder they were sad, and it is singular that not a man, even of those who had before deserted, asked permission to go back. It was a mournful scene there in the wilds of Africa, and on that mysterious river, and Stanley said it was the saddest day in his whole life.

The casting of their fortunes in this desperate venture of his, shows what wonderful influence he had acquired over them, and with what devotion he had inspired them. No wonder his heart clung to them to the last, and he would never leave them, until he saw them safe again in their homes. In order to rouse the men, he shouted, "Sons of Zanzibar, lift up your heads and be men. What is there to fear? Here we are all together, like one family, with hearts united, all strong with the purpose to reach our home. See this river, it is the road to Zanzibar. When saw you a road so wide? Strike your paddles deep, and cry out 'Bismillah,' and let us forward." No shout greeted this appeal, as with sickly smiles they paddled downward. Uledi tried to sing, but it was such a miserable failure that his sad companions could not restrain a smile.

CHAPTER XXIII

DESCENT OF THE CONGO

Stanley was now like Cortez when he burned his ships behind him—there was no returning—one and all must move on together to a common fate. All danger of desertion, for the present, was over, and he felt that the consciousness of there being no possible escape, and that one destiny awaited them all, not only bound them closer together, but would make them better fighters.

At first, on their downward march, they met a peaceful tribe, and then a hostile one which would listen to no terms, and whose reply to every request for peace was, "We don't want you; we will eat you." They, however, passed by unmolested, and swept down the river, astonished to see its banks so thickly populated. That night they encamped in a dense jungle, which was found to be the home of the hippopotamus in the dry season. Tipo-tipo had left with

Stanley two cannibals that he had captured, to be used by him in conciliating the savages, as they knew their language. These tried their arts this night on the natives on the farther bank, who, no sooner espied the strangers, than they beat their drums and advanced to attack them. The cannibals talked so eloquently and plausibly to them, that the savages withdrew and left them in peace. The next morning they came to the mouth of a large river named Lowwa, one thousand yards wide, and seemingly quite deep.

On the last day of the year, they were moving quietly down stream—the heavens bright above them and the banks green beside them—when they suddenly heard the hated war-drum sound; and soon the canoes of the natives shot out from both shores, and for a moment a collision seemed inevitable; but the two cannibals shouted Sennennch! "peace," so plaintively, that they desisted and the little fleet passed on unmolested. But the next day they met other boats which advanced, their crews shouting "we will eat you," but they were easily driven off. It produced a novel sensation in Stanley to be hailed every day and ordered to give himself up for a good roast. At length they came to a peaceful tribe, from whom they obtained provisions.

Gathering such information as they could from the natives, they now continued on very quietly, when they were suddenly attacked by savages in canoes of immense size. One, eighty-five feet long, singled out the Lady Alice and made for it. The crew of the latter waited till it came within fifty feet, and then, pouring in a deadly volley, made a dash to run it down. The frightened crew, just before the collision, jumped overboard, leaving the big boat in the hands of Stanley.

Keeping on, after this little fight, they passed small tributaries, and at length heard the roar of a cataract below. But while they were listening to the unwelcome sound, there suddenly rose over it the wild, shrill war-cries of the savages from both sides of the river. There was no escape for the expedition now—they must turn and fight. Dropping their stone anchors near the bank, they poured in their volleys, but, not being able to dislodge this new foe, they pulled up their anchors and rowed up stream where Stanley divided his forces, and while one attracted the attention of the enemy in front, the other landed, and marching across the land, took them in the rear. As soon as Stanley heard the first shot announcing its arrival, he landed and attacked the enemy in front and routed them, and camped for the night undisturbed.

Next morning, however, the natives appeared again in strong numbers and attacked the camp. The fight was kept up for two hours, when a sally was ordered, and they charged on the enemy, who, though giving way, kept up the fight for four or five hours more. Two of Stanley's men were killed and ten wounded. The former were thrown into the river, for Stanley had determined to bury no more men till out of the cannibal country. This defeat of the natives gave the expedition a few days' rest, so that this first of the series of "Stanley falls," as they were named, could be thoroughly explored, not only for geographical purposes, but to ascertain the best way of getting around them. He found that the falls could not be run, and that a carry around them some two miles long must be made. A path was cleared with axes, and boat and canoes were taken from the water and carried with great labor, yet safely, overland, and launched once more on the stream without accident, and anchored in a creek near its entrance into the main river. Not wishing to remain here, the order to advance was given, and soon they were again afloat on the great river. Sweeping downward they heard the roar of another cataract, and, although the war-horns were resounding on every side, they encamped on an island in the middle of the river. The hostile natives on the island, filled with terror, escaped to the mainland. In the morning Stanley explored the island, and found it contained five villages, all now deserted, and in them was such a variety of implements as showed that the inhabitants were adepts in the manufacture of all kinds of iron tools.

The river was full of islands, winding among which, day after day, Stanley often found to be the only means of escape from the pertinacious cannibals. These islands presented a beautiful appearance with their luxuriant foliage, but while the eye was resting on loveliness, the ear would be saluted with the sound of war-drums and hideous shouts. Whenever Stanley landed and visited a village from which the inhabitants had fled, he would see human bones scattered around, flung aside like oyster-shells, after the meat was removed, and at times the whole expedition felt as if they were destined to make a grand luncheon for these ferocious man-eaters.

The next day Stanley began to make preparations to get around the falls. The first thing was to clear himself of the savages that crowded the left bank and were ready to pounce on him any moment. So taking thirty-six men he led them through the bushes and drove the natives back to their villages, a mile distant, and after a desperate struggle he drove them out of these. He next cut a narrow path, three miles long, around the cataract. This was slow work, and as haste was imperative the men were kept at work all night, flaming torches lighting up the way and making the gloomy shadows of the strange forest deeper still. Camps were distributed at short intervals along the route, and to the first of these the canoes were carried before daylight. The savages made a rush on them but were driven back. At night another stretch of path was made, to which the canoes and baggage were hurried before the cannibals were astir in the morning. There was less hostility and the work went steadily on, and at last, after seventy-eight hours of unceasing labor and almost constant fighting the river was again reached and the boats launched.

This was accomplished on January 14th, but though the river had been reached, new perils awaited them. There was a stretch of two miles of rapids that must be passed. After six canoes had been passed safely, one was upset, and one of those in it, Zaidi, instead of swimming ashore, as the others did, clung to it and was borne helplessly down to the cataract below. But on the very verge was a solitary rock on which the boat drifted and split—one part jamming fast. To this the poor wretch clung with the strength of despair, while all around leaped and whirled and roared the boiling water. Those on shore shrieked in agony, and Stanley was hastily sent for. He immediately set to work making a rattan rope, in order to let down a boat to him by which he could be pulled ashore. But the rope was not strong enough, and snapped asunder as soon as the boat reached the heavy suck of water just above the falls, and it was whirled into the vortex below. Other and stronger ropes were then made and another canoe brought up and three ropes lashed to it. A couple of men would be needed to paddle and steer the boat so that it could reach the unfortunate wretch on his perilous perch, and volunteers were called for. But one glance at the wild and angry waves was enough, and no one responded. Stanley then appealed to their feelings, when the brave Uledi stepped forward and said "I will go." Others of the crew followed, but only one was needed. The two stepped calmly into the boat and pushed off—watched with intense anxiety by those on shore. Reaching a certain distance above the falls, it drifted rapidly down toward them, guided by those holding two of the cables on shore. The third floated from the stern of the boat for the poor wretch on the rock to seize. Attempt after attempt was made to get this within Zaidi's reach, but the whirling waters flung it about like a whip-lash. At length the boat was lowered so close to the brink of the falls that he was able to reach it, but no sooner had he seized it and flung himself loose, than he was borne over the edge and disappeared below. But he held on to the rope and soon his head appeared above the boiling waves, when the word was given to haul away. The strain, however, was too great, and the cables parted and away dashed the canoe toward certain destruction, and a cry of horror arose from those on shore, for all three now seemed inevitably lost. But Zaidi below, by hanging on to the rope, pulled the boat against the rock where it lay wedged. He was then pulled up, and the three crouched together on the rock. A stone was now tied to about three hundred feet of whip-cord and flung to them, but they failed to catch it. Again and again was it thrown only to be pulled in and recast, but at last it whirled so close to them that they caught it. A heavy rope of rattan was then tied to it and drawn across and fastened, and a bridge thus secured.

But this had taken so much time that night came on before the work could be finished; the three wretched men were left therefore, to crouch on the rock, and wait for the morning. All night long they held on to their wild perch, while the water rushed, and boiled, and roared around them, and the deep thunder of the cataract rose in one deep monotone over all, so that they could not hear each other speak.

The next morning, early, the Arabs were set to work making more ropes, which were finally hauled across, and fastened round the waist of each man, and then, one by one, they leaped into the water and were drawn safely ashore, amid the joyous shouts of the people.

They now set to work cutting a road three miles long through the woods. Over this the canoes were hauled with great labor before the savages on the farther side knew what was going on. But the moment the canoes were afloat, the foe discovered them, and rushing forward with their canoes the battle commenced. Stanley dashed through them, and sweeping down stream for a mile, landed on the island where the tribe lived, and quietly detaching twenty men, sent them to the villages, while he kept the savages at bay. In a short time, the detachment returned, bringing with them a crowd of women and children as prisoners, and a large herd of sheep. The savages, when they saw these marching down to the landing-place, were taken so completely aback, that they stopped fighting at once, and withdrew to consult what was best to do in this extraordinary turn of affairs. They sat in their canoes, waiting to see their friends massacred. Negotiations for peace were soon opened and concluded, and the ceremony of blood-brotherhood was gone through with, the captives and herds were then surrendered up and friendly terms were established.

The fifth cataract was at the foot of this island and was safely passed, and the expedition encamped on the bank of the river, on a green plat of ground, and slept undisturbed. In the morning, to their unbounded surprise, they found themselves inclosed in a net of cord, reaching from the shore above the camp, to the shore below it, passing through the bushes. Stanley knew what this meant—that they were to be speared, when they approached it, like so many wild beasts. He at once ordered one of the chiefs, Manwa Sera, to take thirty men and row up the river a short distance and land, thence to march inland, and come up behind those lying in wait outside of the net. At the end of an hour he ordered men forward to cut the nets, when the firing commenced. The savages soon turned and fled, but to their astonishment, met the enemy advancing on them by the road leading from their villages, at which discovery they fled in every direction. Eight prisoners were, however, captured and brought into camp. On being questioned, they confessed that they were after man-meat and said that their tribe, which lived about a day's journey inland, ate old men and women and every stranger that fell into their hands.

They now kept down the river for several miles unmolested, until they heard the sullen roar of the sixth cataract rising over the woods, when they camped on the right bank, near an island covered with villages. Stanley knew what was before him here, and ordered a stockade to be commenced immediately. But, before this was finished, the everlasting drum and horn pealed through the woods and soon the savages were upon them. After a short fight, they retreated, followed by Stanley's soldiers to a large village, but there were only three or four old women in it, who were brought into camp. In a short time a heavier force approached and made a furious attack, but it was quickly driven back and two wounded men were taken prisoners. A part of Stanley's force was all this time cutting a path around the cataract. The next morning they set to work with a will and by noon passed it safely. Stanley having wormed out of his captives all the information he could of the surrounding country and the various tribes that inhabited it, set them free. Passing some rapids, they came to a village in which there was but a single old man, solitary and alone, who had been there for several days. The next day they halted to repair the boats. The persistent course of the river, till within the last few days to the north, and sometimes northeast, had troubled Stanley, and but for the immense volume of water that he knew had no eastern outlet, would have shaken his faith in its being the Congo. But, since he passed the last cataract he had noticed that it gradually deflected to the northwest, and now swept by almost due west, having evidently at last started on its journey for the sea. Long islands still divided the river, making, most of the time, two streams and shutting out the opposite banks. Keeping down the right channel, they passed through enchanting scenery, undisturbed by war-drums and savage shouts. Though the water was smooth on their side, over the island, on the other, they could hear the roar of rapids, and a few miles farther down the loud roar of the seventh and last cataract of the "Stanley Falls" burst on their ears, filling the solitude with its loud thunder. The river here was over a mile wide, and the fall of such an immense body of water over a high ledge made the earth tremble.

It was one incessant fight, either with the savages or with nature, and it seemed as if fate determined to wear out these indomitable men. Soon the loud war-drums, and horns, and battle-shouts were mingled with the roar of the cataract, showing that here, too, they must fight before they could get below it. Dropping down as near as it was safe to the commencement of the rapids, they pulled ashore and pitched their camp in a dense forest. Fearful of being attacked before they could intrench, they immediately set to work with their axes to throw together a brushwood fence, while thirty soldiers were stationed in front toward the river, to repel assault. They had hardly completed it before the naked cannibals were upon them with a fury that threatened to break through their defenses. All this time out from the woods, adown the gorge through which the river plunged, war-drums and horns were heard summoning the thickly-scattered villages to the scene of combat. Before the steady fire of the musketeers the savages suffered so severely that at sunset they abandoned the attack and withdrew. Stanley now secured his boats and strengthened the brushwood fence, and laid his plans for the morning.

The camp was roused at five o'clock, and they pushed on to a point nearer the falls, so that the work of carrying around them was completed before the Wangas opened battle. Everything being made secure, they waited for the expected attack to begin, but, no enemy appearing, Stanley sent out scouts to ascertain what they were about. They brought back word that no savages were to be seen. On advancing to the villages, Stanley found to his astonishment that they were all deserted. Why, or whither they had fled was a profound mystery. Here was a town or cluster of villages, each with four or five streets running through it, and capable of containing two thousand inhabitants, deserted in a single night. The silence of death reigned over it.

Left thus at peace, he began to turn his attention to the falls. He found the river here in this terrific gorge was contracted to less than one-third of its breadth a short distance above, and hence flowed with a power and strength that can hardly be conceived. Crowded together, the waters struggled and leaped, and tore onward with a wildness and fury like the Niagara River below the falls. He here found baskets tied to long poles set to catch fish. They emptied some of these and found about thirty fish, of a different species from any known in our waters. These fish-baskets showed that they were now among savages that did not depend wholly on human flesh for subsistence. The villages, houses, and various implements and articles of household furniture were far in advance of those among the cannibals above them. At the same time the people here seemed more alert, fearless and determined.

The carry around these falls was not interrupted, and the immense labor of transporting so many boats and so much baggage along a rough-cut path was cheerfully performed. The next day, however, while congratulating themselves on the changed condition of things, they saw a large number of canoes approaching, and soon a musket-shot rang over the water, and one of Stanley's men fell. A new peril now threatened them—they found the natives armed with Portuguese muskets. Though it was a sure sign that they were approaching the coast, it showed also that hereafter it was to be fire-arms against fire-arms, not rifles against spears and arrows; and if the natives continued hostile, the destruction of the expedition seemed certain with such odds against it. Heretofore, in every combat the men picked up a number of native shields, almost as big as doors, which they preserved. In battle, the women and children would hold these before the soldiers, which was the chief reason why there had been so few casualties when fighting from the boats; but if bullets hereafter were to be fired, these would be of no use. Still there was nothing left but to fight to the last.

This changed condition of things caused Stanley the greatest anxiety. He, however, formed his boats in line of battle and the firing commenced—the natives after every discharge retiring to reload. Stanley's soldiers fired so rapidly, and with such deadly effect, that after an hour had past the natives withdrew, and the expedition moved off and was soon lost to sight amid the innumerable islands that studded the river, and each of which was loaded with the most luxuriant vegetation.

The next day they floated down the river undisturbed, the islands growing more numerous as it expanded, until now it had become several miles wide. On one island they saw an immense elephant standing amid the trees, but no one proposed to stop and kill him, though his huge tusks were a tempting sight; there was too much at stake to think of hunting the great crocodiles and hippopotami and other amphibious monsters, who made the channels around these islands their home.

The next day, the 13th of February, they suddenly came upon a large number of villages. They were hidden from view, till the boats were so close upon them that it was too late to retreat. The next minute the forest resounded with the loud war-drums and ivory horns, while the fierce war-cries had changed their character and sounded like nothing human Stanley had ever heard. Bright gun-barrels gleamed above the light, graceful boats as they came swiftly on. But as they drew near the natives seemed to be filled with such strange wonder at the novel spectacle of two white men, that they did not fire, but sat and stared at them as if they had been ghosts. They followed for five miles in dead silence, when one of them fired and killed an Arab. In an instant, the boats wheeled and opened such a rapid fusillade that the savages retreated. But, when Stanley again resumed his downward course they turned and followed again, hovering like hawks around him for five miles, but making no attack.

They were now just above the equator, and were moving south-west. The next morning the islands were so thick that they shut out both banks, but keeping on down stream they at length came upon a village, and attempted to pass it unobserved, but the tap of a drum showed that they were observed, and their hearts sank within them at the prospect of another fight. In a few minutes drum was answering drum in every direction, and soon the savages were seen manning their canoes. Stanley, seeing his men were worn down by this incessant fighting, made them a short speech, telling them if they must die it should be with their guns in their hands. He had come to have great contempt for the natives on the water so long as they were without fire-arms. He could soon scatter them and keep them at a respectful distance with his rifles, but when it should be five hundred muskets against his forty guns, the whole character of the struggle would be changed.

As they quietly floated down, canoe after canoe filled with gayly-decorated savages shot out into the river, till an immense fleet of them was in pursuit. Stanley ordered his men to cease paddling and wait their approach, determined, if possible, to make peace. But, while he was standing up holding out cloth and wire and making peaceful gestures, the crew of one canoe fired into his boat, wounding three men.

There was nothing left now but to fight, and soon the crash of fire-arms awoke the echoes of the forest-covered shores. The men had raised their shields, and to their joy found them a perfect protection, as the enemy fired bits of iron and copper, that could not penetrate them any more than the native arrows. As the fight went on other canoes arrived, until Stanley counted sixty-three canoes which he estimated carried five guns apiece, which would make three hundred and fifteen to his forty-four—a desperate odds truly, and if the Africans' guns had been loaded with bullets, they would have doubtless then and there ended the expedition. It is a little curious that whenever Stanley gets into a desperate strait that even his boldness and pluck cannot help him out of, some unforeseen thing comes to his aid, and he escapes.

In this case his rifles had much longer range and greater penetrating force than the old-fashioned muskets, so most of the enemy kept at a distance of a hundred yards. One brave fellow, however, kept dashing up to within fifty yards and firing, till he was wounded. It was a lucky thing for Stanley that their guns were poor, their cartridges feeble and their aim bad. At length the fire began to slacken, and dwindling down to now and then a random shot, before six o'clock it ceased altogether.

The fight being over, the men laid down their guns and once more took up their paddles and were soon out of sight of their enemies, and at sunset they camped on an island that lay amid a nest of islets.

The next day, the 15th, they continued their journey and for three days were unmolested and allowed to enjoy the magnificent scenery amid which they floated; but they had little inclination to admire scenery, for they were half-starved, not having been able to purchase a particle of food for a week. On the 19th they came to a great river, the largest tributary they had yet seen, pouring an enormous volume of black water into the Livingstone.

It now began to look as if, having escaped death by battle and the cataracts, they were about to yield to famine. They met fishermen, but these would have nothing to do with them. On the 19th, nine days since they had been able to purchase any provisions, they came to Ikengo, where to their great joy they found friendly natives. The next day Stanley held a market on the island where he had encamped, to which the neighboring chiefs came, as well as the villagers. Trade was brisk and before night he had a bountiful supply of sheep, goats, bananas, flour, sweet potatoes and various tropical fruits, for which he exchanged cloth, beads and wire. The men revelled in the unexpected abundance, and hope and joy took the place of gloom and discontent. The next day they resumed their apparently endless journey, and floated peacefully amid green islands, scattered like gems over the broad bosom of the now friendly stream.

On the 23d, while floating quietly down, word was brought Stanley that the wife of one of the Arab chiefs, who had been sick for some time, was dying, and he pulled his boat alongside of the one in which she lay. She knew she was going, and bade him an affectionate good-bye. Soon after she expired. At sunset a weight was tied to her body, and she was dropped into the waters of the river, and left to sleep in this lonely bed, far away from the cocoanuts and mangoes of her native land.

Their course now led them among beautiful islets, made gay by the rich plumage of tropical birds. Occasionally they met a few canoes, but no hostility was exhibited. On the 27th, they came upon natives fishing, who at once showed themselves to be friendly, and exhibited no distrust at all. It was a new revelation to the wanderers. Hitherto, it was only after the most patient waiting and persevering efforts that they could gain the confidence of the savages, if, indeed, they secured it at all. Here it was freely given, and they directed them to a good camping place, on an island from whence they looked across to the fields and villages of Chumbiri, where these fishermen belonged. The fishermen then departed, to report to their king, who sent them back with presents of food, and a promise that he would visit the camp. True to his word, he appeared next day, escorted by five canoes filled with soldiers, carrying muskets. He wore a curious hat, was very cool and self-possessed in his manner, and inclined to be sociable. He took snuff incessantly, and in enormous quantities. After a long conversation, he invited them to make his village their home, and Stanley, wishing to learn all he could of the river below, accepted the invitation, and the expedition crossed the river and was received in savage pomp. A grand market was held, and exchanges freely made. The women did not seem to be of the pure African blood, being brown instead of black, with large eyes, beautifully shaped shoulders, and altogether very pretty. They were fond of ornaments, some of them wearing thirty pounds of brass wire around their necks. Stanley estimated that the forty wives, six daughters and the female slaves of the king carried on their necks about one thousand four hundred pounds of brass wire.

He stayed here a week, enjoying the hospitality of the king, who, in addition to all his other kindnesses, gave him three canoes, as an escort, and on the 7th of March he turned the prows of his boats again down stream. That night they encamped in a jungle, into which two immense serpents crawled, one of which was killed just as he began to twine his folds about a woman. It measured thirteen feet and a half in length, and fifteen inches round the body. Having passed tributary after tributary, they went ashore on the morning of the 9th to cook breakfast. The women were busily engaged in preparing it, when they were startled by loud musket shots and six of the men fell. They had been taken completely by surprise, but springing to their guns, they dashed into the woods and a fierce fight followed, which lasted an hour. It was one incessant crack of musketry, each one sheltering himself as best he could. The savages were finally driven off, but not until they had wounded fourteen of Stanley's men. This was the sharpest fight he had yet had, and if it were a fair prelude to what was to follow, the expedition would soon consist of nothing but wounded men. It is astonishing, that in all these fights, of which this was the thirty-second and last, neither Stanley nor Pocoke should receive a wound.

After the wounded men had been attended to, they again set out and floated peacefully down, not suspecting any danger, until they approached a settlement which suddenly swarmed with excited armed men. Rowing away as fast as possible, they soon got clear of the village, and encamped three miles below. The next day the voyage was charming, taking them through beautiful and ever-changing scenery. Nothing occurred to mar their pleasure the following day except a fierce south wind, which now began to set in regularly every day, making the river exceedingly rough for the canoes, especially at this point, where the river expanded to nearly two miles in width. This great breadth extended as far as the eye could reach, and, hemmed in by cliffs, it resembled a pool, which young Pocoke christened "Stanley Pool."

Paddling slowly down this pool, they passed several villages. Makoneh, the chief of one, proved very kind and hospitable, and offered to conduct Stanley to the next cataract. As they swept down, they halted at a friendly village, the chief of which inquired how they expected to get over the mighty falls below. He was a bluff, genial, good-souled negro, who seemed glad to assist them in any way in his power, and finally offered to guide them to the cataract. Moving down, soon its low roar was heard swelling over the forest, gradually increasing as they advanced till it rose like a continuous thunder-peal from the solitude below.

Makoneh led the way, and just skirting the first line of breakers he landed on a pebbly beach. The village of Itsi was in sight, he being the petty king of a neighboring tribe. Some canoes soon crossed from it, and were received so kindly that the natives went back with such wonderful stories to their king that next day he paid Stanley a visit. He came in a large canoe carrying eighty-six persons. It was over eighty-five feet long, and propelled by sixty paddlers. These, standing up and keeping time with their strokes to the steady beat of a drum, sent the boat like an arrow through the water and made a stirring picture as they dashed up to Stanley's camp. There were several gray-headed men present, one of whom was introduced to Stanley as the king. The latter noticed that the rest laughed heartily at this, which afterwards turned out to be a practical joke. However, Stanley sat down with the venerable person in amicable conversation, while a young native and Frank seemed to strike up a warm friendship for each other, or at least the native for Pocoke, judging by the way he pressed presents on him.

It seemed strange to Stanley that the young savage should

180

give twice as much to Frank as the king gave to him, but it now came out that this young man was the king, and the aged man Stanley had been conversing with was merely one of his counselors. Stanley at once changed his attention, and asked him what present would please him. The royal young savage had been looking about at the various things in camp, and seeing a very large goat, told Stanley that he wished "big goat." Now this happened to be the last thing the latter wished to part with. A lady in England had requested him to bring back a goat of this very breed, and he had purchased several, of which this alone had survived the long and dangerous journey. He therefore endeavored to bribe the young king by doubling the other presents he had prepared. No, he would have the "big goat." Stanley then offered to give him an ass instead. At this the savage seemed to hesitate. The donkey was very desirable, but at this critical moment the animal sent up a huge bray, which so frightened the women that he would not take him. Other tempting offers were made but nothing would do but the "big goat," and as Stanley was short of provisions (the men having squandered those the king of Chambiri had given them), and as he must have these, he reluctantly turned over the big goat and the young king departed highly delighted. The next day he returned bringing three ordinary goats in exchange and some provisions. Soon the kings or chiefs of other neighboring tribes came in bringing fruit, and everything was harmonious, and treaties of amity were made with all. The one with Itsi was quite ceremonious. Among other things, he gave Stanley a white powder as a charm against evil, in return for which, the latter, with all due gravity, presented him with a half-ounce vial full of magnesia as the white man's charm. This and blood-brotherhood closed the formal proceedings of the treaty-making powers—quite as important, in their way, as similar councils in civilized countries.

Stanley found by observation that though he had traveled from Nyangwe over one thousand two hundred miles, he had descended not quite a thousand feet.

CHAPTER XXIV

AMONG THE CATARACTS

It is a little singular, that in this age of inquiry and persistent effort to get at the cause of things, no one has yet attempted to explain the reason of tribal differences. Aborigines occupying the same parallels of latitude and longitude, subject to the same influences of climate, living on the same diet, are different in color, features, and more than all, in disposition. The real, or supposed influences, that lie at the bottom of the different races, do not apply here. Difference of origin, of climate, of food, all these must have great effect in changing color, features and character, and hence, to a certain extent, explain how such distinct nationalities exist, but they do not in the least account for tribal differences where all these are the same, and where there are not even barriers of mountains and rivers separating them. Why should our western Indian tribes, roaming over the same prairies, living on the same food, and similar in all their modes of life, be yet so different in form, feature and disposition? Is there really no way of getting a satisfactory, true explanation of all this?

So in Africa, Stanley crossed the continent in the same general range of latitude. The savages he met were all dwellers of the equatorial region, and hence lived in the same climate, used the same food, dressed in the same way, and lived the same life, and yet they were as dissimilar as different nationalities. If any educational influences had been brought to bear upon them one could understand this, but none have been exerted. These same tribal differences Stanley found on the Congo. Fierce cannibals and gentle agricultural people were living side by side. Suspicious, faithless men, differing very little from the better class of monkeys, lived neighbors to tribes unsuspicious and trustful, and wonderfully advanced in the arts of mechanism. At the falls, which were named "Stanley Falls," the natives were suspicious, faithless, cruel, but when he reached the Livingstone Falls, he found the people hospitable, kind and trustful. When this difference burst on Stanley practically, he felt it sensibly, but he philosophically dismissed it with the simple remark, such "is the effect of trade." We cannot accept this explanation at all, for they had no trade with the outside world, and they showed the same kindly natures before he commenced trading with them. The only evidence of their connection with civilized life was that they had muskets, and yet the very first tribe which possessed them was the most fierce, implacable and relentless he met with. This ethnological question has never yet been settled. Still it is not singular that Stanley did not just then trouble himself with it. As long as the difference existed and was now in his favor he was content, as well he might be. The friendly natives at the head of these falls assured him that he had passed the cannibal country, but they differed materially as to the number of falls below—one making them three, another a half dozen or more. No matter whether they were few or many, they must be passed, though he dragged his canoes over lofty mountains to do it.

But if the differences in the character of the natives was great, that in the character of the scenery and aspect of the river was no less so. The wild, fierce savages had become tame, while the gently flowing river, studded with green islands, had become wild and fierce and angry. The gradually descending plain was transformed into the terrific gorge over which hung beetling cliffs, and the placid current into a roaring torrent dashing amid rocks, plunging over precipices, and filling the solitudes with an ever-angry voice. Hostile savages were behind, but hostile nature was before the adventurers, to whom there would be no rest till they found the restless sea.

Immediately before them were two stretches of rapids and then a cataract. The first was a mere piece of broken water that was easily passed. Having no fear of hostile natives, Stanley leisurely explored both river and shore to ascertain the best way of getting around the second rapids. The goods, asses, women and children were taken overland, while the boats were led with hawsers from rock to rock along the shore. Fortunately not a rope broke, and by five o'clock the rapids were passed and all were in camp together.

The last of the rapids Stanley declared to be the wildest stretch of water he had ever seen. For four miles the river looked as if thrown upward by volcanic action beneath and at the same time swept by a fierce hurricane above, and all the while it was dashing madly on at the rate of thirty miles an hour. Huge troughs would be formed, as if the stream was yawning asunder, and then the divided water would come together with a crash, sending up columns twenty feet high to dissolve in foam and spray. The crash of colliding waves and the steady roar of the rapids were awful. It was literally a "hell of waters." The land carriage around this wild stretch was a rough piece of work. Paths of brushwood were made, and the canoes slowly hauled up rocky heights and slid down into deep gullies—the women and children toiling after. They were nearly four days getting around this four miles of impassable rapids. The men were fainting for want of food when smooth water was at last reached. This, however, continued but a short distance, when they had to take to land again and haul their boats over a rocky point for three-quarters of a mile. This task took three days to accomplish. When it is remembered that one of the canoes was eighty-five feet long, and another seventy-five and dug out of a solid tree, we can get some conception of the tremendous effort it required to transport them over rocks and hills. When smooth water was again reached, it gave them only a short respite. Stanley, however, found it necessary to halt and give the people rest, for the tremendous strain of the last week was telling fearfully on them.

On the 25th, they found themselves once more confronted by ugly rapids. In endeavoring to lead the boats around them, the best canoe was dragged by the mere force of the current from the hands of fifty men and whirled down the mad stream and dashed to pieces. Toiling amid the rocks several men were injured, one having his shoulder dislocated, while Stanley fell into a chasm thirty feet deep, but fortunately struck on his feet, and thus escaped with some slight bruises, though he was very much stunned. On the 27th, they succeeded in getting past this "cauldron," as it was called, although they narrowly escaped losing their largest canoe. The next day they had smooth water for a short distance and then they came to "Rocky Falls." These, however, were passed with comparative ease and two men were sent forward to explore. They reported, on their return, that about a mile below was another cataract, and that at its head was an excellent camping place in a sheltered bay. Stanley determined to reach this spot before dark, and so, manning his seventeen remaining canoes, he led the way, hugging the shore, so as not to get into the suction of the water above the falls. All were told to follow him and by no means to venture out into the middle of the stream. Keeping close to the right bank, he felt his way carefully onward and at last floated into the tranquil bay, at the head of the fall. Three canoes followed him, and as he was waiting for the others to come in he saw, to his horror, the largest canoe in midstream and coming down like a race-horse. Kalulu had charge of this, and deceived by the smooth, glassy surface of the stream, he had pulled out into midcurrent. The moment he was caught by it his doom and that of the four men with him was sealed. There was nothing to be done by those on shore but to watch the swiftly-gliding boat till it shot over the edge of the falls to disappear in the tumult below. Three of the men were Stanley's especial favorites, and he felt their loss keenly. While his eyes was yet resting on the spot where they had gone down, another canoe shot in sight, driving straight for the falls. Fortunately, it struck them at the least dangerous point and went over safely, then, skillfully working the canoe toward the shore, its two inmates sprang overboard and swam to land. Stanley immediately dispatched his boat's crew up-stream to tell the rest to hug the shore, and in no case to venture out into the stream. Before they reached the canoes, another one, with only the lad Soudi, shot by, he crying, as he was borne swiftly onward, "There is but one God—I am lost, master," and the next moment he too dropped out of sight. Strange to say, though the canoe was whirled about at the bottom like a spinning-top, it did not sink, and was finally swept out of sight behind an island. The rest of the canoes arrived safely.

The next day Stanley sent Frank to bring over the goods to where he was encamped, while he himself traded with the natives, whom he found very friendly, and from whom he obtained abundant provisions. After resting one day, they got everything round the falls and encamped on the 1st of April. In the afternoon, to the surprise and joy of all, young Soudi walked into camp. He had a strange story to tell. He was borne helplessly down the rapids, confused and dizzy, till at last the boat drifted against a rock, when he jumped out and got on shore. Before he had time to think where he was, he was seized from behind and pinioned, and dragged to the top of the mountain by two men, who stripped and examined him with great curiosity. The next day several of the tribe came to see him, one of whom had been in Stanley's camp when King Itsi visited it, and he told such terrible stories about Stanley and of his gun that could shoot all day, that they became frightened and took Soudi back to the place where they had found him, and told him to speak well of them. The other two men who had gone safely over the fall, and also joined the camp.

Proceeding on down-stream they came to more rapids, in passing which they met many narrow escapes. It was, indeed, a succession of rapids, and while Stanley conducted the boats through them, Frank took the rest of the party and goods overland. The former examined every inch of the way carefully before starting. Thus day after day passed, they continually fighting the relentless river. Sometimes the water was too rough to admit the passage of the boats, and then they had to be carried overland. It was slow and tedious work, and but little progress was made. The question each one kept asking himself was, how long will this last and when shall we see smooth water again?

Each day was but the repetition of its predecessor, and if the natives had been as hostile as those farther up the river, they could not have got on at all. The only variation was when the river took some new whim or the formation of the country required more effort and new modes of getting on. Thus one day they undertook to lead the canoes by hawsers around a rocky point where the eddies set up-stream with the strength and velocity of a torrent, so that it seemed impossible to get them down-stream. To add to the difficulty, the cliffs on the top of which the men with the hawsers stood, were fifty feet high and their jagged edges sawed the ropes till they parted one after another.

So creeping along the shore to-day, and daring the midstream, which, though boisterous, was clear of rocks, to-morrow, they kept on, hoping after the next stretch to reach a quiet flowing river. The Lady Alice fared hard in this perilous navigation, and once came near being lost. All this time the resources of the expedition were being exhausted, for though the natives were friendly everything had to be paid for, and it was not difficult to answer the question, "How long will our remaining currency last?"

The next rapids they came to Stanley named the "Lady Alice Rapids," because, as we suppose, both he and the boat escaped almost by a miracle from sharing one sad fate in the wild and mad waters of the Livingstone. The cables lashed to bow and stern, to let the boat down, parted, or were snatched from the hands on shore, and away she dashed down the foaming current. Above, the naked cliffs rose three hundred feet high—around boiled and tossed the tumultuous waters, and certain destruction seemed to await the man who had triumphed over so many obstacles and who at last was nearing the goal of his ambition. The Arabs, whose life depended on his life, were in despair—their master was gone—there was no one left to lead them out of this strange wilderness. Nothing but the coolness of Stanley saved him and his crew. Watching every change in the flow of the current—resigning himself to the wild will of the mad waters when struggling was useless—taking advantage of every favorable change of the current and bidding his men row for life at the right time, he at length reached shore, and at once sent messengers to his despairing camp to tell them he was safe. He knew, and they knew, that all their lives hung on his. He had a narrow escape, and the natives on shore, as they watched his boat flung about like a cockle-shell in the boiling surge, looked upon him as lost.

If Stanley wanted any new proof of the affection of his Arabs for him, he had it now. He had been able, after his fierce struggle with the rapids and being carried, in the meantime, over one fall, to reach land at least two miles below his camp, in which he was looked upon as lost. When, therefore, the message was received that he was alive and safe, his followers streamed forth in one confused mass, and hastening down the river, came in a long, straggling line in sight of Stanley, waving their arms on high, shouting words of welcome and overwhelming him with expressions of exuberant joy.

This involuntary outburst of feeling and gratitude that their "master" was safe, repaid him tenfold for all the suffering and peril he had endured. It is strange, when such momentous results hang on a single life, how we go on as though nothing depended upon it till the moment comes when we are about losing it.

The men, women and children had joined in this grand exodus to congratulate Stanley on his deliverance from what appeared certain death, and the men now returned to bring the goods to this point where the new camp was pitched. Not twenty rods from it the Nikenke River came foaming and tumbling into the Livingstone from a precipice one thousand feet high, with a terrific roar and rumble. Almost as near, another tributary dashed over a ledge four hundred feet high, while just above was the wild rapids he had just passed, and just below another stretch of swift and tumbling water. The din of these surrounding cataracts made a fearful, terrific music in these mysterious solitudes, and awakened strange feelings in Stanley, as he lay and listened and wondered what would come next.

The sharp crash of the near cataract tumbling from its height of a thousand feet, the low rumble of the lower fall and the deep boom of the mighty river made up a grand diapason there in the wilds of Central Africa. West from the great lakes the continent seemed to stretch in one vast plateau, across which the river moved in placid strength, its gently sweeping current parted with beautiful islands, that filled the air with perfume exhaled from countless flowers and tropical plants, and making a scene of loveliness that intoxicated the senses. But all this was marred by the presence of blood-thirsty cannibals, whose war-drums and savage cries filled this world of beauty with terrific sounds and nameless fears. But the moment the stream reached the edge of this plateau, where man seemed to become more human, it rolled into cataracts and rapids, down a steep incline, till it came to the sea. Canoes were upset and lost, and men were barely saved from death by expert swimming during these fearful days, and yet Stanley could get no reliable information from the natives how far down this remorseless stretch of water extended. This terrible struggle, which the party underwent, and the exhausting nature of their work may be faintly imagined when it is stated that for thirty-seven consecutive days they made less than a mile a day. It was a constant succession of rapids from the middle of March to the latter part of April.

At length, on the 22d, they came to the "big cataract," called by the natives Inkisi, which Stanley fondly believed would be the last. The table-land here is one thousand feet high, and the natives occupying it flocked into Stanley's camp, curious to know how he

187

was to get his canoes past the falls. When he told them he was going to drag them over that table-land one thousand feet high, they looked at him in speechless astonishment. His own men were thunderstruck when he announced to them his determination. But they had become so accustomed to believe he could do anything he resolved upon, that they silently acquiesced. The natives, as they looked at the heavy canoes and then on the lofty height, with its steep, craggy ascent, took their departure and began to climb back to their homes to secure their property, for they said, if the white man intended to fly his boats over the mountains, they did not know what terrible things might next happen.

Having settled on the undertaking, Stanley immediately set to work to carry it out, and the first day built a road nearly a mile long. The next day the Lady Alice and a small canoe were resting on the high summit. The work was done so quietly and without any disastrous results to life and property, that the native chiefs were dumb with admiration and offered to bring six hundred men next day to help haul up the heavy canoes. They kept their word, and soon boats and baggage were in camp on the top of the mountain. Sending off a party ten miles ahead to prepare the natives for his coming, Stanley took the women and children, with the goods and boat's crew, on to the next tribe to make a camp near the river, for the purpose of exploring the defile through which he was finally to work his way.

He had found many articles of English make among the natives, showing that he was approaching the coast from which these must have been obtained. They had not, however, been brought there by traders, but had worked their way up from market to market along the river. The sight of them was encouraging to the members of the expedition who were getting worn out, while disease also prevailed to a large extent and threatened to increase. Still they might be a great way off from the coast yet, in time if not in distance, if they continued to make but one mile a day. Hence Stanley had to be very economical in everything, especially in the use of meat, though the constant and terrible mental and physical strain on him made it necessary that he should have the most nourishing food. For lack of this in a simple form, he concocted a dish out of vegetables, fruit and oil, which proved to him a great benefit.

CHAPTER XXV

EXPERIENCES BY THE WAY

It was the 29th of April when Stanley gave his last instructions to his Arab chiefs about getting the canoes down the mountain to Nzabi, the home of the next tribe west. On his way he entered a magnificent forest—the tall and shapely trees of which reminded him of his early wanderings in the wilds of Arkansas and on our western frontiers. It was not strange, while looking at them, that he should be reminded of the "dug-outs" of the Indians which he had so often seen, and that the thought should occur to him to make some canoes, to take the place of those which he had lost in the passage of the rapids and falls above. It seems as if his early life had prepared him especially for all the contingencies that were to occur in his long and varied explorations in Africa. After thinking the matter over a short time, he resolved that the boats should be built, and having obtained permission of the chief of the district, he at once commenced operations. The first tree selected was more than three feet in diameter and ran up sixty feet straight before it reached a limb. As soon as it was prone on the ground the men were set to work in sections upon it, and in a week it was finished. In a week more another was completed, measuring forty-five feet in length and eighteen inches deep. All this time the canoes were advancing over the land at the rate of a little more than a third of a mile a day, and finally they reached camp the day before the second boat was finished.

Things, however, had gone badly in the camp on the mountain-top after Stanley left, for the Arabs, following their apparently natural propensity, began to steal. One man, who had been caught in the act, was seized and made a prisoner by the natives who resolved to keep him as a slave. Stanley spent an entire day negotiating for his redemption, and finally had to give one hundred and fifty dollars' worth of cloth to get him released. It was plain that he could not afford to redeem many men at this price, and he distinctly told them that if after this any of them were caught stealing, they would be left in the hands of the natives, to be held as slaves for life. A terrible punishment, yet as it proved not great enough to deter them from committing the same crime afterwards, as opportunity offered.

The labor of the men engaged in hauling the canoes over the high mountain had been so great, that Stanley felt that some days of rest were demanded to recuperate them. But as idleness was always the fruitful source of all kinds of evil with the Arabs, he determined to keep the men who had hewed out the two boats still at work, and set them to making a third canoe.

The chief of this district now informed Stanley, greatly to his surprise and disappointment, that there were five falls immediately below him, while how many lay between these and the sea no one could tell. No matter; he must still move on, and, for the present, cling to the river on account of the sick, if for no other reason.

On the 18th, he sent off a man to get some axes repaired by a native blacksmith. While the latter was engaged in the work, a spark flew from the anvil against the body of one of his children playing near by, burning him slightly. The enraged man asserted that the accident was owing to a wicked charm of the stranger, and, running out, he beat the war-drum, at which the excited natives assembled in great fury, and the poor Arab was in danger of immediate immolation, when the chief happened to arrive and saved him.

On May 22d, the great teak canoe, the third which had been built, and which Stanley named Livingstone, was launched in the creek just above its entrance into the river amid the shouts of the natives. It could carry forty-six people. So far as means of transportation was concerned, Stanley was now at ease—but would there ever be a peaceful river on which these twelve canoes could float?

It was now the 22d of May, and since the 24th of February there had been forty rainy days, and hence for the month they had been working their slow, tedious way over the ridges and mountains, the river had been continually rising and now, more than eleven feet above its usual height, it was rolling in a grand, resistless flood through the gorges. Thunder and lightning had accompanied the storms, lighting up the wild river, drowning its fierce roar and drenching the wanderers, till it seemed as if heaven itself was leagued with the natives and the cataracts to drive them to despair and to destruction. The river was still rising, and the rush and roar of the waters were only less terrific than the deafening thunder-peels that shook the chasm in which they were confined. Still they must move on, even though it should be to greater horrors and more desperate conditions and a darker fate. So on the 23d of May they set out, and carrying around a short fall in the creek on the banks of which they had been encamping, and ascending a mountain, they pushed slowly on for three miles over a plateau—the sick and suffering complaining bitterly, while the well were almost ready to give out and die then and there on the shores of the river.

Every fall was expected to be the last, and yet each proved the forerunner only of a worse one to come.

From this creek Stanley led those of the expedition who could walk to the head of the Mowwa Falls. Frank, whose lame foot did not permit him to walk, took the Lady Alice, followed by the canoes, out of the mouth of the creek, to coast carefully along down the river to the same camping-place. In the meantime, Stanley, who had arrived first, took a long and anxious survey of the terrific scene before him. At the head of the falls, where he stood on a grassy plot, a ledge of rock twelve feet high ran straight across the river like a wall for a mile and a quarter and then stopped. From the end to the opposite shore it was a clear space of a little more than a quarter of a mile, through which the compressed river rushed with a strength and shout and fury that were appalling. This wall of rock, however, was not solid—here and there it was cut through as if by some mighty blow, making separate channels that had a fall of twelve feet. Below, as far as the eye could reach, treeless mountains arose nearly a mile into the heavens, while halfway up from the mad river, that tore with the sound of thunder along their bases, perpendicular cliffs stood walling in this awful embodiment of power.

A scene of more utter desolation cannot be imagined than was here presented to his view in this solitary spot. The camp seemed a mere speck amid these gigantic outlines of mountain and river. As he thus looked and listened, awe-struck and subdued, he saw Frank in the Lady Alice coming through the rapids at a terrific pace. This was the first time Frank had attempted such a feat, and he got confused, and was finally thrown into the worst part of the rapids, and in his frantic struggles to release himself, he struck a rock and stove a hole six inches square into the boat. However, all were landed in safety, though Stanley mourned greatly over the severe injury to his boat, which thus far had escaped all harm. It took him a whole day to repair it. Two days after, the goods were transferred below and the boats dropped carefully through the ledge near the shore, where the water was less rough, and reached the camp below the great falls in safety.

While resting here there occurred one of the most interesting scenes of this whole remarkable journey. In the transportation of goods over the mountains robberies of beads, etc., had been committed, and now the last man in the whole party Stanley would wish to have accused of theft was found guilty—the noble, brave, reliable and kind Uledi. True as steel in the hour of danger, quiet, obedient, thinking nothing of his life if Stanley asked him to risk it, he had yet stolen—not things of ordinary value, but that on which their very existence might depend. Cloth was getting so plenty among the natives that its value was very much decreased, but beads were worth ten times their weight in gold, and these Uledi had stolen and hidden in his mat. Of course this must be stooped at all hazards and at whatever sacrifice, still Stanley would almost as soon have lost his hand as to leave Uledi, as he had threatened he would the next man he caught stealing, in the hands of the savages as a slave forever. He therefore called the chiefs together and made them a speech, in which he clearly showed them that their lives depended on putting a stop to theft, for if they were left without anything to buy provisions with they all would inevitably perish of famine before they reached the sea. He also asked them what should be done with Uledi, on whom stolen goods had been found.

The principal chief would not answer for some time, but being urged to give his opinion said at last: It was very hard, seeing it was Uledi. Had it been anybody else he declared he would vote to pitch him into the river, but now he gave his vote for flogging. The rest of the chiefs concurred with him. Stanley then turned to the boat's crew, of which Uledi was coxswain and by whom he was dearly loved. The principal one and the most relied on, the watchman of the boat, replied, "Ah, it is a hard question, master. He is like our elder brother; but, as the fathers of the people have spoken, be it so; yet, for our sakes, master, beat him just a little." He next accosted Zaidi, by whose side Uledi had clung all night in the midst of the cataract, and had saved his life by risking his own. He replied, "Remember it is Uledi, master." Next he addressed Uledi's brother, who cried "Spare Uledi, but, if he must be flogged, give me half of it, I shall not feel it if it is for Uledi." Last of all he asked the poor culprit's cousin, when he replied in a speech that the London Athenæum, in quoting it, said would stand beside that of Jeanie Dean's when pleading for her sister. It occurred thus:

The poor fellow asked, "Will the master give his slave liberty to speak?" "Yes," replied Stanley. He then came forward, and kneeling before him and clasping his feet with his hands, said: "The master is wise. All things that happen he writes in a book. Each day there is something written. We black men know nothing, neither have we any memory. What we saw yesterday is to-day forgotten. Yet the master forgets nothing. Perhaps, if the master will look into his book, he may see something in it about Uledi. How Uledi behaved on Lake Tanganika; how he rescued Zaidi from the cataract; how he has saved many men, whose names I cannot remember, from the river—Bill Ali, Mabruki, Kom-kusi and others. How he worked harder on the canoe than any three men; how he has been the first to listen to your voice always; how he has been the father of the boat-boys. With Uledi, master, the boat-boys are good

192

and ready, without him they are nothing. Uledi is Shumari's brother. If Uledi is bad, Shumari is good. Uledi is my cousin. If, as the chiefs say, Uledi should be punished, Shumari says he will take half of the punishment; then give Saywa the other half, and set Uledi free. Saywa has spoken."

All this was uttered in a low, humble tone, with his head bowed to Stanley's feet. Stanley could not resist such an appeal, and said: "Very well, Uledi, by the voice of the people, is condemned; but as Shumari and Saywa have promised to take the punishment on themselves, Uledi is set free and Shumari and Saywa are pardoned." The moment the poor fellow was set free, he stepped forward and said: "Master, it was not Uledi who stole—it was the devil which entered into his heart."

This touching scene is given, not merely for its pathos, but because these untutored natives, here in the wilds of Africa, illustrated the principles that lie at the very foundation of the Christian religion. First, they recognized the great fundamental doctrine of atonement—of expiation—the suffering of the innocent in the place of the guilty, by which the offender can be pardoned. In the second place, Uledi uttered over again the sentiments of Paul— when a man's whole nature revolts at the wrong he has done, and hates himself for it, it is not he that commits it, but "sin that dwelleth in him," when he would do good, evil was present with him. It was a happy termination of the affair, for it would have been a cruel act to have had the noble, true, unselfish and brave Uledi suffer the indignity of a whip.

Another scene occurred, while in camp, that shows on what an insignificant, nay, ridiculous, thing the fate of a great expedition may turn. One day, Stanley being at leisure took out his note-book and began to write, as was his custom when he had a few hours to himself. The natives who flocked into camp in great numbers daily, noticed him and began to whisper among themselves. The crowd around him gradually increased and began to be strangely agitated, as the word "tara tara" passed from lip to lip, and presently, as if seized by a single impulse, they all ran away. Stanley merely observed the fact without stopping to think what the cause of this sudden abandonment of the camp might be. He therefore went on writing, when suddenly he was startled by loud war-cries ringing far and near over the mountain top, and, two hours after, he saw between five and six hundred natives fully armed rushing down the table-land toward the camp. He quickly mustered his men to be prepared for what seemed an unprovoked attack, but determined, if possible, to avoid a collision. He therefore advanced toward them as they drew near, and, sitting down on the ground, in a friendly tone asked what it all meant and why they had come in such a warlike manner to their friends. A large savage, acting as spokesman, replied that they had seen him make marks on some "tara tara." Those black lines he had drawn on paper, he said, would bring sickness and death and utter ruin on the land, and the people, and animals, unless the book containing them was burnt up.

Here was an unexpected dilemma. He must burn up that note-book or fight these five or six hundred armed, desperate savages. But that note-book, the gathered results of nearly three years of exploration, was the most precious thing on earth to him. He was astounded and sorely perplexed at the strange demand—burn up that note-book! He might as well burn up himself. Even if he could remember his main adventures, he could not recall all the observations, plans of maps and routes, and statistics of every kind it contained, and without which the whole expedition was a failure. No, he could not give it up, but what then—fight one against four, all armed with muskets, to retain it? Suppose he could put them to rout, it could not be done without a serious loss of life to himself as well as to them. But this was not the worst of it—with the natives friendly and aiding him as they had done, and supplying him with provisions, it would be almost a miracle if he ever reached the sea-shore; but with them hostile, even if he could fight his way through them, he would certainly perish from famine, for he could obtain no provisions, without which, he and the book would perish together. But, still, he could not give up that book, and he turned over in his mind every conceivable plan of averting the catastrophe. Finally, he told them to wait a moment, while, in the meantime, he stepped back to his tent as if to fetch it.

All at once it occurred to him that he might substitute another book for it, if, among his scant collection, he could find one at all resembling it. Turning them over, he came across a volume of Shakespeare of just about the same size. True the binding was different, but those savages knew as little of the peculiar binding of a book as they did of its contents. Besides it lay open on Stanley's knee when they saw it, and they observed only the black lines. However, the attempt to pass it off on these wild savages for the real book was worth making. So taking it in his hand, he walked back to where they stood with ferocious looks waiting for his decision, and handing it to them, told them to take it. No, they would not touch it, he must burn it. Well, Stanley said, he would do anything to please such good friends as they were. So together they went to a camp-fire near by, and solemnly consigned poor Shakespeare to the flames.

The natives were delighted at this evidence of Stanley's good-will, and became faster friends than ever. What he would have done

194

had it come to the issue—burn that note-book or fight—he does not tell us.

The river had been thoroughly explored for two miles below where they were encamped to the head of Zinga Falls. It was a rough, wild stretch of water, but it was thought it might be passed safely by using great caution and keeping out of the midstream rapids. At all events, Stanley had determined to try it first himself in his own boat—a resolution that nearly cost him his life. The next day, the 3d of June, the attempt was to be made, and Frank passed the evening in Stanley's tent in great spirits, talking and singing songs of merry old England. He was always singing, and most of the time religious songs which he had learned at home. The wilds of Africa had equalized these men, and they held sweet communion together this last night on the banks of the wild river. Frank seemed unusually exhilarated, little dreaming, alas, that the next night his lifeless body would be tossing amid the rocks that lined the bed of the fierce torrent below—his merry songs all hushed—nevermore to while away the weary hours in this dreary solitude of Africa or brighten the life of his England home.

CHAPTER XXVI

DEATH OF FRANK POCOKE

Frank Pocoke, as stated previously, joined the expedition under Stanley as a servant, and his brother had fallen at what proved to be the mere outset of the real main expedition, subsequently Frank, by his intelligence, geniality, ability and courage, and perhaps quite as much by the necessity of companionship that Stanley felt the need of in that wild region, and which only a white, civilized man could furnish, had risen above the position he had taken till Stanley looked upon him more as a friend than as a servant. This was natural; he was the only man he could talk with in English; the only man who had the taste and manners of civilized life; the only one who in the long halt could in any way be his companion; and, more than all, the only man who could certainly be depended on to stand by him in the hour of danger to the last, and fall, if fall they must, side by side. Whoever else might prove false in these vast untrodden solitudes, Frank Pocoke, he well knew, would not be one of them. Under such circumstances and conditions, Stanley would not have been the true man he is if he had not lifted the servant up to the place of a friend. It was therefore but natural that in the long mental discussion at Ziangwe as to whether he should return or choose some other route than through the hostile tribes whose territory the waters of the Lualaba washed, or push on at all hazards by following its current to the sea, that he should take his quondam servant into his confidence and they should together talk over all the probabilities of the different routes to be adopted. In another place we have shown what those difficulties were, and what the real or imaginable obstacles were that confronted Stanley if he determined to follow the Lualaba at all hazards to the sea.

In speaking of the death of young Pocoke, we wish to show what influence he had at last in fixing the determination that led to his own death and to Stanley's fame as an explorer. One day, while Stanley was discussing with Pocoke the wisest course to pursue, the latter said: "Mr. Stanley, suppose we toss up, to determine whether we shall follow the Lualaba as far as the Lowra, and then strike off for Monbruto, or follow it to the sea?"

Stanley, who had become almost indifferent as to whether one course or the other would end his life, agreed, and a toss-up was made, the result being on the side of following the river to the sea. The drawing of straws was then resorted to. Three trials of chances were made, and the decision of fate, as proposed by Pocoke, was to follow the river to the sea. He little thought that accidental toss was a toss-up for his own life, and that so trivial an affair settled his fate forever. We know what was Stanley's final decision, and though he does not acknowledge that this trial by chances had any effect on his final determination, the experience of human nature, since the world began, proves that it must have had. Even Napoleon, who believed that Providence was on the side of the strong battalions, had an equally strong belief in his "star." While it, doubtless, did have more or less influence on Stanley, it did not weaken his faith in the "strong battalions," which was, in his case, a wise provision, so far as he could make it, against all possible and probable contingencies.

We have said thus much to show the real relations that Frank Pocoke at last sustained to the expedition. In the long and terrible march through the gloomy forest after leaving Zywague, and before finally launching on the Lualaba, to quit it no more till they reached the sea or lay at rest forever on its solitary banks, Pocoke's shoes had become completely worn out. In traversing, half-barefoot, the tangled undergrowth, they had at last given out entirely, and the result was his feet became chafed, and at last, through constant irritation, caused by the necessity of hastening forward at all hazards, the abrasions that would have healed, could they have made a short halt, became ulcers, so that when they again struck the Lualaba he was unable to walk any farther, and Stanley said that if at any time they would have to leave the river and carry around rapids, Frank would have to be carried also. Stanley always led the way over the rapids and selected the paths for hauling around the canoes, while Pocoke superintended the soldiers, distributed the rations, etc. But now he was placed on the sick-list.

On the morning of the 3d of June, they came to the Mowwa Falls, around which they must carry and the men shouldered the goods and baggage and started overland for Zinga, three miles distant, while Stanley attempted to run two small falls, named Massesse and Massassa, with the boat's crew. Hugging the shore for about three-quarters of a mile, they came at last to a lofty cliff, against which the tide threw the down-rushing stream back in such fury that great whirlpools were formed and they steered for the centre of the river and endeavored to stem the tide, but failed. After fighting fiercely against the raging of whirlpools, they tried again to advance in another direction, when Stanley discovered that his boat was fast filling with water, while the surface became still more terribly agitated at a point toward which he had been unconsciously drifting. The danger now became imminent. Shouting to the men to leave off bailing and pull for life for the shore, he threw off his coat, belt and shoes, to be in readiness to swim when the boat should capsize, as he expected it would. A wild whirlpool was near the boat and for a moment it seemed certain that it would drift into the vortex. But by a strong effort it was forced away and they pulled for shore. By the time they had reached it, the leaky boat was half-full of water. Finding it impossible to proceed in it he returned to Mowwa Falls, and after a short rest took a canoe and tried to proceed. But while he was talking with Pocoke, the crew had scattered, and as those who had gone to Zinga had not returned, he determined to go overland and look after the goods, and leave to his chief captain, Manwa Sera, the supervision of the passage of the falls. He told him to first send forward a reserve canoe with short ropes fastened to the sides. "The crew," he said, "will pick their way carefully down the river until near the falls, then let the men judge for themselves whether they are able to take the canoe farther. Above all things stick to the shore and do not play with the river." He then bade Pocoke good-bye, saying he would send him his breakfast immediately with hammock bearers, shook hands and turned to climb the mountain toward the camp.

Sending back the breakfast as he had promised, he paid a visit to the kings of Zinga. Becoming anxious about the boats, as this was the first time he had ever permitted any one but himself to lead the way in any dangerous part of the river, he about three o'clock took his glass and going to the shore began to look up the river that came tearing out of the mountain like a wild animal and shaking the shores with its loud thunder. Suddenly he saw something black tossing amid the turbulent water. Scanning it closely, he saw it was an upturned canoe and to its sides several men were clinging. He instantly dispatched two chiefs and ten men to a bend toward which the wreck was drifting. The crew, however, knowing there was another cataract just below, attempted to right the boat and save themselves; but, unable to do so, got on the keel and began to paddle for dear life with their hands toward the shore. As they got near the far bank, he saw them jump off the boat and swim for shore. They had hardly reached it when the overturned boat shot by Stanley like an arrow and with one fierce leap dashed over the brink of the cataract and disappeared in the foam and tumult below. In a few minutes a messenger arrived out of breath, saying that eleven men were in that canoe, only eight of whom were saved—the other three being drowned, one of whom was Pocoke. Stanley turned fiercely on Uledi, his coxswain, and demanded how he came to let Pocoke, a lame man, go in the rescue canoe. "Ah, master," he replied, "we could not help it, he would not wait. He said, 'since the canoe is going to camp I will go too. I am hungry and cannot wait any longer. I cannot walk and I do not want you to carry me, that the natives may all laugh at me. No, I will go with you;' and refusing to listen to Captain Manwa Sera, who remonstrated with him, he got in and told us to cast off. We found no trouble in forcing our way against the back current. We struck the down current, and when we were near the fall I steered her into the cove to take a good look at it first. When I had climbed over the rocks and stood over it, I saw that it was a bad place—that it was useless to expect any canoe to go over it without capsizing, and I went to the little master and told him so. He would not believe me, but sent other men to report on it. They told the same story: that the fall could not be passed by shooting over it in a canoe. Then he said we were always afraid of a little water and that we were no men. 'All right,' I said, 'if you say cast off I am ready. I am not afraid of any water, but if anything happens my master will be angry with me.' 'Cast off,' the little master said, 'nothing will happen; am I not here?' You could not have counted ten, master, before we were all sorry. The cruel water caught us and tossed and whirled us about and shot us here and shot us there, and the noise was fearful. Suddenly the little master shouted 'Look out! take hold of the ropes! and he was tearing his shirt off when the canoe, which was whirling round and round with its bow in the air, was dragged down, down, down, until I thought my chest would burst; then we were shot out into daylight again and took some breath. The little master and two of the men were not to be seen, but soon I saw the little master with his face upward but insensible. I instantly struck out for him to save him, but we were both taken down again and the water seemed to be tearing my legs away; but I would not give in; I held my breath hard then and I came to the surface, but the little master was gone forever. This is my story, master." Stanley then examined the men separately, to ascertain if it were true and found it was. This man was brave but not foolhardy, and the best and most reliable in the whole party.

Stanley very briefly expressed the sadness and loneliness of his feelings that night as he sat and looked on the empty tent of young Pocoke, but no language can express the utter desolation of his situation. His position, surroundings, prospects, all combined to spread a pall black as midnight over his spirit and fill his heart with the gloomiest forebodings. Sitting alone in the heart of a country never before trod by the foot of a white man, on the banks of a mysterious river, on whose bosom he was to be borne he knew not where, the gloomy forest stretching away beyond him, the huts of strange natives behind him, the water in deep shadows rushing by, on whose foam and whirlpools his friend had gone down, and whose body then lay tossing amid the broken rocks, the strangely silent tropical sky, brilliant with stars, bending over him, the thoughts of home and friends far away caused a sad and solemn gathering of emotions and feelings around his heart till they rushed over it like that rushing water, and made him inconceivably sad there in the depths of the forest. With no one to talk to in his native tongue, no one to counsel with, without one friend on whom he could rely, left all alone to meet the unknown future, was to be left desolate indeed. Before, he knew there was one arm on which he always could lean, one stout, brave heart that would stand unflinchingly by his side in the deadliest peril, share all his dangers, and go cheerfully to the very gates of death with him. But now he was alone, with none but natives around him, with whom he must meet all the unknown dangers of the untrodden wilderness before him—perhaps be buried by them in the gloomy forest or left to be devoured by cannibals. It was enough to daunt the bravest spirit, appall the stoutest heart, and that lonely night on the banks of the Lualaba will live in Stanley's memory forever.

Stanley pronounced a high eulogium on his young friend, saying that he was a true African explorer—he seemed to like the dangers and even the sufferings of the expedition, so well did they harmonize with his adventurous spirit. Quick and resolute, he was always docile and in the heat and excitement of battle would obey Stanley's slightest wish with alacrity. He seemed fitted for an explorer; no danger daunted him, no obstacle discouraged him, while his frame, though slight, was tough and sinewy, and he was capable of undergoing any amount of labor and could endure the heaviest strain. He had so endeared himself to Stanley that the latter said, in a letter to young Pocoke's parents, that his death took away all the joy and exultation he should otherwise have felt in accomplishing the great task the two had undertaken together.

CHAPTER XXVII

THE COMPLETED WORK

The next morning Stanley arose with a sad and heavy heart; the cruel, relentless river seemed more remorseless than ever, and its waves flowed on with an angrier voice that seemed full of hate and defiance.

Eighty men were still behind, at Mowwa, and the next day word reached Stanley that they had mutinied, declaring they would follow the river no longer, for death was in it. He, borne down with his great loss, paid no attention to the report, and stayed and mourned for his friend for three days before he set out for Mowwa. He found the men sullen, sad and reckless. It would be strange, however, if he could not regain his old influence, which, after much effort, he did. But he did not get all down to Zinga till after four days. Meantime Frank's body had been found floating, face upward, some distance below the falls. All the canoes did not reach Zinga till the 19th, more than a fortnight after Frank's death.

On June 20th Stanley began to make preparations to continue on down the river. There had been terribly hard work in passing and getting round the falls where Frank lost his life, but the worst of it was, when they had succeeded, they seemed to have just begun their labors, for it had all to be repeated again. The men had lost all spirit and did not seem to care what became of them; and so, when on the 20th Stanley ordered the men to their work to lay brushwood along the tracks marked out for hauling the canoes from the Pocoke basin around Zinga point into the basin beyond, the men seemed disinclined to move. Stanley, in surprise, asked what was the matter. "We are tired of this," growled a burly fellow, "and that's what's the matter."

Stanley soon discovered that he was not alone in his opinion, and though once he would have quelled this spirit of rebellion with prompt, determined action, he did not feel like using harsh measures now, or even harsh language. He knew he had tasked them to the uttermost—that they had followed his bidding unquestioned so far as he ought to ask them, and so he called them together to talk with them and give them an opportunity frankly to tell their grievances. But they had nothing to say, except that they had gone far enough and did not mean to make another effort. Death and famine awaited them, and they might as well give up first as last. Stanley did not attempt even to appeal to them, except indirectly. He simply told them that he too was hungry, and could have had meat, but saved it for them. He too was weary and sad. They might leave him if they chose—he had his boat still, and if he was left alone he had but to step into it—the falls were near, and he would soon be at rest with his friend. It is most pitiful and sad to see how the indomitable will of this strong man had given way. The bold and confident manner with which he set out from Nyangwe— the healthy, cheery tone in which he addressed them when bowed down with grief at the farewell song of Tipo-tipo's Arabs are gone, and in their place had come a great weariness and despair. To see such a strong man forced at last to yield, awakens the deepest sympathy. No wonder he was weary of life, and longed to die. Under his terrible mental and physical strain of the last six months the toughest nature must give way, while to this was added the feebleness that comes from want of food and the utterly dreary, hopeless prospect before him. As he stood amid his dusky followers, his once sinewy frame looked lean and languid, and his voice had a weary, despairing tone. The star of fame that had led him on was gone down, and life itself had lost all its brightness, and when he had done speaking he turned away indifferent as to the future. The men listened, but their hungry, despairing hearts felt no sympathy. They too had reached the point of indifference as to the future, except they would no longer cling to that cruel river, and thirty-one packed their baggage and filed away up the ascent and were soon lost to view. When it was told to Stanley, he inquired how many had gone. Learning that only thirty-one had left, and that the rest would stand by him to the last, he roused himself, and unwilling that the faithful should perish through the disaffection of a few men he sent messengers after the deserters to plead with them to come back. They overtook them five miles away and urged them to return, but in vain. Setting the faithful to work, he dispatched two men to cut off the fugitives and to tell the chiefs not to let them pass through their territory. They obeyed and beat the war-drum, which so terrified the wanderers that they were glad to return. It would seem strange that men who have been accustomed to obey him implicitly for nearly three years, and had stood by him so staunchly in many a fight and through countless perils, could so easily desert him now. But despair will make even a wise man mad, and these poor creatures had got into that hopeless condition which makes all men reckless. Starting off with no definite aim in view, no point to travel toward, shows how desperate they had become. No wonder they saw no hope in clinging to the river, for they had now been over a month going three miles, and it seemed worse than useless to attempt to push further in that direction.

On the 23d of June, the work of hauling out the canoes to take them over a hill two hundred feet high was commenced, and by noon three were safely on the summit. Next came the Livingstone, which had been recently made. It weighed some three tons, yet, with the aid of a hundred and fifty natives, they had succeeded in getting it twenty feet up the bank, when the cables parted and it shot swiftly back into the river. The chief carpenter clung to it, and being carried beyond his depth, climbed into it. He was only a short distance above the falls when the brave Uledi, seeing his peril, plunged into the river and swimming to the boat, called out to him to leap overboard instantly. The poor wretch replied that he could not swim. "Jump," shouted Uledi, "you are drifting toward the cataract." The terrified creature, as he cowered in the canoe, faltered out, "I am afraid to." "Well, then," said Uledi, "you are lost—brother, good-bye," and struck out with all his might for the shore. A minute's longer delay, and he, too, would have been lost, for, though a strong swimmer, he was able, only by the most desperate effort, to reach shore less than sixty feet from the brink of the falls. The next minute the canoe was shooting over them into the boiling cauldron below. Tossed up and down and whirled about, it finally went down and was seen no more.

The next day the other boats were hauled up and then the process of letting them down commenced. This was done in safety, when the goods were sent overland to the Mbelo Falls beyond, while the boats should attempt to run the rapids There was no abrupt descent, but a wild waste of tumbling, roaring water dashing against the cliffs and rocks in reckless fury. Stanley resolved to try them before risking his men, and embarking in the Lady Alice, with men on shore holding cables attached to bow and stern, he drifted slowly downward amid the rocks. The little boat seemed a mere toy amid the awful surroundings in which it floated, and Stanley realized as it rocked beneath him what a helpless thing it would be in the wild and turbulent midstream. Just as he reached the most dangerous point, one of the cables parted. The boat swung to, when the other snapped asunder and the frightened thing was borne like a bubble into the boiling surge and carried downward like an arrow. Down, down, between the frowning precipices, now barely escaping a huge rock and now lifted like a feather on the top of a wave it swept on, apparently to certain destruction. But death had lost all its terrors to these hard-hunted men, and the six in the boat sat resigned to their fate. The brave Uledi, however, kept his hand on the helm and his steady eye on the hell of waters around and before them. Sometimes caught in a whirlpool that tossed them around and around, and then springing like a panther down a steep incline, the boat continued to plunge on its mad course with death on every side, until at last it shot into the Niguru basin, when they rowed to the sandy beach of Kilanga. Here, amid the rocks, they found the broken boat in which Pocoke went down, and the body of one of the men who was drowned with him jammed among the fragments.

Stanley looked back on this perilous ride with strange feelings. It seemed as if fate, while trying him to the utmost, was determined he should not perish, but that he should fulfill the great mission he had undertaken. His people seemed to think so too, for when they saw his boat break adrift and launch into the boiling rapids they gave him up for lost; but when they caught sight of him coming toward them alive and well, they gave way to extravagant joy and exclaimed, "it is the hand of God—we shall reach the sea." The escape was so wonderful, almost miraculous, that they could not but believe that God had spared him to save them all.

They now pushed on with little trouble to Mpakambendi, the terminus of the chasm ninety-three miles long, in which they had been struggling a hundred and seventeen days. This simple statement conveys very little to the ear, yet what fearful shapes does it conjure up to the imagination! Ninety-three miles of rapids and cataracts, with only here and there a stretch of smooth water! A mile and a quarter a day was all the progress they had made now for nearly four months. No wonder the poor Arabs gave up in despair and refused any longer to follow the river.

Although below the chasm the stream did not flow with that placidity it did through the cannibal region, still it did not present any dangerous rapids, as they glided on toward the sea with new hopes. The natives along the banks were friendly, though difficulties were constantly arising from the thieving propensities of the Arabs. Two were seized by the natives, and Stanley had nearly to bankrupt himself to redeem them, on which he gave the men a talk and told them plainly that this was positively the last time he would redeem a single prisoner seized for theft, nor would he resort to force to rescue him.

It was now the 7th day of July, and although hope had revived in the hearts of the people, some of the sick felt that they should never see their native island again. Two died this day and were buried on the banks of the river whose course they had followed so long. They now had clear, though not smooth sailing for some nine or ten miles, when they came to another fall. This was passed in safety, with the assistance of the natives, who assembled in great numbers and volunteered their services, for which they were liberally rewarded. More or less broken water was experienced, but not bad enough to arrest the progress of the boats. Provisions were getting scarce, and consequently the thieving propensity of the Arabs to obtain them more actively exhibited itself, and one man, caught while digging up roots in a garden, was held as a prisoner. The men asked his release, but Stanley, finding that the price which the natives asked for his redemption was far greater than his means to pay, would not interfere and the man was left to live and die in perpetual slavery. But this did not stop thieving, and soon another man was caught in the act and made prisoner. This case was submitted to the chiefs, and their decision was to let him remain in slavery. But the men were starving, and even this terrible exhibition of the doom that awaited them was not sufficient to deter the men from stealing food. The demands of the stomach overrode all fears of punishment, and three or four days after another man was detected and made a prisoner. He, too, was left a slave in the hands of the natives. Dangerous rapids were now and then encountered, but they were passed without accident, and Stanley at last found that he was close to the sea. He announced the fact to his people, who were intensely excited at the news. One man, a boatman, went crazy over it, and, shouting "we have reached the sea, we are at home," rushed into the woods and was never seen again. The poor wretch, probably, lay down at last in the forest, with the groves of Zanzibar, in imagination, just ahead of him. Sweeping downward, frequent rapids occurred, but the expedition kept on until it reached the district of Kilolo.

Stanley here lay down weary and hungry, but was aroused by musket-shots. His people, starving and desperate, had scattered about, entering every garden they saw to get something to eat, and the natives had attacked them. Soon wounded men were brought in, whom the natives had shot. Several had been captured whom Stanley refused to redeem, and they were left to pine in endless captivity, never again to see the hills of Zanzibar, as he over and over again had promised they should.

Changing from bank to bank, as the character of the river changed, the expedition, on the 30th of July, heard in advance the roar of the cataract of Isingila. Here Stanley ascertained that they were but five days' journey from Embomma, a distance always traveled by land by the natives, on account of the obstructions in the river.

As the whole object of the expedition had been accomplished and the short distance beyond these falls to the sea was known to Europeans, he resolved to leave the river and march by land to Embomma. At sunset the Lady Alice was drawn out of the water to the top of some rocks and abandoned forever. To Stanley it was like leaving a friend behind. The boat had been his companion for nearly three years. It had carried him over the waters of the lakes, dashed at his bidding among hostile canoes, rocked him to sleep amid the storms, borne him all safely over foaming cataracts, and now it must be left ignobly to rot in the wilds of Africa. As he turned to cast a last farewell glance on it resting mournfully on the rocks, the poor boat had almost a human look, as if it knew it was to be left behind and abandoned forever.

On the 1st of August, the famished, weary column took up its line of march towards the sea—the mothers carrying infants that had been born amid the cataracts, and the larger children trudging slowly after. Nearly forty of the one hundred and fifteen were sick, and though it was painful to travel, they were cheered by the promise that in four or five days they should once more look on the sea, towards which their longing hearts had been turned for so many weary months. Coming to a village, the king stopped them and told them they could not pass without they gave him a bottle of rum. Uledi, hastening up, asked Stanley what the old man wanted. "Rum," he replied. Hitting him a severe slap in the face, "there is rum for him," growled Uledi, as the drunken negro tumbled over. The latter picked himself up and hurried away, and Stanley and his worn and wasted band passed on without further molestation. It was hard to get food, for one party would demand rum and refuse to furnish it without, while another wanted them to wait till the next market-day.

On the third day they reached Nsanda, the king of which told Stanley it was but three days' march to the sea. The latter asked him if he would carry a letter to Embomma for him. He replied no, but after four hours of hard urging he agreed to furnish guides for three of Stanley's men.

The next day they set out, carrying the following letter:—

Village Nsanda, August 4th, 1877.

To any gentleman who speaks English at Embomma:

Dear Sir: I have arrived at this place from Zanzibar with one hundred and fifteen souls, men, women and children. We are now in a state of imminent starvation. We can buy nothing from the natives, for they laugh at our kinds of cloth, beads and wire. There are no provisions in the country that may be purchased except on market-days, and starving people cannot afford to wait for these markets. I therefore have made bold to dispatch three of my young men, natives of Zanzibar, with a boy named Robert Ferugi of the English mission at Zanzibar, with this letter, craving relief from you. I do not know you, but I am told there is an Englishman at Embomma, and as you are a Christian and a gentleman, I beg of you not to disregard my request. The boy Robert will be better able to describe our condition than I can tell you in a letter. We are in a state of the greatest distress, but, if your supplies arrive in time, I may be able to reach Embomma in four days. I want three hundred cloths, each four yards long, of such quality as you trade with, which is very different from that we have; but better than all would be ten or fifteen man-loads of rice or grain to fill their pinched bellies immediately, as even with the cloths it would require time to purchase food, and starving men cannot wait. The supplies must arrive within two days, or I may have a fearful time of it among the dying. Of course I hold myself responsible for any expense you may incur in this business. What is wanted is immediate relief, and I pray you to use your utmost energies to forward it at once. For myself if you have such little luxuries as tea, coffee, sugar and biscuits by you, such as one man can easily carry, I beg you, on my own behalf, that you will send a small supply, and add to the great debt of gratitude due to you upon the timely arrival of supplies for my people. Until that time, I beg you to believe me,

Yours, sincerely,

H. M. Stanley,
Commanding Anglo-American Expedition,
for Exploration of Africa.

P. S.—You may not know my name; I therefore add, I am the person that discovered Livingstone.

H. M. S.

After writing this letter, Stanley called his chiefs and boat's crew to his tent and told them of his purpose to send a letter to Embomma for relief, and wanted to know which were the most reliable men—would travel fastest and least likely to be arrested or turned back by obstacles. The ever-ready Uledi sprang to his feet and exclaimed, as he tightened his belt, "O master, I am ready now!" The other volunteers responded as quickly, and the next day, the guides appearing, they started off. In the meantime, the expedition resumed its slow march, having eaten nothing but a few nuts to stay their stomachs. Coming to a village, the chief demanded payment for passing through his country, and armed his followers; but on Stanley threatening to destroy every man in the place, his rage subsided, he shook hands, and peace was made and sealed by a drink of palm wine and the promise of a bottle of rum.

In the meanwhile, Uledi and his companions pressed swiftly on, but when about halfway the guides, becoming frightened, deserted them. Unable to obtain others, they resolved to follow the Congo. All day long they pressed steadily forward, and, just after sunset, reached Boma, to which the name Embomma had been changed, and delivered the letter. The poor fellows had not tasted food for thirty hours, and were well-nigh famished. They soon had abundance, and the next morning (August 6th), while Stanley was leading on his bloated, haggard, half-starved, staggering men, women and children, Uledi started back with carriers loaded down with provisions.

At nine o'clock, the expedition had to stop and rest. While they lay scattered about on the green sward, suddenly an Arab boy shouted, "I see Uledi coming down the hill!" and sure enough there were Uledi and Kacheche leaping down the slope and waving their arms in the air. "La il Allah, il Allah!" went up in one wild shout—"we are saved, thank God!" Uledi had brought a letter to Stanley, who had scarcely finished reading it when the carriers appeared in sight laden with provisions. The sick and lame struggled to their feet and, with the others, pressed around them. While Stanley was distributing them, one of the boat-boys struck up a triumphant song, that echoed far over the plain. They then set to and ate as only starving men can eat.

When all were supplied, Stanley turned to his tent, to open the private packages sent to him. Heavens! what a vision met his astonished sight! A few hours before, he had made his breakfast on a few green bananas and peanuts, washed with a cup of muddy water, and now before him were piled champagne, port and sherry wines, and ale, and bread and butter, and tea, and sugar, and plum-pudding, and various kinds of jam—in short, enough luxuries to supply half a regiment. How Stanley felt that night as he looked on his happy, contented followers, may be gathered from the following extract from a letter he sent back next day to his kind-hearted deliverers. After acknowledging the reception of the bountiful supplies, he says:

"*Dear Sirs—Though strangers I feel we shall be great friends, and it will be the study of my lifetime to remember my feelings of gratefulness when I first caught sight of your supplies, and my poor faithful and brave people cried out, 'Master, we are saved—food is coming!' The old and the young men, the women and the children lifted their wearied and worn-out frames and began lustily to chant an extemporaneous song in honor of the white people by the great salt sea (the Atlantic), who had listened to their prayers. I had to rush to my tent to hide the tears that would come, despite all my attempts at composure.*

"*Gentlemen, that the blessing of God may attend your footsteps, whithersoever you go, is the very earnest prayer of*
"*Yours faithfully,*
"*Henry M. Stanley.*"

That day was given up to feasting and rejoicing, and the next morning—a very different set of men—they started forward. All this and the next day they marched cheerfully over the rolling country, and on the third, while slowly descending a hill, they saw a string of hammocks approaching, and soon Stanley stood face to face with four white men, and so long had he been shut up in a country of blacks that they impressed him strangely. After some time spent in conversation they insisted on his getting into a hammock, and borne by eight stout bearers he was carried into Boma, where rest and abundance awaited him. He stayed in this village of a hundred huts only one day and then embarked on a steamer for the mouth of the river, a hundred or more miles away. Turning northward he reached Kabinda, where one of the expedition died. The reaction on these poor creatures after their long and desperate struggle was great, and they fell back into a sort of stupor. Stanley himself felt its influence and would fall asleep while eating. The sense of responsibility, however, aroused him and he attempted in turn to arouse his men. But, notwithstanding all his efforts, four died of this malady without a name after he reached Loanda, and three more afterwards on board the vessel that carried them to Cape Town.

Stanley gave his poor followers eight days' rest at Kabinda and then in a Portuguese vessel proceeded to Loanda. Here the governor-general offered to send him in a gun-boat to Lisbon. This generous offer was very tempting, and many would have accepted it, but Stanley would not leave his Arab friends who had shared his toils and hardships, and shown an unbounded trust in his promise to see them back to Zanzibar. A passage being offered them in the British ship Industry, to Cape Town, Stanley accepted it, and, instead of going home where comfort and fame awaited him, turned southward with his Arab followers. At Cape Town he was received with every mark of distinction, and delivered a lecture there giving a brief account of the expedition, especially that part of it relating to the Congo. A British vessel here was placed at his disposal, and while she was refitting Stanley gave his astonished Arabs a ride on a railroad, on which they were whirled along at the rate of thirty miles an hour. Of all the wonders they had seen since they left Zanzibar, nearly three years before, this was the greatest. Entertainments were prepared for them, suitable garments for that cold latitude provided, till these poor, simple children of nature were made dizzy by the attentions they received. Among other things a special evening was set apart for them in the theatre, and they were thrown into raptures at the performance of the acrobats and made the building ring with their wild Arab shouts of approval.

At length, on the 6th of November, nearly two months from the time they reached the Atlantic coast, they set sail for Zanzibar. Stopping for two days at Natal to coal, where every possible attention was lavished on them, they again put to sea and stretched northward through the Indian Ocean.

Day after day these now contented people lay around on deck, drinking in health from the salt sea air. All but one was shaking off every form of disease contracted in their long wanderings. This one was a woman who was slowly dying, and who was kept alive alone by the thought of seeing her home once more. At last the hills of Zanzibar arose over the sea, and as these untutored Arabs traced their well-known outline, their joy was unbounded, and Stanley felt repaid for the self-denial that had refused a passage home from Loanda to stay by his faithful followers to the very last. Their excitement increased as the caves and inlets grew more distinct, and at last the cocoanut and mangrove-trees became visible. As the vessel entered port their impatience could not be restrained, and the captain of the vessel, sympathizing with their feelings, had no sooner dropped anchor than he manned the boats, while the eager creatures crowded the gangway and ladder, each struggling to be the first to set foot on their native island. As boat-load after boat-load reached the shore, with a common feeling they knelt on the beach and cried "Allah!" and offered up their humble thanksgiving to God, who had brought them safely back to their homes.

The news of their arrival spread like wild-fire on every side, and soon their relatives and friends came flocking in from all directions, and glad shouts, and wild embracings, and floods of glad tears made a scene that stirred Stanley's heart to its profoundest depths. Still, there was a dark side to the picture. Scores of those that came rushing forward to greet them, fell back shedding tears, not of gladness, but of sorrow, for they found not those whom they fondly hoped to meet. Of the three hundred that had set out, nearly thee years before, only one hundred and twelve were left—and one of these, the poor sick woman, lived only long enough to be clasped in her father's arms, when she died.

The great journey was ended, and Stanley, after paying off the living and the relatives of the dead, at last started for home. As he was about to enter the boat that was to bear him to the ship, the brave Uledi and the chiefs shoved it from shore, and seizing Stanley, bore him through the surf on their shoulders. And when the latter stood on the deck, as the vessel slowly steamed away, the last object he saw on shore through his eyes filled with tears, was his Arab friends watching him till he should disappear from sight.

An enthusiastic reception awaited him in England, while from every part of the continent distinguished honors were bestowed upon him.

He had performed one of the most daring marches on record—traced out, foot by foot, one of the largest lakes of Central Africa, followed its mightiest river, which, from the creation, had been wrapped in mystery, from its source to its mouth, and made a new map of the "dark continent."

Among the testimonials of the estimation in which the great work he had accomplished was held, may be mentioned the gift of the portrait of King Humbert of Italy, by himself, with the superscription:

"ALL' INTREPEDO VIAGGATORE,
ENRICO STANLEY.
UMBERTO RE.

TO THE INTREPID TRAVELER,
HENRY STANLEY.
KING HUMBERT."

The Prince of Wales also complimented him warmly on his achievements, while the Khedive of Egypt conferred on him the high distinction of the Grand Commandership of the Order of Medjidie, with the star and collar. The Royal Geographical Society, of London, gave him a public reception, and made him Honorary Corresponding Member, and the Geographical Societies and Chambers of Commerce of Paris, Italy and Marseilles sent him medals. He was also made Honorary Member of the Geographical Societies of Antwerp, Berlin, Bordeaux, Bremen, Hamburg, Lyons, Marseilles, Montpelier, Vienna, etc., etc. Honorary membership of almost every distinguished society in England and on the continent were conferred on him, and all seemed to vie with each other in heaping honors on the most intrepid traveler of modern times.

As Americans, however, it gives us great pleasure to record the following sentiment, showing that Stanley takes especial pride in being an American. He says: "For another honor I have to express my thanks—one which I may be pardoned for regarding as more precious than all the rest. The Government of the United States has crowned my success with its official approval, and the unanimous vote of thanks passed in both houses of legislature, has made me proud for life of the expedition and its success."

CHAPTER XXVIII

THE FRUITS OF VICTORY

After victory, the fruits of victory; and to secure the latter is often more difficult than to win the former. The soldier may conquer a realm; it requires the statesman to organize and establish sovereignty. We may be entranced with enthusiasm at the daring of the explorer; we must bow with respect to the man who transformed a wilderness into a peaceful field of industry and commerce. Doubtless, at the end of his great Congo campaign, in 1878, Mr. Stanley longed for rest and home. Up to that time all his life had been a wandering, chiefly amid dangers and discomforts. He had written his name among those of the world's foremost explorers. Well might he have considered his task accomplished, and have turned his way toward scenes of rest and pleasure. Instead of that, all these great deeds were but the prelude to his real life-work.

Early in November, 1878, Mr. Stanley was invited by Leopold, King of the Belgians, to visit the royal palace at Brussels, on a certain day and at a certain hour. He went. He found assembled to meet him a large number of persons of note from all parts of the world, mostly men interested in commerce and finance. The object of the meeting was to promote the enterprise of studying what might best be done with the Congo River and its vast basin. Mr. Stanley was to tell them of the country, and they were to consider how to open it up to trade and civilization. "I have," said the explorer, "passed through a land watered by the largest river of the African continent, and that land knows no owner. A word to the wise is sufficient. You have cloths and hardware, and glassware and gunpowder, and those millions of natives have ivory and gums and rubber and dyestuffs, and in barter there is good profit!"

This was a tempting prospect, and a course of action was soon fixed upon. A company was formed, one hundred thousand dollars capital was subscribed on the spot, and Mr. Stanley was commissioned to organize, equip and lead an expedition. He was to open up a road through the Congo country to the heart of Africa. He was to erect stations, according to the means furnished, along the overland route for the convenience of the transport and the European staff in charge, and to establish steam communication wherever available and safe. The stations were to be commodious, and sufficient for all demands that were likely to be made on them. Ground was to be leased or purchased adjoining the stations, so as to make them in time self-supporting. Land along each side of the route was also to be secured, to prevent persons ill-disposed toward the company from interfering with its plans. The whole scheme was founded on the ideas of peace and equity. The expedition was to make its way by paying, not by fighting.

Mr. Stanley went to work promptly and energetically. This meeting was held on November 25th. The directors of the enterprise met again on December 9th. On January 2d, 1879, Mr. Stanley laid before them plans and estimates for the first six months' work, and on January 23d he was on his way to Zanzibar. It was, of course, desirable to have experienced men associated with him, so he sought out as many of his old comrades as possible. In that work some time was spent, but in the latter part of May he left Zanzibar in the steamer "Albion," which had been chartered for the use of the expedition. He had with him sixty-eight men, recruited at Zanzibar, of whom forty-five had accompanied him on his former journey down the Congo. At nine o'clock in the morning of August 14th he sighted land at the mouth of the Congo, and soon after was at anchor near the Dutch settlement at Banana Point. Here he met, for the first time, the other officers chosen to go with him on the expedition. There were one American, two Englishmen, two Danes, five Belgians, and one Frenchman. In the harbor was a small fleet of steamers intended for the expedition, and on shore was a considerable store of goods for bartering with the natives.

On August 21st, seven days after Mr. Stanley's arrival at Banana, the vessels of the expedition, consisting of the "Albion" and eight other craft of various sizes (the largest being the steel twin screw steamer "La Belgique," sixty-five feet long and eleven feet beam; and the smallest the "Jeune Africaine," a screw launch, twenty-five feet long and five feet ten inches beam) steamed out of Banana Haven, and began the ascent of the noble river. Boma, once the horrible emporium of the slave-trade, was reached after a sail of eight days; a depot was formed at Mussuko, four hours higher up the stream on the south bank; and the "Albion," after making one or two trips between Mussuko and Banana Point, in order to bring up the goods which had been left behind, was released from river duty, taken down to Banana Point, coaled, and sent home, on September 17th.

So far, all had gone well. In thirty-four days it had reached its first base of operations, ninety miles from the sea. All its supplies had been brought hither in safety, and the outlook for the future was promising. Soon after the departure of the "Albion" steps were taken to advance still further up-stream, and the next station was made at Vivi. This was six hours' sail in a nine-knot steamer above Boma. The site was carefully chosen, and Vivi has since become the most important station on the river. But before Mr. Stanley could commence operations in September, 1879, a palaver had to be held, and terms required to be arranged with the neighboring chiefs, of whom there were five. At the palaver the five chiefs formed a somewhat motley group. The introductions being over, the object of the expedition was explained through the medium of a lingster or interpreter; proposals were made on the part of the association; and the chiefs, after begging a bottle of gin apiece, returned to their houses to consider what the Mundelé, or trader, as Mr. Stanley was now called, had said to them.

On the following day they returned, and as the conference which followed was, in its general features, similar to many others that were held, we may as well use Mr. Stanley's description of it:—

"The conference began by the lingster, Massala, describing how the chiefs had gone home and consulted together for a long time; they had agreed that if the Mundelé would stay with them, that of all the land unoccupied by villages, or fields and gardens, I should make my choice, and build as many houses, and make as many roads, and do any kind of work I liked; that I should be considered as the 'Mundelé' of Vivi, and no other white man should put foot on Vivi soil, which stretched from the Lufû up to the Banza Kulu district, and inland down to the Loa river, without permission from me; no native chief of inland or riverside should molest any man in my employ within the district of Vivi; help should be given for work, and the people of Vivi, such as liked, should engage themselves as workmen; anybody, white or black, native or foreign, passing to and fro through the land, should do so freely, night and day, without let or hindrance; if any disagreement should arise between any of my people, white or black, and the people of Vivi, they, the chiefs, would promise not to try and revenge themselves, but bring their complaint before the Mundelé of Vivi, that he might decide upon the right and the wrong of it; and if any of their people were caught in the act of doing wrong, then the white man shall promise that his chief shall be called to hear the case against him, and if the crime is proved the chief shall pay the fine according to custom.

"'All this,' continued Massala, 'shall be set down in writing, and you shall read it, and the English lingster shall tell it straight to us. But first we must settle what the chiefs shall receive in return for these concessions.'"

This was not so easily settled. Four hours were spent before the bargain was concluded, and Mr. Stanley found himself obliged to pay one hundred and sixty dollars down in cloth and a rental of ten dollars per month. The papers confirming the agreement were then drawn up in due form, and signed by the various parties concerned in the matter.

Mr. Stanley, as "Mundelé of Vivi," had no good reason to congratulate himself upon his bargain. He had, of course, secured a site for his station, but he had been compelled to pay a big price for it, and his land was a mere wilderness of rocky and barren hillsides. All the really good land at Vivi was already occupied, and the natives would not part with it. On the evening of the day on which his contract was signed he wrote in his diary: "I am not altogether pleased with my purchase. It has been most expensive, in the first place, and the rent is high. However, necessity has compelled me to do it. It is the highest point of navigation of the Congo, opposite which a landing could be effected. The landing-place is scarcely three hundred yards long, but if the shores were improved by leveling, available room for ships could be found for fifteen hundred yards." On the plateau near the river was room for a town of twenty thousand people, and the situation seemed salubrious. So a road was made up to the plateau, buildings erected, and a large quantity of goods brought up from Mussuko, and safely housed.

So far the expedition had had plain sailing. The Congo affords a magnificent waterway from the ocean, at Banana, up to Vivi. But a little distance above Vivi are the Livingstone Falls, rendering further navigation impossible. It was therefore necessary to build a road and make further progress overland. So work was begun on a new road, from Vivi to Isangila, fifty-two miles above, which had been chosen as the site of the next station. The country was wild and rugged, and ruled by thirty or forty different chiefs. Each of these chiefs had to be negotiated with and won over, and each in his own way. Moreover, the individual owners of farms and gardens had to be dealt with, and often paid exorbitant prices for their land. Surveying the route was a long and toilsome job. The work of clearing and grading would have been stupendous had it been designed merely to make it a wagon-road. But it was to be more than that. It was to be a road over which several of the steamboats could be transported, to be relaunched on the river above the falls. Mr. Stanley never faltered, however, and at noon of March 18th, 1880, the work of making the road was begun. On January 2d, 1881, within ten months from the actual beginning of the work, the road, fifty-two miles in length, was completed, the boats were on the shore at Isangila waiting to be repaired, scraped, and painted, and the "Royal," a small screw steamer presented to the expedition by the King of the Belgians, was steaming on the river.

From Isangila there was smooth navigation up-stream for eighty-eight miles, to the Falls of Ntombo Mataka. Adjoining the latter is the district of Manyanga, where Mr. Stanley decided to erect the next station, and on May 1st, 1881, the whole expedition was safely encamped there. Of his achievements thus far Mr. Stanley speaks thus: "We were now one hundred and forty miles above Vivi, to accomplish which distance we have been employed four hundred and thirty-six days in road-making and in conveying fifty tons of goods, with a force of sixty-eight Zanzibaris and an equal number of West Coast and inland natives. During this period we had travelled four thousand eight hundred and sixteen English miles, which, divided by the number of days occupied in this heavy transport work, gives a quotient of over eleven miles per day!"

This expedition was intended to reach, as its farthest point, Stanley Pool, which was still ninety-five miles away, and every mile was full of difficulties. The river was not navigable, so an overland road had to be surveyed, "palavered" for, purchased and built, and the boats dragged over it. Worse still, Mr. Stanley was stricken down with fever, and for a long time lay on the brink of the grave. But even from his sick-bed he continued to direct affairs and to inspire his followers with his own unshaken faith in the success of the enterprise. So, by December 3d, 1881, the expedition was safe at Stanley Pool with the steamer "En Avant" launched in the Bay of Kintamo, beyond which were thousands of miles of navigable water. The new station was founded on Leopold Hill, a fine site overlooking the river, and was named Leopoldville, in honor of the royal patron of the enterprise. Doubtless this place will become the chief centre of Central African commerce. Its situation is magnificent. The climate is salubrious. The surrounding natives are friendly. Other stations have since been founded, further up the river, all tributary to Leopoldville. The most distant of them is on the island of Wané Rusari, at the foot of Stanley Falls, one thousand and sixty-eight miles from Leopoldville.

CHAPTER XXIX

THE CONGO FREE STATE

Mr. Stanley's discoveries, and the enterprise of the "Committee for the Study of the Upper Congo"—which was the real name of the company under which he was sent out—soon attracted universal attention, and that, too, of a most practical kind. It became evident that the Congo Valley must have a fixed and potent government. King Leopold did not desire to assume the sole responsibility, nor, indeed, would the other European powers have agreed to his transform so large a slice of the African continent into a Belgian colony. Accordingly, an international conference was summoned to meet at Berlin, and the result of its deliberations was the erection of the entire valley into a potentially independent commonwealth, called the Congo Free State. On February 25th, 1885, treaty was signed by the representatives of the United States and the chief European powers. A Constitution and Government were provided for the new state, with King Leopold at its head, under the protection of the treaty-signing powers. Thenceforward civilization made rapid progress. The state was admitted to the International Postal Union, and post-offices were opened at

Banana, Boma, Vivi, and elsewhere. Courts, schools, etc., were also established. A railroad has been constructed over the route of Mr. Stanley's roads around the cataracts, connecting with the steamer routes, and making an unbroken line of steam transportation from Stanley Falls to the Atlantic Ocean.

The entire area of the Congo basin is estimated by Mr. Stanley at one million five hundred and eight thousand square miles. Some of it is claimed by France, some by Portugal, and some is yet unapportioned. But the overwhelming bulk, one million sixty-five thousand and two hundred square miles, belongs to the Congo Free State. It has not all yet been surveyed, of course, but its character is pretty well known. It has vast forests, extensive and fertile plains, and unsurpassed systems of lakes and rivers. Its lakes cover thirty-one thousand seven hundred square miles; among them being Lakes Leopold II., Muta Nzige, Tanganyika, Bangweola, and Mweru. The Congo, of course, is the principal river. It is one of the five or six longest streams in the world, and in point of volume surpasses all but the Amazon.

Unlike the Amazon, Mississippi, Nile, Ganges, Volga, and, indeed, almost all other great rivers, the Congo has no delta. It discharges itself by a single unbroken estuary seven miles and a half broad, in many places over two hundred fathoms deep, and with a current of from five to seven knots an hour. The volume of water brought down has been variously estimated; the lowest estimate being two million cubic feet per second. The Mississippi, when at the height of its March flood, has an outflow of one million one hundred and fifty thousand cubic feet per second; so that its volume must be very greatly exceeded by that of the Congo.

The scenery along the banks of the Congo is affirmed by all who have seen it to be magnificent. Mr. Stanley has seen none to equal it. In his opinion neither the Indus nor the Ganges, the Nile nor the Niger, nor any of the rivers of North or South America has any glories of mountain or foliage or sunlight which are not greatly excelled by those of his favorite river, and many of the finest passages in his volumes are devoted to descriptions of the beauty and magnificence seen along its banks.

The population of the Free State of the Congo Mr. Stanley estimates at about forty-five millions. According to the latest trustworthy calculations, the population of the whole of Africa is represented by two hundred millions. Some place it at one hundred and seventy millions. The data on which these calculations are based are, of course, imperfect, and Mr. Stanley's seem to have been based chiefly upon the density of population he found on the banks of the upper Congo. But in other parts, and especially away from the rivers, there must be large tracts of country where the population is much less dense than it is along the banks of the Congo, and any generalization for the whole of the country, based upon the latter, must manifestly give too high a figure.

Of the climate of the country, Mr. Stanley is entitled to speak with authority, and justly, as no European has had so large an experience of it. With care as to food, clothing, and exposure, Europeans, it would seem, may live as long, and enjoy as good health on the banks of the Congo as they may in most other places. But care is absolutely requisite; without it the climate proves as hurtful as the climate of the west coast of Africa is generally said to be.

As a field for commerce, Mr. Stanley speaks of the country in the most glowing terms, and believes that it excels all other known lands for the number and rare variety of precious gifts with which nature has endowed it. He says: "The forests on the banks of the Congo are filled with precious redwood, lignum vitæ, mahogany, and fragrant gum-trees. At their base may be found inexhaustible quantities of fossil gum, with which the carriages and furniture of civilized countries are varnished; their boles exude myrrh and frankincense; their foliage is draped with orchilla-weed, useful for dye. The redwood, when cut down, chipped and rasped, produces a deep crimson powder, giving a valuable coloring; the creepers, which hang in festoons from tree to tree, are generally those from which india-rubber is produced (the best of which is worth fifty cents per lb.); the nuts of the oil palm give forth a butter, a staple article of commerce; while the fibres of others will make the best cordage. Among the wild shrubs is frequently found the coffee-plant. In its plains, jungle, and swamp luxuriate the elephants, whose tusk furnishes ivory worth from $2.00 to $2.75 per lb.; its waters teem with numberless herds of hippopotami, whose tusks are also valuable; furs of the lion, leopard, monkey, otter; hides of antelope, buffalo, goat, cattle, etc., may also be obtained. But, what is of far more value, it possesses over forty millions of moderately industrious and workable people. The copper of Lake Superior is rivaled by that of the Kwilu-Niadi Valley, and of Bembé. Rice, cotton, tobacco, maize, coffee, sugar, and wheat would thrive equally well in the broad plains of the Congo. I have heard of gold and silver, but this statement requires corroboration, and I am not disposed to touch upon what I do not personally know. A large portion of the Congo basin, at present inaccessible to the immigrant, is blessed with a temperature under which Europeans may thrive and multiply. There is no portion of it where the European trader may not fix his residence for years, and develop commerce to his own profit with as little risk as is incurred in India."

Such is the country which the skill, tact, courage, and, in brief, the genius of Mr. Stanley have rescued from the degradation and barbarism of ages, and given a place among the great nations of the world. It is his fame to have been not merely an intrepid explorer, not merely a peaceful and almost bloodless conqueror, but in fully equal measure a civilizer, a trade-bearer, a statesman; the finder, the founder, and the builder of a great and mighty state.

CHAPTER XXX

EMIN, THE LAST OF THE SOUDAN HEROES

Mr. Stanley returned to civilization, and in 1886 revisited America for the first time in thirteen years. He was received with the highest honors, and the lectures which he delivered were attended by crowded and delighted audiences. It seemed at last as though he were to enjoy a considerable period of rest. He had opened up the Dark Continent, and founded the Congo Free State on a secure basis. He might now direct its operations from London or Brussels, and spend his years in well-won ease. But this was not to be. He was abruptly summoned to undertake one of the most arduous of all his tasks, which was to lead an expedition to the relief of Emin Pasha at Wadelai, on the Nile.

The history of Emin Pasha is a most romantic and noble one. His real name is Edward Schnitzer, and he was born in 1840 at Oppeln, in Silesia. His father, a merchant, died in 1845, and three years before that date the family removed to Neisse. When Edward Schnitzer had passed through the gymnasium at Neisse he devoted himself to the study of medicine at the University of Breslau. During the years 1863 and 1864 he pursued his studies at the Berlin Academy. The desire for adventure and an exceptional taste for natural sciences induced the young medical student to seek a field for his calling abroad. He, therefore, at the end of 1864, left Berlin with the intention of obtaining a post of physician in Turkey. Chance carried him to Antivari and then to Scutari. Here he soon managed to attract the attention of Valis Ismael Pasha Haggi, and was received into the following of that dignitary, who, in his official position, had to travel through the various provinces of the empire. When, in this way, Dr. Schnitzer had learned to know Armenians, Syrians, and Arabians, he finally reached Constantinople, where the Pasha died in 1873. In the summer of 1875 Dr. Schnitzer returned to Neisse; but after a few months the old passion for travel again came over him, and he betook himself to Egypt, where favorable prospects were opened out to him. With the beginning of the year 1876 he appears as "Dr. Emin Effendi," enters the Egyptian service, and places himself at the disposal of the Governor-General of the Soudan. In the post there given him Dr. Emin met with Gordon, who two years before (1874) had been intrusted with the administration of the newly-created Equatorial province. Gordon sent him on tours of inspection through the territory and on repeated missions to King M'tesa at Uganda. When Gordon Pasha, two years later, became administrator of all territory lying outside the narrower limits of Egypt, Dr. Emin Effendi received the post of commander at Lado, together with the government of the Equatorial province. With how much fidelity and self-denial he devoted himself to his task is well known.

During the first three years of his term he drove out the slave-traders from a populous region with six million inhabitants. He converted a deficiency of revenues into a surplus. He conducted the government on the lines marked out by General Gordon, and was equally modest, disinterested, and conscientious. When the Mahdi's rebellion broke out, a governor-general of another stamp was at Khartoum. Emin's warning from the remote South passed unheeded. Hicks' army, recruited from Arabi's demoralized regiments, was massacred; the Egyptian garrisons throughout the Soudan were abandoned to their fate; atrocious campaigns of unnecessary bloodshed were fought on the seaboard, and General Gordon was sent to Khartoum to perish miserably while waiting for a relief expedition that crawled by slow stages up the Nile, and was too late to be of practical service. During all these years of stupid misgovernment and wasted blood Emin remained at his post. When the death of General Gordon and the retreat of Lord Wolseley's army wiped out the last vestige of Egyptian rule in the regions of the Upper Nile, the Equatorial Provinces were cut off, neglected, and forgotten.

It then became impossible for Emin to communicate with the Egyptian Government, and he was practically lost to the world. He was dependent upon his own resources in a region encompassed by hostile tribes. He might easily have cut his way out to safety, by the way of the Congo or Zanzibar, with the best of his troops, leaving

220

the women and children behind to their fate. But this he scorned to do. He stood at his post, and bravely upheld the standard of civilization in Africa. He had with him about four thousand troops at the outset. He organized auxiliary forces of native soldiers; he was constantly engaged in warfare with surrounding tribes; he garrisoned a dozen river stations lying long distances apart; his ammunition ran low, and he lacked the money needed for paying his small army. But, in the face of manifold difficulties and dangers, he maintained his position, governed the country well, and taught the natives how to raise cotton, rice, indigo, and coffee, and also how to weave cloth, and make shoes, candles, soap, and many articles of commerce. He vaccinated the natives by the thousand, in order to stamp out small-pox; he opened the first hospital known in that quarter; he established a regular post-route with forty offices; he made important geographical discoveries in the basin of the Albert Lake; and in many ways demonstrated his capacity for governing barbarous races.

The last European who visited him was Dr. Junker, the German traveller, who parted from him at Wadelai on January 1st, 1886. His position was then more favorable, but he had been reduced at one time to extremities, his soldiers having escaped by a desperate sortie, cutting their way through the enemy after they had been many days without food, and "when the last torn leather of the last boot had been eaten." Letters written by him in October, 1886, at Wadelai, describing his geographical discoveries, were received in England in 1887, with a contributed article for a Scotch scientific journal. The provisions and ammunition sent to him by Dr. Junker had had a very encouraging effect upon his troops. He wrote: "I am still holding out here, and will not forsake my people."

The betrayal of Gordon at Khartoum by the British Government had so disgusted and exasperated decent public opinion in England that a popular demand was made for the rescue of Emin. The Government took no step other than to allow a small grant of money to be made from the Egyptian treasury. But private subscriptions furnished an ample sum, and an "Emin Relief Committee" was formed to press the work.

CHAPTER XXXI

STANLEY TO THE RESCUE

Mr. Stanley arrived in New York, after his thirteen years' absence, on November 27th, 1886. On December 12th of the same year he was requested by the King of the Belgians to return immediately to Europe. He did so, and was commissioned to head the expedition then being formed for the relief of Emin Pasha. There was much discussion as to the route to be taken, most authorities favoring that overland from Zanzibar. But Mr. Stanley determined upon the Congo, and he described the character of the expedition as follows:

"The expedition is non-military—that is to say, its purpose is not to fight, destroy, or waste; its purpose is to save, to relieve distress, to carry comfort. Emin Pasha may be a good man, a brave officer, a gallant fellow deserving of a strong effort of relief, but I decline to believe, and I have not been able to gather from any one in England an impression, that his life, or the lives of the few hundreds under him, would overbalance the lives of thousands of natives, and the devastation of immense tracts of country which an expedition strictly military would naturally cause. The expedition is a mere powerful caravan, armed with rifles for the purpose of insuring the safe conduct of the ammunition to Emin Pasha, and for the more certain protection of his people during the retreat home. But it also has means of purchasing the friendship of tribes and chiefs, of buying food and paying its way liberally."

Mr. Stanley went from England to Egypt, where he stopped for a time at Cairo, completing his arrangements with the Egyptian government. On reaching Zanzibar he found that his agents had already recruited a force of six hundred men for the expedition, and that Tippu-Tib, who had escorted his caravan in 1877, when the first descent of the Congo was made, was waiting for him. Tippu-Tib was the Zobehr of the Upper Congo, commanding two of the best roads from the river to Wadelai. He agreed to supply six hundred carriers at thirty dollars a man; and as Emin was reported by Dr. Junker to have seventy-five tons of ivory, the expenses of the expedition might be largely defrayed by the return of the Zanzibaris to the Congo with their precious loads. Tippu-Tib was also offered the position of governor at Stanley Falls at a regular salary. He consented to accompany Mr. Stanley on these terms. The steamer set out on February 25th for the mouth of the Congo with about seven hundred men of the expedition, reaching its destination in four weeks. He was then twelve hundred and sixty-six miles from Aruwimi, whence he was to march four hundred miles through an unknown country to Emin's capital. It was as late as April 26th before he could leave Leopoldville, on Stanley Pool, and it was not until the second week in June that the explorer himself was at Aruwimi, much delay having been caused by defective transportation.

He left men at Stanley Falls, with instructions to rebuild the storehouses, to open negotiations with the tribes, and to provide convoys of provisions for the relief expedition. A rear-guard was left at Yambouya, and the advance column passed on to the limits of navigation, whence the overland march was taken up. Few difficulties were encountered apart from the natural obstacles presented by a country very difficult to traverse. About July 25th the expedition had ascended the River Aruwimi as far as an elevated tract of country forming a portion of the Mabodi district.

Thus, Mr. Stanley and his comrades plunged into the wilderness, and were lost to the sight of the world. From time to time thereafter countless rumors came from Africa regarding them, rumors varied in tone as in number. At one time they had reached Emin in safety. Again they were all massacred long before they got to Wadelai. Now, Mr. Stanley had put himself at the head of Emin's army and was marching on Khartoum to avenge Gordon and overthrow the Mahdi; and then he and Emin were captured by the Mahdist forces at Lado. Stories came of a mysterious "White Pasha" who was leading a conquering army through the Bahr Gazelle country, and it was very generally believed that it was Mr. Stanley, who had reached Wadelai and was returning to the coast by the way of the Niger. But on December 15th, 1888, startling news came from Suakim, on the Red Sea coast of Egypt. Osman Digna, the Frenchman who had turned Arab and was leader of the Mahdist army there, under a flag of truce informed the British commander that Emin's province had fallen into Arab hands, and that Emin and Stanley were prisoners. In proof of this he sent a copy of a letter just received from a Mahdist officer in the Soudan, as follows:

"In the name of the Great God, etc. This is from the least among God's servants to his Master and chief Khalifa, etc. We proceeded with the steamers and army. Reached the town Lado, where Emin, Mudir of Equator, is staying. We reached this place 5th Safar, 1306. We must thank officers and men who made this conquest easy to us before our arrival. They caught Emin and a traveller staying with him, and put both in chains. The officers and men refused to go to Egypt with the Turks. Tewfik sent Emin one of the travellers, whose name is Mr. Stanley. This Mr. Stanley brought with him a letter from Tewfik to Emin, dated 8th Jemal Aowal, 1304, No. 81, telling Emin to come with Mr. Stanley, and gave the rest of the force the option to go to Cairo or remain. The force refused the Turkish orders, and gladly received us. I found a great deal of feathers and ivory. I am sending with this, on board the 'Bordain,' the officers and chief clerk. I am also sending the letter which came to Emin from Tewfik, with the banners we took from the Turks. I heard that there is another traveller who came to Emin, but I heard that he returned. I am looking out for him. If he comes back again, I am sure to catch him. All the chiefs of the province with the inhabitants were delighted to receive us. I have taken all the arms and ammunition. Please return the officers and chief clerk when you have seen them and given the necessary instructions, because they will be of great use to me."

This was accompanied by what appeared to be a letter written by the Khedive at Cairo to Emin, which had been intrusted to Mr. Stanley to deliver, and this convinced many of the truth of Osman Digna's story. But, as a matter of fact, as will be seen later, it was all an ingenious lie, concocted for the purpose of frightening the British into abandoning Suakim to the slave-traders. Meantime there was true news of actual disasters on the Congo. Major Barttelot, commanding the rear guard of the expedition, was murdered; and Mr. Jamieson, who succeeded to the command, died of fever. Under these circumstances, the gloomiest and most anxious views prevailed regarding Mr. Stanley's fate.

It was in December, 1888, that the dark views concerning Stanley's fate most prevailed, but ten days later positive and authentic news of Mr. Stanley's safe arrival at Emin Pasha's capital was received, and on April 3d, 1889, full details of the campaign, written by Mr. Stanley himself, were published. His letter to the chairman of the Emin Pasha Relief Committee was dated at Bungangeta Island, Ituri or Aruwimi River, August 28th, 1888, and gave full accounts of the varying fortunes of the expedition, with its disasters and successes.

CHAPTER XXXII

STANLEY AND EMIN

In his letter to the Emin Pasha Relief Committee Mr. Stanley closes by saying: "Let me touch more at large on the subject which brought me to this land—viz., Emin Pasha.

"The Pasha has two battalions of regulars under him—the first, consisting of about seven hundred and fifty rifles, occupies Duffle, Honyu, Labore, Muggi, Kirri, Bedden, Rejaf; the second battalion, consisting of six hundred and forty men, guard the stations of Wadelai, Fatiko, Mahagi and Mswa, a line of communication along the Nyanza and Nile about one hundred and eighty miles in length. In the interior west of the Nile he retains three or four small stations—fourteen in all. Besides these two battalions he has quite a respectable force of irregulars, sailors, artisans, clerks, servants. 'Altogether,' he said, 'if I consent to go away from here we shall have about eight thousand people with us.'

"'Were I in your place I would not hesitate one moment or be a second in doubt what to do.'

"'What you say is quite true, but we have such a large number of women and children, probably ten thousand people altogether. How can they all be brought out of here? We shall want a great number of carriers.'

"'Carriers! carriers for what?' I asked.

"'For the women and children. You surely would not leave them, and they cannot travel?'

"'The women must walk. It will do them more good than harm. As for the little children, load them on the donkeys. I hear you have about two hundred of them. Your people will not travel very far the first month, but little by little they will get accustomed to it. Our Zanzibar women crossed Africa on my second expedition. Why cannot your black women do the same? Have no fear of them; they will do better than the men.'

"'They would require a vast amount of provision for the road.'

"'True, but you have some thousands of cattle, I believe. Those will furnish beef. The countries through which we pass must furnish grain and vegetable food.'

"Well, well, we will defer further talk till to-morrow."

"May 1st, 1888.—Halt in camp at Nsabé. The Pasha came ashore from the steamer 'Khedive' about one P. M., and in a short time we commenced our conversation again. Many of the arguments used above were repeated, and he said:

"'What you told me yesterday has led me to think that it is best we should retire from here. The Egyptians are very willing to leave. There are of these about one hundred men, besides their women and children. Of these there is no doubt, and even if I stayed here I should be glad to be rid of them, because they undermine my authority and nullify all my endeavors for retreat. When I informed them that Khartoum had fallen and Gordon Pasha was slain, they always told the Nubians that it was a concocted story, that some day we should see the steamers ascend the river for their relief. But of the regulars who compose the first and second battalions I am extremely doubtful; they have led such a free and happy life here that they would demur at leaving a country where they have enjoyed luxuries they cannot command in Egypt. The soldiers are married, and several of them have harems. Many of the irregulars would also retire and follow me. Now, supposing the regulars refuse to leave, you can imagine that my position would be a difficult one. Would I be right in leaving them to their fate? Would it not be consigning them all to ruin? I should have to leave them their arms and ammunition, and on returning all discipline would be at an end. Disputes would arise, and factions would be formed. The more ambitious would aspire to be chiefs by force, and from these rivalries would spring hate and mutual slaughter until there would be none of them left.'

"'Supposing you resolve to stay, what of the Egyptians?' I asked.

"'Oh! these I shall have to ask you to be good enough to take with you.'

"'Now, will you, Pasha, do me the favor to ask Captain Casati if we are to have the pleasure of his company to the sea, for we have been instructed to assist him also should we meet?'

"Captain Casati answered through Emin Pasha:

"'What the Governor Emin decides upon shall be the rule of conduct for me also. If the Governor stays, I stay. If the Governor goes, I go.'

"'Well, I see, Pasha, that in the event of your staying your responsibilities will be great.'

"A laugh. The sentence was translated to Casati, and the gallant Captain replied:

"'Oh! I beg pardon, but I absolve the Pasha from all responsibility connected with me, because I am governed by my own choice entirely.'

"Thus day after day I recorded faithfully the interviews I had with Emin Pasha; but these extracts reveal as much as is necessary for you to understand the position. I left Mr. Jephson thirteen of my Soudanese, and sent a message to be read to the troops, as the Pasha requested. Everything else is left until I return with the united expedition to the Nyanza.

"Within two months the Pasha proposed to visit Fort Bodo, taking Mr. Jephson with him. At Fort Bodo I have left instructions to the officers to destroy the fort and accompany the Pasha to the Nyanza. I hope to meet them all again on the Nyanza, as I intend making a short cut to the Nyanza along a new road."

CHAPTER XXXIII

IN THE HEART OF AFRICA

It was in April, 1889, that the thrilling narrative of Mr. Stanley's march from the Congo to the Lakes was made known. Then he disappeared again from view, but not for long. Early in November following he was heard from again, authoritatively, and in the same month the story of his work in the Equatorial Province was rehearsed to the listening world. It was on November 24th that Mr. Marston, of London, the well-known publisher, received this letter from the explorer, dated at a mission station at the southern end of Victoria Nyanza, September 3d, 1889:

"It just now," wrote Mr. Stanley, "appears such an age to me since I left England. Ages have gone by since I saw you, surely. Do you know why? Because a daily thickening barrier of silence has crept between us during that time, and this silence is so dense that in vain we yearn to pierce it. On my side I may ask, what have you been doing? On yours you may ask, and what have you been doing? I can assure myself, now that I know you live, that few days have passed without the special task of an enterprising publisher being performed as wisely and as well as possible.

"And, for the time being, you can believe me that one day has followed another in striving strifefully against all manner of obstacles, natural and otherwise. From the day I left Yambuya to August 28th, 1889, the day I arrived here, the bare catalogue of incidents would fill several quires of foolscap; the catalogue of skirmishes would be of respectable length; the catalogue of adventures, accidents, mortalities, sufferings from fever, morbid musings over mischances that meet us daily, would make a formidable list.

"You know that all the stretch of country between Yambuya and this place was an absolutely new country except what may be measured by five ordinary marches.

"First there is that dead white of the map now changed to a dead black—I mean that darkest region of earth confined between east longitude 25 deg. and east longitude 29 deg. 45 min.—one great, compact, remorselessly sullen forest, the growth of an untold number of ages, swarming at stated intervals with immense numbers of vicious, man-eating savages and crafty, undersized men, who were unceasing in their annoyance.

"Then there is that belt of grass land lying between it and Albert Nyanza, whose people contested every mile of our advance with spirit, and made us think that they were the guardians of some priceless treasure hidden on the Nyanza shores, or at war with Emin Pasha and his thousands. Sir Percival, in search of the Holy Grail, could not have met with a hotter opposition.

"Three separate times necessity compelled us to traverse these unholy regions, with varying fortunes. Incidents then crowded fast. Emin Pasha was a prisoner, an officer of ours was his forced companion, and it really appeared as though we were to be added to the list. But there is a virtue, you know, even in striving unyieldingly, in hardening nerves and facing these everclinging mischances, without paying too much heed to reputed danger. One is assisted much by knowing that there is no other coup and danger.

"Somehow, nine times out of ten the diminished rebels of Emin Pasha's government relied on their craft and on the wiles of a 'heathen Chinee,' and it is rather amusing now to look back and note how punishment has fallen upon them.

"Was it Providence or luck? Let those who love to analyze such matters reflect on it. Traitors without the camp and traitors within were watched, and the most active conspirator was discovered, tried and hanged. Traitors without fell foul of one another and ruined themselves. If not luck, then surely it is Providence, in answer to good men's prayers far away.

"Our people, tempted by extreme wretchedness and misery, sold our rifles and ammunition to our natural enemies, the Manyema slave-holders. True friends, without the least grace in either their bodies or souls! What happy influence was it that restrained me from destroying all those concerned in it?

"Each time I read the story of Captain Nelson's and Surgeon

228

Parkes' sufferings I feel vexed at my forbearance, and yet again I feel thankful, for a higher power than man's severely afflicted the cold-blooded murderers by causing them to feed upon one another a few weeks after the rescue and relief of Nelson and Parkes. The memory of those days alternately hardens and unmans me.

"With the rescue of Emin Pasha, poor old Casati, and those who preferred Egypt's flesh pots to the coarse plenty of the province near Nyanza, we returned, and while we were patiently waiting the doom of the rebels was consummated.

"Since that time of anxiety and unhappy outlook I have been at the point of death from a dreadful illness. The strain had been too much, and for twenty-eight days I lay helpless, tended by the kindly and skilful hand of Surgeon Parkes. Then little by little I gathered strength and ordered the march for home.

"Discovery after discovery in this wonderful region was made. The snowy ranges of Ruevenzoni, the 'Cloud King' or 'Rain Creator,' the Semliki River. Albert Edward Nyanza, the plains of Noongora, the salt lakes of Kative, new peoples, Wakonju of the Great Mountains, dwellers of the rich forest region, the Awamba, the fine-featured Wasonyora, the Wanyoro bandits, and then Lake Albert Edward, the tribes and shepherd races of the Eastern uplands, then Wanyankori, besides Wanyaruwamba and Wazinja, until at last we came to a church, whose cross dominated a Christian settlement, and we knew that we had reached the outskirts of blessed civilization.

"We have every reason to be grateful, and may that feeling be ever kept within me. Our promises as volunteers have been performed as well as though we had been specially commissioned by the government. We have been all volunteers, each devoting his several gifts, abilities and energies to win a successful issue for the enterprise. If there has been anything that clouds sometimes our thoughts, it has been that we were compelled by the state of Emin Pasha and his own people to cause anxieties to our friends by serious delays.

"At every opportunity I have endeavored to lessen these by despatching full accounts of our progress to the committee, that through them all interested might be acquainted with what we are doing.

"Some of my officers also have been troubled in the thought that their government might not overlook their having overstayed their leave, but the truth is that the wealth of the British treasury could not have hastened our march, without making ourselves liable to an impeachment for breach of faith, and my officers were as much involved as myself in doing the thing honorably and well."

The same mail brought to Sir William Mackinnon a letter from Stanley, dated Kafurro, Arab Settlement, Karagwa, August 5th, 1889, from which the following is taken:

"On the 13th of February a native courier appeared in camp with a letter from Emin Pasha with news which electrified us. He was actually at anchor just below our plateau camp; but here is his formal letter:

"'In Camp, February 13th, 1889.

"'To Henry M. Stanley, Commanding the Relief Expedition:

"'Sir—In answer to your letter of the 7th inst., for which I beg to tender my best thanks, I have the honor to inform you that yesterday, at three, I arrived here with my two steamers, carrying the first lot of people desirous to leave this country under your escort. As soon as I have arranged for the cover of my people the steamships have to start for Mswa station, to bring on another lot of people awaiting transport. With me there are some twelve officers anxious to see you, and only forty soldiers. They have come under my orders to request you to give them some time to bring their brothers, at least such as are willing to leave from Wadelai, and I promised them to do my best to assist them.

"'Things having to some extent now changed, you will be able to make them undergo whatever conditions you see fit to impose upon them. To arrange these I shall start from here with my officers for your camp, after having provided for the camp, and if you send carriers I could avail myself of some of them. I hope, sincerely, that the great difficulties you have had to undergo, and the great sacrifices made by your expedition on its way to assist us, may be rewarded by full success in bringing out my people. The wave of insanity which overran the country has subsided, and of such people as are now coming with me we may be sure.

"'Signor Casati requests me to give his best thanks for your kind remembrance of him. Permit me to express to you, once more, my cordial thanks for whatever you have done for us until now, and believe me to be yours, very faithfully,

"'Dr. Emin.'"

On the 17th of February Emin Pasha and a following of about sixty people, including several high officials, arrived at Stanley's camp. They seemed unanimously in favor of departure from their position; but they pleaded for time, and finally the 10th of April was

230

decided upon as the final day of the delay, which now had aggregated nearly a year. Emin Pasha throughout this interview insisted that it all remained with his people, but still April 10th was agreed to as a day when all could be ready for the start. This decision was emphasized by a council of Stanley's officers, all of whom agreed that no delay beyond the appointed day should be thought of. After much hesitation and questioning on Emin's part, lest he should do a wrong in abandoning any of his people, his final muster was made and the march was begun on the day set by Mr. Stanley.

CHAPTER XXXIV

FORWARD MARCH!

"At muster this curious result was returned: There were with us one hundred and thirty-four men, eighty-four married women, one hundred and eighty-seven female domestics, seventy-four children above two years, thirty-five infants in arms—making a total of five hundred and fourteen. I have reason to believe that the number was nearer six hundred, as many were not reported from fear probably that some would be taken prisoners.

"On the 10th of April we set out from Kavallis, in number about one thousand five hundred, for three hundred and fifty native carriers had been enrolled from the district, to assist in carrying the baggage of the Pasha's people, whose ideas as to what was essential for the march were very crude.

"On the 11th we camped at Masambonis, but in the night I was struck down with a severe illness, which well nigh proved mortal. It detained us at the camp twenty-eight days, which, if Selim Bey and his party were really serious in their intentions to withdraw from Africa, was most fortunate for them, since it increased their time allowance to seventy-two days. But in all this interval only Shukri Aga, the chief of Mswa Station, appeared. He had started with twelve soldiers, but they, one by one, disappeared, until he had only one trumpeter and one servant. A few days after the trumpeter absconded. Thus only one servant was left out of a garrison of sixty men who were reported to be the faithfullest of the faithful.

231

"On the 8th of May our march was resumed. The route skirted the Mega Mountains at their southern end, and encountered the King of Uyoro. The first day's encounter was in our favor, and it cleared the territory as far as the Semliki River, of the Wanyoro. Meantime we had become aware that we were on the threshold of a region which promised to be very interesting, for daily, as we advanced to the southward, the great snowy range which had so suddenly arrested our attention and excited our intense interest on May 1, 1888, grew larger and bolder into view. It extended a long distance to the southwest, which would inevitably take us some distance off our course, unless a pass could be discovered to shorten the distance to the countries south.

"Much, however, as we had flattered ourselves that we should see some marvellous scenery, the 'Snow Mountain' was very coy and hard to see. On most days it looked impending over us like a tropical storm cloud, ready to dissolve in rain and ruin. On its snowy cap shot into view jagged clouds, whirling and eddying round. Often at sunrise Ruwenzori would appear like a crag deeply marked and clearly visible, but presently all would be buried under mass upon mass of mist until the immense mountain was no more visible than if we were thousands of miles away; and then, also, the 'Snow Mountain' being set deeply in the range, the nearer we approached the base of the range the less we saw of it.

"It took us nineteen marches to reach the southwest angle of the range, the Semliki Valley being below us on our right, and which, if the tedious mist had permitted, would have been exposed in every detail. That part of the valley traversed by us is generally known under the name of Awamba, while the habitable portion of the range is principally denominated Ukonju. The huts of the natives, the Bakonju, are seen as high as 8,000 feet above the sea.

"A few days later we entered Unyampaka, which I had visited in January, 1876. Ringi, the king, allowed us to feast on his bananas unquestioned. After following the lake shore until it turned too far to the southwest, we struck for the lofty uplands of Aukori, by the natives of which we were well received, preceded as we had been by the reports of our great deeds in relieving salt lake of the presence of the universally obnoxious Warosura.

"If you draw a straight line from Nyanza to the Uzinja shores of Victoria Lake it would represent pretty fairly our course through Aukori, Karagwe and Uhaiya to Uzinja.

"Aukori was open to us because we had driven Wanyaro from the salt lake. The story was an open sesame. Here also existed a wholesome fear of an expedition which had done that which all the power of Aukori could not have done. Karagwe was open to us, because free trade is the policy of Wanyamba and because the Wateanda were too much engrossed with their civil war to interfere with our passage. Uhaiya admitted our entrance without cavil, out of respect to our numbers, and Wakwiya guided us in a like manner, to be welcomed by Wazinja.

"Nothing happened during our long journey from Albert Lake to cause us any regret that we had taken this straight course, but we have suffered from an unprecedented number of fevers. We have had as many as one hundred and fifty cases in one day. In the month of July we lost one hundred and forty-one Egyptians.

"Out of respect to the first British Prince who has shown an interest in African geography we have named the southern Nyanza, to distinguish it from the other two Nyanzas, Albert Edward Nyanza. It is not a very large lake compared to Victoria, Tanganika and Nyassa. It is small, but its importance and interest lie in the sole fact that it is the receiver of all the streams at the extremity of the southwestern or Left Nile basin, and discharges these waters by one river, the Semliki, into Albert Nyanza. In a like manner Lake Victoria receives all streams from the extremity of the southeastern or Right Nile basin and pours these waters by the Victoria Nile into Albert Nyanza. These two Niles amalgamate in Lake Albert, under the well-known name of White Nile.

"By the route taken I traversed the Semliki Valley, the Awamba, the Usongora, the Toro, the Utraiyana, the Unyampaka, the Antrosi, the Karagive, the Uhaiya, the Uzimza, the South Victoria and the Nyanza. No hostile natives were met. Since we left Kabbarega we travelled along the base of the snowy range Ruwenzori. Three sides of the Southern Nyanza or Nyanza of Usongora, which is called now Albert Edward Nyanza, are about nine hundred feet higher than Albert Nyanza, having an exit at Semliki which receives over fifty streams from the Ruwenzori and finally enters the Albert Nyanza, making the Albert Edward the source of the southwest branch of the White Nile, the Victoria Nyanza being the source of the southeast branch."

The relief committee at once made arrangements for the forwarding of supplies to meet Stanley at Mpwapwa. It was thought that he could not reach the coast before the beginning of next year. Mpwapwa is a station about one hundred and fifty miles from the coast, on the road from Zanzibar and Bagamoyo to Lake Tanganika. But the expedition made rapid progress. On November 20th Captain Wissmann telegraphed from Zanzibar that Stanley had reached Mpwapwa on November 10th, and simultaneously there came a despatch which Captain Wissmann had written at Mpwapwa on October 13th, as follows:

"Four of Stanley's men and one of Emin's soldiers have arrived here. They left Stanley at Neukmma on August 10th, and came by way of Noembo and Mwerieweri north to Mgogo in thirty-three days, including nine days on which they rested. Emin and Casati had three hundred Soudanese soldiers and many other followers with them. They had in their possession a large quantity of ivory. Stanley had a force of two hundred and forty Zanzibaris and was accompanied by six lieutenants—Nelson, Jephson, Stairs, Parke, Bonny and William. The expedition struck camp as soon as the messengers started. Therefore the party should reach Mpwapwa by November 20th. Emin and Stanley repeatedly fought and repulsed the Mahdists, capturing the Mahdi's grand banner. A majority of Emin's soldiers refused to follow him southwards, asserting that their way home did not lie in that direction. Emin left two Egyptian officers in charge of stations."

This prediction that the expedition would reach Mpwapwa by November 20th was more than verified. He got there on November 10th. On November 11th Sir William Mackinnon received a despatch from Stanley announcing his arrival there, and stating that he expected to reach Zanzibar in a few days.

To the British Consul at Zanzibar Mr. Stanley wrote, under the same date:

"We arrived here yesterday on the fifty-fifth day from Victoria Nyanza and the one hundred and eighty-eighth day from the Albert Nyanza. We number altogether about seven hundred and fifty souls. At the last muster, three days ago, Emin Pasha's people numbered two hundred and ninety-four, of whom fifty-nine are children, mostly orphans of Egyptian officers. The whites with me are Lieutenant Stairs, Captain Nelson, Mounteney, Jephson, Surgeon Parke, William Bonny, Mr. Hoffman, Emin Pasha and his daughter, Captain Casati, Signor Marco and a Tunisian, Vitu Hassan, and an apothecary. We have also Pères Girault and Schinze, of the Algerian mission. Among the principal officers of the Pasha are the Vakeers, of the Equatorial province, and Major Awash Effendi, of the Second battalion.

"Since leaving Victoria Nyanza we have lost eighteen of the Pasha's people, and one native of Zanzibar, who was killed while we were parleying with hostile people. Every other expedition I have led has seen the lightening of our labors as we drew near the sea, but I cannot say the same of this one. Our long string of hammock bearers tells a different tale, and until we place these poor things on shipboard there will be no rest for us. The worst of it is we have not the privilege of showing at Zanzibar the full extent of our labors. After carrying some of them one thousand miles, fighting to the right and left of the sick, driving Warasura from their prey, over range and range of mountains, with every energy on the full strain, they slip through our hands and die in their hammocks. One lady, seventy-five years of age, the old mother of the Valkiel, died in this manner in North Msukuma, south of Victoria Nyanza.

"We had as stirring a time for four days as we had anywhere. For those four days we had continuous fighting during the greater part of daylight hours. The foolish natives took an unaccountable prejudice to the Pasha's people. They insisted that they were cannibals and had come to their country for no good. Talking to them was of no use. Any attempt at disproof drove them into white hot rage, and in their mad flinging of themselves on us they suffered."

CHAPTER XXXV

AT THE COAST AT LAST

A special correspondent of the New York Herald reached Msuwah at 5 P. M., on November 29th, and immediately sent to that paper the following despatch:

"I have just met Henry M. Stanley, Emin Pasha, Casati, Lieutenant Stairs, Mr. Jephson, Dr. Parke, Nelson and Bonny and five hundred and sixty men, women and children.

"I have found Stanley looking exceedingly hearty. He wears a Prussian cap, linen breeches and canvas shoes.

"I presented him with the American flag with which I was intrusted, and it is now flying from Mr. Stanley's tent.

"The great explorer's hair is quite white and his moustache is iron gray.

"Emin Pasha is a slight, dark man. He wears spectacles. In a short conversation which I had with him he told me he did not wish for any honors for what he had done. He simply desired to be employed again in the Khedive's service.

"I have given Captain Casati his letters. He looks well, but the hardships which he has undergone seem to have quite undermined his constitution.

"All the other Europeans are well. We shall proceed toward the coast the day after to-morrow.

"Stanley, Emin and Casati were entertained at dinner last night in this camp by Baron Gravenreath. Speeches were made by the Baron and by Stanley. The Baron complimented Stanley, Emin and their companions on their march from Central Africa. Stanley responded and praised German enterprise and civilizing abilities."

Mr. Stanley and his comrades moved steadily forward, and on December 3d were met by Major Wissmann at Atoni on the Kinghani River. The occasion was duly celebrated by the drinking of healths and loyal toasts in bumpers of champagne. Major Wissmann provided horses, and Mr. Stanley and Emin Pasha made a triumphal entry into Bagamoyo at 11 o'clock on Wednesday morning, December 4th. The town was profusely decorated with bunting and verdant arches, and palms were waving from every window. Major Wissmann's force and the German man-of-war "Sperber" fired salutes. All the vessels in the roadstead were handsomely decked with flags.

Major Wissmann entertained the party at luncheon, when the captain of the "Sperber" formally welcomed Mr. Stanley, and then congratulated Emin on behalf of Emperor William. During the afternoon many Europeans came to greet the explorers.

In the evening there was a champagne banquet. The German Consul offered a toast in honor of Queen Victoria. Major Wissmann toasted Stanley, calling him his master in African exploration. Mr. Stanley made an eloquent reply. He thanked God that he had done his duty, and referred with emotion to the soldiers whose bones were bleaching in the forest. He said his motto had always been "Onward." He testified to the divine influence that had guided him in his work. Emin Pasha toasted Emperor William. Lieutenant Stairs responded to a toast to Stanley's officers. Major Brackenbury proposed the health of Major Wissmann, which was drunk with all honors, the company heartily singing "He's a jolly good fellow."

The festivities of the evening had, however, a sad ending. A great crowd gathered outside, lustily cheering the illustrious guests. Emin Pasha went to a window and stepped out upon the balcony to acknowledge the compliment. Being nearly blind, he stumbled and fell over the low parapet to the street, a distance of twenty feet. He was picked up terribly bruised, the blood streaming from his ears, and it was feared that his skull was fractured. All the physicians present declared his injuries fatal, excepting Stanley's comrade, Dr. Parke. He took a more hopeful view of the case. Next day it was found that the skull was not broken, although Emin had sustained various severe internal injuries. Mr. Stanley telegraphed to England that the Pasha's condition was most critical, and that the German naval surgeons there declared that only twenty in a hundred of such cases ever recover, this percentage including all the cases of men in the vigor of life. Emin's age was not great, but his physical condition was not good. In addition to other bad symptoms, the hemorrhage from the ears continued, and this, though it prevented the immediate formation of a large clot in the brain, menaced life by loss of strength. He was lying in the German hospital at Bagamoyo. Dr. Parke still had some hope. Day by day news of the patient grew better, and soon he was regarded as on the sure though slow road to recovery.

Mr. Stanley was conveyed from Bagamoyo to Zanzibar by the German warship "Sperber," which had been placed at his disposal by the Emperor. This was a compliment without precedent.

On December 5th the German Emperor telegraphed to Emin:

"Now you have at last returned from your post, where you have remained over eleven years, with truly German loyalty and devotion to duty, I am glad to greet you, sending my congratulations and imperial appreciation. I have felt special satisfaction from the fact that it was through territory under our protection that German forces were able to smooth the way to the coast for your return."

At the same time the Emperor cabled to Stanley as follows:

"Thanks to your perseverance and inflexible courage, you have now, after repeatedly crossing the Dark Continent, overcome a new and long succession of exceeding perils and almost unendurable hardships. That, after surmounting those, your return journey should lead you through lands covered by my flag, affords me great satisfaction, and I welcome you heartily to civilization and security."

Stanley cabled the following answer:

"Imperator et Rex: My expectation has now reached its end. I have had the honor to be hospitably entertained by Major Wissmann and other of your Majesty's officers under him. Since arriving from Mpwapwa our travels have come to a successful conclusion. We have been taken across from Bagamoyo to Zanzibar by your Majesty's ships 'Sperber' and 'Schwalbe' and all honors, coupled with great affability, have been accorded us.

"I gratefully remember the hospitality and princely affability extended to me at Potsdam, and am profoundly impressed with your Majesty's condescension, kindness and gracious welcome. With a full and sincere heart I exclaim, Long live the noble Emperor William!"

The Emperor was immensely pleased with Stanley's reply. He read it aloud, encircled by a brilliant party, at a supper given by the

Grand Duke of Hesse. Then he again cabled to Stanley, urging him to make an early visit to Berlin, and giving him hearty assurance of a warm German greeting.

In England Mr. Stanley was the hero of the day. Tributes to his worth abounded on every hand. The Royal Geographical Society took in charge the arrangements for a formal welcome on his return.

www.ingramcontent.com/pod-product-compliance
Lightning Source LLC
LaVergne TN
LVHW030633080426
835509LV00022B/3451